Praise for *Yankee Lawyer*

"If you wondered all these years about the reality of Mr. Tutt, about his background, his romance, and his private life, the answer is here. . . . Very much a human being, he has enjoyed clubs and diversions and the society of men who also were looking askance at the economic and social ills of the day. He grew apart from his boyhood friend, Calvin Coolidge, and close to Theodore Roosevelt, Lincoln Steffens, Mark Twain, Booth Tarkington, and many other humanists. His autobiography is every bit as fascinating as Mr. Train's stories have led us to expect it would be."

—*New Orleans Times-Picayune*

"As a lawyer, Ephraim Tutt needs no introduction to the American public. . . . His life has been spent in the court room, battling for justice on behalf of the weak and the helpless. His career has been a mixture of Sir Galahad, Robin Hood, and Don Quixote, with a strong dash of Izaak Walton and the whole thoroughly shaken. Now, at seventy-five, Ephraim Tutt the lawyer has given us a full-length portrait of Ephraim Tutt the man. If there is such a thing as a typical American he will be found between the pages of this humorous and charming book."

—*The New York Times*

"Ephraim Tutt . . . has written a book about himself at last. . . . His autobiography at the ripe old age of seventy-five not only rounds off a notable career but also gives his public a chance to glimpse the rungs of his particular ladder of fame."

—*The Washington Post*

The Myth of Ephraim Tutt

Arthur Train and His Great Literary Hoax

MOLLY GUPTILL MANNING

FOREWORD BY JOHN TRAIN

THE UNIVERSITY OF ALABAMA PRESS
Tuscaloosa

Typeface: Garamond

Cover photograph: Arthur Train in his study with a portrait of Ephraim Tutt
behind him. Photo by Underwood & Underwood. Photo courtesy of Princeton
University Library.
Cover design: Erin Kirk New

∞

The paper on which this book is printed meets the minimum requirements of American
National Standard for Information Sciences—Permanence of Paper for Printed Library
Materials, ANSI Z39.48-1984.

Library of Congress Cataloging-in-Publication Data

Manning, Molly Guptill, 1980-
The myth of Ephraim Tutt : Arthur Train and his great literary hoax / Molly Guptill
Manning ; foreword by John Train.
p. cm.
Includes bibliographical references and index.
ISBN 978-0-8173-1787-4 (hardback) — ISBN 978-0-8173-8657-3 (e book)
1. Train, Arthur Cheney, 1875-1945.—Criticism and interpretation. 2. Train, Arthur
Cheney, 1875-1945. Yankee lawyer. 3. Train, Arthur Cheney, 1875-1945.—Authorship.
4. Literary forgeries and mystifications—History—20th century. I. Title.
PS3539.R23Z78 2012
813'.52—dc23
2012020090

For my wonderful husband, Chris

Contents

Foreword

Train and Tutt

Let me begin by introducing myself: John Train, son of Arthur Train, and thus, as it were, stepbrother of Ephraim Tutt. When I was a boy, Eph Tutt practically lived in our house. He was always there, in that my father was usually thinking about the next Tutt story. He wrote them one after another, whereupon they reappeared in print after a while when the *Saturday Evening Post* came to the door. I am not aware of any other American publication so universally enjoyed by almost every household in the country as the *Post,* which claimed, incidentally, to have been founded by Benjamin Franklin. It was, so to speak, the reading of both upstairs and downstairs. (In our house, the situation was more complicated, since the stories were being *created* upstairs and then *read* downstairs.)

My father, following the habit of a lifetime, wrote everything with a very soft pencil on yellow legal pads. Having corrected the text, he mailed off the sheets to a man named Frank George, who worked in the Department of Agriculture in Washington. George's advantage was not that he could refine any references to agriculture in the tales, since there were none; rather, he had the gift of being able to decipher my father's handwriting, which he then typed up and mailed back. Once reviewed, the typed sheets went on to the *Post* in Philadelphia. This roundabout system worked very well for many years.

My father had a room in our house on Seventy-Third Street where he did his writing—and enjoyed an afternoon nap. Alas, my mother took up painting in her middle age and liberated my father's writing room to be her studio, so from then on he would walk down each morning to the University Club to do his writing in its wonderful barrel-vaulted library. Thereafter, for lunch, he would continue to the Century Club, which he found extremely congenial.

In the summer the household moved to Mount Desert Island in Maine, where my father built a small, square, separate "writing house" with morning and afternoon desks to cope with the changing angle of the sunlight. There was also a deliciously comfortable daybed for the necessary post-prandial snooze and a potbellied stove for the cold days late in the season. Bits of Tutt memorabilia cropped up here and there, such as a stove-pipe hat and fishing gear. (Like his creation, my father was a keen salmon fisherman.)

He loved walking around the hills of Mount Desert and could be found up there many afternoons. In the city, the stroll from Seventy-Third Street to lunch and back was most of the exercise he got.

Mr. Tutt's experiences and ideas and ideals were my father's, but physically they were quite unlike. Tutt was tall, while Train was short. And their upbringings could not have been more different. Far from Tutt's origins in upstate New York, my father grew up in Boston, where his father, a lawyer, served for seven terms as attorney general of the state, until he was elected to Congress.

So there we have two generations—my father and grandfather—dedicated to the furtherance of justice. And actually there was a third. Arthur Train's grandfather graduated from Harvard, then a theological seminary, in the class of 1805, whose twenty-three members were intended for the ministry, which indeed he entered. However, he converted to the Baptist denomination, which meant that his parishioners, who were already paying tithes to the state to support the established church there, had to pay more all over again to support him and his church. This was the First Baptist Church of Framingham, Massachusetts, a handsome structure where its founder, "Father" Train, is well remembered. Those, then, are the moral forebears of my own father, and thus of his creation, Mr. Tutt.

The ordinary citizen encounters the law at every turn. Laws to do with marriage, children, education, housing, urban organization, taxes, elections, government, crime. There's no end to the laws we must have if we are going to live together. However, there are many quite different philosophies of law. (I encountered thirteen of them in a course at the Harvard Law School.) Some seek to give the citizen wide latitude in life—freedom—others strengthen the state's power to guide him on a moral or political path. Some are very specific, others general. The very general Ten Commandments go back to ancient Babylon, while today Congress is cranking out new laws and regulations by the minute. In the cat's cradle of laws that surround us, there are many that were useful once and are now irrelevant, many that are outright contradictory.

One of my father's—and Mr. Tutt's—central ideas, therefore, was the inevitable differences and indeed collisions between law and justice. What most people feel to be right today may be in conflict with laws of an earlier time that are still on the books. Above all, to be useful, law must be predictable, so that we can know how we are supposed to conduct ourselves, and yet in the variety of complex circumstances in which we may be entangled, unpredictable legal imbroglios are inevitable.

In the Greek drama these problems are central, and their resolution sometimes requires the intervention of a divinity, the deus ex machina. In my father's tales the perversion of justice through the abuse of law by some rascal often required a different deus ex machina to restore the right, notably that all too human quasi-divinity Mr. Tutt. Watching someone rescue a victim of injustice and frustrating the machinations of a scoundrel is always satisfying to watch, which is what makes the Tutt morality tales so gratifying. In the end, Arthur Train wrote many non-Tutt books over the course of his life, which were at least as popular as his collected volumes of Tutt stories, but the public (and the editors) knew what they wanted: more Tutt stories.

John Train
New York, New York

Acknowledgments

This book would never have been written if it were not for Richard Hamm, who is responsible for introducing me to both Arthur Train and Ephraim Tutt. In addition to being a wonderful professor and instilling in me a lasting interest in the field of legal history, I will forever be grateful for his enthusiasm for this project and his assistance in tracking down the truth about Ephraim Tutt.

This book has also been the product of the encouragement, support, and feedback from several colleagues. It was through the many conversations that I had with Edward Pekarek, a former coworker and current friend, that I decided to begin the daunting task of writing this book. Through our many discussions about Train and Tutt, Edward became very familiar with these two characters, and I am grateful for the helpful feedback he provided on the manuscript as well as his excitement for the topic.

I am also indebted to Elizabeth Duwe, who was kind enough to read an early draft of the book and provide constructive comments on how it might be improved. Her suggestions and review of the manuscript were extremely useful, as was her fresh perspective on the material.

Christopher Manning, my husband, was also a wonderful help throughout the book-writing and publication process. I am thankful for his valuable advice and for providing motivation and encouragement when I needed it most.

I would also like to thank my mother, Nancy Anne Guptill, for being so supportive of my desire to write this book.

The Myth of
Ephraim Tutt

Introduction

May 23, 1945, was a grueling day for the infantrymen of the Seventh Division. As "wind and rain lashed at the[ir] camouflaged bodies," they slowly advanced through mud and enemy fire to gain control of strategic hills on Okinawa Island, Japan. Servicemen stationed nearby reported trudging through a "stream of death," as they faced some of the "fiercest fighting of the Pacific war." In fact, the mixture of rain and blood that covered the ground was so deep that the "infantrymen almost swam through the red pools of liquefied earth," and the mud below was so thick that it "seemed determined to pull off the shoes of the plodding doughboys." Despite the challenging terrain and menacing attacks, by nightfall the Seventh Division added two more hills to the territory American forces controlled. The Seventh Division's conquest was front-page news in the United States—with each victory, World War II seemed closer to an end.[1]

After the Seventh Division retired to their camp that night, it was not long before a familiar debate arose, transforming the otherwise united group into two competing factions. Since they had already endured countless discussions on the topic, many of which grew rather heated, the unit decided that their disagreement had smoldered long enough. The following day, a sergeant, captain, and technician fifth grade (T/5) wrote a joint letter to Charles Scribner's Sons, the publisher of *Yankee Lawyer: The Auto-*

biography of Ephraim Tutt, in the hopes of securing an answer to the controversy that had long vexed their infantry division.

"Dear sirs," they began, "having read your published book, *Yankee Lawyer* . . . we have started a never ending discussion. The question raging back and forth is whether Ephraim Tutt is a real or a[n] imaginary character."

They explained: "We have read many magazine stories written by Arthur Train [about Ephraim Tutt] for the *Saturday Evening Post* which we have readily taken for fiction, however your published book has divided us into two camps as to the authenticity of the character." On the one hand, some of the men believed that Ephraim Tutt was not a real person, and his "autobiography" was just another story written by Arthur Train. Those on the other end of the debate were certain that the book could not possibly have been a work of fiction. Having reached an impasse, the men playfully reported, "At the moment we are fighting two battles, one with the Jap[anese] on Okinawa and the other among ourselves about your particular book. We have no doubt as to the outcome of the argument with the Jap[anese] but are certainly up in the air about Ephraim Tutt." The men asked for clarification so that the matter would be settled and peace might be restored to the Seventh Division's leisure hours.

Considering the danger the men faced each day, it is rather surprising that one of their most pressing concerns was to determine whether Ephraim Tutt was a real person. However, the significance of the book transcended the issue of whether Tutt existed; the principles that Tutt represented galvanized the men and renewed their sense of purpose in fighting the war. As the men of the Seventh Division remarked, "Real or imaginary, Ephraim is a hell of a lot better ideal and inspiration to fight for than blue berry pie and a chance to boo the Brooklyn Dodgers."[2]

For a quarter of a century, Tutt had accompanied Americans through prosperous times as well as some of the most challenging events in the nation's history. He provided entertainment during the lighthearted 1920s, he was a source of comfort and hope to Americans as they persevered through the Great Depression, and, by the time World War II commenced, Tutt had attained the status of an American icon and was considered as historically significant as Uncle Sam and Paul Bunyan. By midcentury

Tutt was so popular that he was on the radio and had a television program, books about him were on national best-seller lists, his "life" story was written into a script for the New York stage, and he was asked to endorse certain products. To his fans, however, Tutt was not a mere literary luminary but an old soul they had come to know over the years who felt like a longtime friend. In fact, Tutt felt like such a familiar part of people's lives that after reading his autobiography many confused him for a former college classmate, an acquaintance from the past, or even a long-lost relative. Tutt's longevity in print caused many people to feel as though he were much more than a character.

When his autobiography was published, readers were suddenly unsure of whether Tutt was a living person, or if the book was actually written by Tutt's faithful chronicler, Arthur Train. Spirited disagreements about who wrote *Yankee Lawyer* abounded. Letters filled the mailboxes of Charles Scribner's Sons, Arthur Train, and Ephraim Tutt, as the book seemed to inflict on its readers either confusion or amusement. For example, one reader reported that "the identity of Mr. Tutt has been the subject of discussion . . . for several days with more basis for argument than the 'Baker Street Irregulars' have for the actual existence of Sherlock Holmes." Other letters reported that disputes over Tutt's existence had resulted in all sorts of contention and strife—countless bets and wagers were made, friendships were compromised, tension developed between members of literary groups and bar associations, and even a federal judge complained that he was at a loss of what to make of the book (it did not help when he called local booksellers and one said the book was fiction by Train and the other said it was an autobiography by Tutt). For some, it seemed that their sanity hung in the balance. "Who, in Heaven's name, wrote *Yankee Lawyer*," one woman demanded, seemingly at her wits' end.[3]

Yet other readers congratulated Arthur Train for having written such a wonderful tribute to the Ephraim Tutt character; they found his "hoax" gloriously clever. One enchanted reader remarked: "Are you not a pioneer in your field? Has any previous writer of fiction turned the tables on himself as you have done? I cannot think of any other writer whose books, over so considerable [a] span of years, have set the stage so perfectly for such a performance. And how admirably you have pulled it off!" In another letter, a woman wittily requested Train's autograph: "While 'Mr. Tutt' is my old friend—it is through Mr. Train 'we met.' So—I'd rather, if you please, have Mr. Train autograph this book." Train typically satisfied such requests (though he had a tendency to sign whatever name a reader requested—his own or Tutt's).[4]

The answer to the question asked by members of the Seventh Division and countless others is that Ephraim Tutt never existed—at least not in a physical sense. However, by my own conservative estimate, upward of tens of thousands of people around the world sincerely believed he was a living lawyer who practiced in New York during the first half of the twentieth century. Although it was not Arthur Train's intention to mislead anyone, Tutt's autobiography was so masterfully written, with so many historically accurate details and realistic flourishes (such as providing actual photographs of people who were identified as Tutt and his parents), that a significant number of people became unsure whether Tutt was just an imaginary character or if he had actually lived the life Train had given him. For those who wished that Tutt was a real person, his "autobiography" provided the little encouragement needed to transform their wish into (what seemed to be) a reality.

In the end, Train's publication of *Yankee Lawyer* proved to be one of the greatest and most unique literary hoaxes in the history of that mischievous tradition. While the literary hoax has taken many forms over the years—from Jonathan Swift's 1708 prank publication of a false almanac that predicted that a townsperson who irked him would die on an appointed date (followed by the publication of an elegy confirming that this vexatious individual had passed away when he had not) to James Frey's recent publication of his embellished and fabricated "memoir," *A Million Little Pieces*—it has never featured an established creature of fiction writing his own autobiography. Train's feat is also unparalleled because he did not intend for it to be a hoax; he genuinely believed that it would have been impossible for anyone to confuse Tutt, who was such a well-known character, for a real person. After all, the truth was hiding in plain sight the whole time—Train's creation of a fictitious Ephraim Tutt was common knowledge. As a result, even readers who wanted to believe in the existence of a living Ephraim Tutt often had their doubts, and these readers were generally amused when their suspicion that Tutt was a creature of fiction was confirmed. In fact, one reader—who had mailed a fan letter to Tutt one morning, discovered Tutt did not exist by the afternoon, and wrote a second letter to Tutt's publisher the same day—wrote: "Go ahead. Laugh. I have laughed at myself since writing early this morning." He described Train's hoax as "superb" and wished he could obtain Train's autograph.[5]

However, not all people approached Train's ruse with such lightheartedness. Some were so upset when they learned Tutt was not real, they shed tears and wrote angry letters to the guilty parties. One woman, who had written to Tutt and then learned he did not exist, demanded that Scribner's return her prior letter to her and noted "you will perhaps forgive a feeling of profound sadness that a character so fine should be a travesty of all that it proclaimed to champion!" She even commented that "Train should not have worked so hard and done such a good job," for Train "would have been a greater advocate of justice had his character Tutt stood on the honest legs of fiction."[6] Other letters expressing sadness, shock, disappointment, and irritation were mailed. One reader felt so outraged by Train's literary mischief that he even sued for fraud.

It is often difficult to identify at what point a literary hoax crosses the proverbial line. However, in the case of Arthur Train, his unprecedented stunt of publishing his own character's autobiography is one hoax that should not go down in history as a reprehensible one. Train wrote *Yankee Lawyer* to impart vitality on his most popular and beloved character and to ensure that Tutt would live beyond the limited years that Train—a mere mortal—had left. On both points, Train succeeded, and for the most part, Tutt's fans—whether they were fooled or not—were grateful to have read the story of Tutt's extraordinary life.

1
Arthur Train

I enjoy the dubious distinction of being known among lawyers as a writer, and among writers as a lawyer.

—Arthur Train

On March 13, 1944, Arthur Train was at the height of his literary career. His most recent book had become a best seller, and he could hardly believe the storm of publicity that surrounded it. Although his exact actions on that date have been lost to history, he likely followed his usual schedule and awoke early, dressed in his signature outfit—a dark blue pinstripe suit, a silk shirt, an unassuming tie, and brown shoes—and prepared to devote the next several hours to the welcome chore of writing at either Manhattan's University Club or Century Club.[1] As he left his home, located at 113 East Seventy-Third Street, he bid his wife goodbye, grabbed his creased-brim hat and deposited it on his head, reached for his cane (as was the fashion at the time), and greeted the cantankerous early spring weather.

As mundane as it may have started, this day proved to be a remarkable one, for, by sunset, a handful of papers were delivered to Train that changed the course of the rest of his life. The papers were a summons and complaint; Train was being sued for fraud, along with his publisher and longtime editor. While the prospect of a lawsuit might ordinarily cause one to feel panic, I am nearly certain that upon reading these documents a look of amusement spread across Train's face, his lips formed a sly grin, and his eyes twinkled—he was absolutely delighted. In fact, the only matter that likely bothered him was that he had not considered how advantageous a lawsuit would be until he had already become a party to one.

Boyhood and Beyond

Arthur Cheney Train was born in Boston, Massachusetts, on September 6, 1875, to Charles and Sarah Train.[2] His father attended Brown University and the Dane Law School of Harvard College, and after graduating with his law degree, he became district attorney of the northern district of Middlesex County, Massachusetts, in the late 1840s. Thereafter, Charles Train devoted his career to government service, working in a litany of positions. To name a few, he served as a Republican representative for the Thirty-Sixth and Thirty-Seventh US Congresses, which sat from 1859 to 1863. While Congress was recessed in 1862, Charles Train volunteered to serve in the Union army and worked "as assistant adjutant-general" during the Battle of Antietam. Charles Train was a delegate to the national Republican convention at Baltimore, which nominated Abraham Lincoln for the presidency in 1864, and was even honored with the distinction of being offered a seat as an associate justice on the US Supreme Court (which he declined). At the conclusion of his federal congressional term, Train returned to Massachusetts, where he worked within his local government, first as a member of the common council and later in the state legislature.[3]

In 1871 he was elected attorney general of Massachusetts and was reelected annually to that position for seven years. During this time, Charles Train prosecuted an assortment of cases, including "several celebrated capital cases." By the 1870s, Train was known as "a criminal lawyer [who] unquestionably stood at the head of his profession, while as an attorney in civil cases he ranked among the most eminent attorneys in the State."[4] According to Arthur Train, one of his father's schoolmates once described his father as "a genial, large-hearted, impulsive boy; sarcastic, transparent; never attempting to conceal his faults; nourishing no ill will; seeking no revenges; always ready to meet all consequences; just the boy—as in years after he was just the man—one would most like to have for a friend, or an enemy."

Despite Charles Train's successful and lucrative career, Arthur's mother—whom Arthur described as a "sweet little woman" who "had the charity and self-effacement of a saint"—governed their household with a strict sense of frugality, imparting a feeling on young Arthur that his "family came from a lower economic stratum than most of [his] fellows." In fact, Arthur claimed this "early sense of social inferiority" "dominated [his] life." As a child Train recalled turning to moneymaking enterprises such as digging for dandelions—which he sold for five cents per quart—and engaging in a "negligible trade in old iron and bottles" in order to have some spending money. The insecurity he felt regarding his social status "bred in [him] a recalcitrant individualism, that led [him] to question and challenge everything that was conventional and authoritative." This sense of rebellion may have proved especially problematic since Train was raised amid a strict Puritan tradition, to which his family, at a minimum, paid homage. Train recalled that during his childhood he spent many miserable Sundays "cooped up in a long high-backed pew during long, dreary hours, without occupation except to draw surreptitious pictures of the minister in the back of [his] prayer book" and to play with small toys he had "smuggled" into church, which his father unfailingly discovered and confiscated.[5]

Although Charles Train died when Arthur was only nine years old, Arthur had a few opportunities to travel from court to court—riding circuit—with his father, during which Arthur had his first experiences with the law. Apparently, these trips left quite an impression on Arthur, for, when he was only seven years old, while pretending to be a "prosecuting attorney, [he] sentenced all his schoolteachers to prison for life." In addition to what appears to be an early interest in the law, Arthur also loved writing stories. "[Writing] was a passion even in [his] childhood." Train also enjoyed reading whatever he could get his hands on. As a child he recalled reading his parents' magazines, one of which included a baffling column that told thrilling tales of "love and adventure" that often ended "abruptly with [a] laconic statement." Before he "gave [them] up . . . in view of the inevitable disappointment attending the denouement," Arthur would sometimes amuse himself with writing a "more literary ending" to these sagas.[6]

When Arthur turned twelve years old, he entered St. Paul's School, in Concord, New Hampshire, where, for the next four years, he spent "the happiest days of [his] youth," enjoying country life and "freedom from parental restraint." Although discipline was no small matter, "the presence of boys of [his] own age from all parts of the country opened up vistas into a new and exciting world." During this time, Arthur overcame some of his self-consciousness and insecurities; however, when he was admitted to Harvard University in 1896, they resurfaced. "My four years at Harvard were years of frustration, embittered by my inability to achieve the social recognition from my classmates to which I felt entitled. Whether or not there be (or was) such a thing as Harvard indifference, I found Harvard almost wholly indifferent to my own existence, and this intensified all the characteristics that engendered my upbringing." Train described his undergraduate years as resulting "in nothing more but a complete intellectual demoralization," believing he had "left Cambridge with a less well-trained mind than when [he] entered it." Although he graduated magna cum laude and was a commencement speaker, he believed his success was based upon his selections of easy, "snap" courses and "sporadic cramming for examinations." Train claimed that he "loafed" through his four years, "sitting on the steps of [his] dormitory, smoking innumerable stogies."[7]

After taking so little satisfaction with his years spent earning his undergraduate degree, it is no small wonder that Arthur remained at Harvard to attend its law school. Arthur was driven by an obligation to follow in his father's footsteps, and thus earned an LLB degree from Harvard Law School in 1899. While studying the law, Train dated Ethel Kissam, and the two were married on April 20, 1897, at St. Bartholomew's Church, in Manhattan. After Arthur's law school graduation, the Trains initially stayed in Boston, during which Arthur briefly worked in a "conventional . . . law office."[8]

In 1900 Arthur and Ethel moved to New York City. During the early years of their marriage, Ethel devoted herself to her writing career and succeeded in publishing several novels as well as stories in popular periodicals. Arthur, on the other hand, paid little attention to his writing and set out to make a name for himself in the legal world. His first job in New York was at Robinson, Biddle & Ward, located in lower Manhattan. Try as he might, however, Train found himself "bored, impatient and unhappy." Train's memory of his employment at this firm was far from ideal:

> My desk looked out into a narrow and gloomy airshaft. Only by sticking my head out of the window on a clear day could I glimpse a patch of blue far, far above. It made me feel as if I were imprisoned at the bottom of a well. Across the shaft on the story next above was another window—just like mine—at which sat an ancient with sunken cheeks and wisps of white hair encircling his parchment-covered skull. His profile was side-ways to me, looking down, presumably at a desk, motionless. So far as I could see, he neither moved nor spoke. He was there every morning when I came; and he was there when I went home. Perhaps he is there yet;—if so, he looks the same. I used to wonder if he had ever been young. "There," I said to myself one day, "but for the grace of God goes Arthur Train!"[9]

Train knew something had to change; however, he was unsure of when or how such change would come about.

On January 11, 1901, Train was at home, sick with a bad case of the flu. As he passed the time reading a stack of newspapers in bed, Train glanced at a headline that "eventually . . . determine[d] the whole future course of [his] life." Flu be damned, Train dressed and headed to downtown Manhattan, hoping his fate was about to change. The newspaper had reported that New York State governor Theodore Roosevelt had removed New York County district attorney Asa Bird Gardiner from office because it had become clear that he was no longer fit to serve. According to the *New York Times,* "certain leading politicians" had threatened to manipulate elections and revert to violence at the polls if necessary to get the votes they wanted. Gardiner, inexplicably, threw his support behind the chief of police, who indicated he would not try to stop such criminal violation of the law. Since the district attorney, by the very nature of his position, was to oversee the observance of the laws, Governor Roosevelt simply could not tolerate Gardiner's stance on this issue. Thus Governor Roosevelt fired Gardiner and named Eugene A. Philbin to be his successor. Since with a new district attorney there would be new jobs, Train saw this as an opportunity to leave his unsatisfying law firm career and try his hand at public service.[10]

Train secured a letter of introduction to Philbin from Lewis L. Delafield, an esteemed member of the New York bar, and then made his "first visit to the grimy old building on Lafayette Street where [he] was destined to spend so many active years." Unfortunately, Train was too late. Philbin had already filled all the vacancies on his official staff and had exhausted the salary appropriations earmarked for his office. It was no small consolation, however, when Philbin noted that he was terribly sorry since he would "have been glad to appoint any one so highly recommended by Mr. Delafield." Undeterred and certain of his destiny, Train offered to work "for nothing," and explained, "this is the kind of work I want to do and I think I can do it. Give me a chance and I promise you faithful service. If I don't make good, fire me. It won't have cost you anything." Maybe it was Train's tenacity and earnestness, or some other virtuous trait apparent to the new district attorney, but Philbin agreed, and Train began his work in the New York County District Attorney's Office on that fateful day. Train was led to a room on the fourth floor, which became his office. For the next ten years, "on and off," Train would call this office his "official home."

The district attorney's office "was as depressing an environment as could be found anywhere," but it was the first place after Train's years at Harvard where he felt truly alive, interested, and engaged. "A daily succession of melodramas was enacted before my eyes, in which every human passion was laid bare, quivering in the raw—love, hate, lust, revenge, jealousy, cupidity. Every case was a tragedy; every trial a detective story." Over the course of the next decade, Train tried "thousands of all sorts of cases," and his name became well known as it appeared in headlines and news stories with frequency.[11]

In June 1908, Train tendered his resignation as assistant district attorney in order to enter private practice, though Train continued to try cases on behalf of the district attorney's office over the course of the next several years. Private practice did not suit Train; he had difficulty finding clients and was unable to earn a salary even close to that which he earned in public service (during his first year of private practice, Train earned $900; during his first year at the district attorney's office, he earned $7,500). In 1909 Train formed a partnership with Richard B. Olney, who served as US attorney general under President Grover Cleveland, and opened an office at 30 Broad Street in Manhattan. One of Train's few cases that received publicity while he was partnered with Olney involved a notorious affair implicating several members of high society. Mrs. Catherine K. Blake alleged that Train's client Katherine Mackay had "enticed" Dr. Blake away from her, causing Mrs. Blake to suffer damages in the amount of $1 million. Within a month of the sordid details of this suit being smeared across the pages of New York newspapers, Mrs. Blake elected to drop her suit. (Within one year of forfeiting her suit, the Mackays divorced in Paris, Mrs. Blake obtained a decree of divorce in Connecticut, and the day after Mrs. Blake's divorce decree was executed, Dr. Blake married the former Mrs. Mackay.) While the scandalous details of the case captured the interest of the public (it was often front-page news), it was not the type of case that inspired Train's practice of law. Perhaps save one matter while operating as Train & Olney, Train found neither financial success nor fulfillment in the legal matters brought before the firm.[12]

The benefit to financial catastrophe and dull employment was that Train focused more on his writing, and during his days at Train & Olney he came to create and develop one of the foremost organizations for writers in the twentieth century. It all began when, around 1911, Train wrote a serial for *McClure's Magazine,* titled *"C. Q." or, in the Wireless House,* for which Train had made an "arrangement . . . by letter" to sell the "serial rights" to *McClure's* for $3,000. However, Train learned that *McClure's* sold the English serial rights to the story to a magazine in London. Since "at the moment [he] had no clients but plenty of time to ponder technicalities," Train decided to investigate whether *McClure's* had the right to do this. After all, what were "serial rights"? To Train they meant "the right to publish *once* serially—in a specified magazine—[and] nothing else." Apparently "serial rights" meant something much more liberal to *McClure's*. Train decided to call Cameron McKenzie, the editor of *McClure's* at the time, and "innocently congratulate him on having sold 'my English rights,' [and] inquire how much he had received for them." According to Train, the conversation went something like this:

[Cameron] hemmed and hawed and finally said $600—"but they don't belong to you, you know—they belong to us!" he added.

"Oh, no!" I assured him. "I only sold you the right to print the story once serially in *McClure's*."

"But I hold the copyright!" he protested.

"What of it?" I argued. "You might hold my watch in your hand and yet it wouldn't be yours! That $600 belongs to me and if you don't send me a check for it I'll take legal steps to enjoin publication in England."

That was rot, but it worked. You see, I was a lawyer. Finally, gagging, he agreed to send me a check—largely, I believe, to avoid having to consult counsel. I hung up the telephone receiver and whooped for joy.

"What the hell is all the noise about?" asked Olney.

"I've got a client!"

"Who?"

"Myself! I got a fee of $600!"

Olney came over and sat sideways on my desk.

"How about that copyright stuff?" he suggested.

"I don't know anything about it!"

"Well, I advise you to find out!" he warned. "I don't believe any of you writing fellows know what you're doing. If you saved $600, maybe you can save $6000!"

Train did some research and soon discovered a federal court case that proved that not only did the editor of *McClure's* have every right to sell Train's story, but he could do it again and again. Train could hardly stomach the practical effect of the case's holding: that "every story ever published in an American magazine was at that moment without a copyright and free to be pirated." Train also learned that "the outright sale of a manuscript to a publisher, no reservations being made, was held to transfer every right of every sort and kind that the author might now have, or in the future possess, therein—including all serial rights, all 'second' (newspaper) rights, book, theatrical, movie, reprint, everything—he had sold the shirt off his back!"[13]

Train was "appalled at the horror of it." He quickly began calling his friends, warning them not to sell another piece of writing until a way to protect writers' interests could be implemented. The offices of Train & Olney were soon filled with concerned authors. Train studied the activities of writers' organizations in France and England and held a conference to discuss the predicament of American writers; his efforts led to the creation of the Authors' League of America. According to the papers of incorporation, the object of the league was "to procure adequate copyright legislation, both international and domestic, to protect the rights of all authors, whether engaged in literary, dramatic, artistic, or musical composition, and to advise and assist all such authors voluntarily in the disposal of their productions." In the league, authors found a place where they could voice their woes, discuss unscrupulous editors and publishers and "blacklist" them, and determine under what terms they should sell their manuscripts or rights to publishers. Train's legal expertise proved invaluable in this endeavor, since the league was responsible for revising "the old stereotyped contract whereby the author, not only parted with everything he owned but sold himself into bondage as his publisher's galley-slave for succeeding books," and Train "drafted a memorandum to accompany manuscripts offered for serial publication, by which the editor was to copyright *all* rights but act as trustee of the author for all save what he had paid for." By the 1940s, "there [we]re comparatively few authors of any standing who [we]re not members of the League and heartily in accord with its purpose and policies." Even in 1912 the members of the board of directors of the league included such notable personalities as Ida Tarbell and Samuel Hopkins Adams, and in 1913 Theodore Roosevelt became vice president of the league. In 1927 Arthur Train was honored by being elected vice president, and the following year he was elected president. The league not only meant a great deal to Train as it allowed him to protect the interests of his fellow writers, but it also bridged his two vocations—writing and law.[14]

Throughout the next few years, Train continued to practice law; however, his writing career began to take greater precedence in his life. It became increasingly clear that "at heart, [Train] was a writer rather than a lawyer—a writer . . . with a legal mind."[15] Although as assistant district attorney he helped secure noteworthy convictions and demonstrated his natural talent for practicing law, Train did not feel that he earned great distinction for his role in the courtroom. He was skilled at law and was an excellent courtroom lawyer, yet his attitude toward his legal practice reveals that he was not emotionally invested in it and he lacked the motivation to fully devote himself to that vocation. When it came to writing, however, he felt more engaged and challenged than he did with the law. Writing made Train feel alive, while the law seemed to demoralize and exhaust him. As Train allowed himself to consider writing as a full-time career, his writing flourished and he became more comfortable with his ultimate decision of leaving the practice of law.

In the early 1920s, Train succumbed to his destiny. Although he became a lawyer because it "was a family tradition" and, at the turn of the century, "the writing of fiction was looked upon as, at best, a frivolous and even as a rather scandalous vocation," by the 1920s Train's legal career was effectively over. He no longer went to court, he no longer represented clients, and he no longer kept a law office. Instead, Train turned his full attention to writing. The only legal battles Train fought over the next decades, save one, were in his works of legal fiction. Although Train left the law and did not look back, for the rest of his life he seemed to "enjoy the dubious distinction of being known among lawyers as a writer, and among writers as a lawyer."[16]

Family Life and Leisure Time

During the two decades that Train transitioned from being a full-time lawyer to a full-time writer, his family grew to include three daughters—Lucy, Helen, and Margaret—and a son, Arthur Kissam Train Jr. During their marriage, Arthur and Ethel enjoyed traveling, and they embarked on many trips that usually involving hiking and camping. In fact, much to Arthur's delight, Ethel proved to be a formidable outdoorswoman. (After a particularly rigorous trip to the Sierra Nevada, which the Trains took with their friends and frequent travel companions, Marshall Bond and his wife, Mr. Bond wrote to Train expressing how impressed he was with Ethel's "splendid nerve.")[17] However, in 1923 Ethel suddenly passed away after a bout of bronchial pneumonia. Although Train went on to remarry, he forever carried with him a gold pocket watch, which was a gift to him from Ethel.

In the winter of 1926, Train wed Helen Coster Gerard, who had three sons from a previous marriage, Sumner, James, and C. H. Coster. In 1928 Helen and Arthur Train had their first and only child together, John Train. Throughout his years in New York, Arthur and his family lived in a five-and-one-half-story white stone and redbrick home on East Seventy-Third Street. He also vacationed regularly in Maine and built a home on a tract of land he purchased, nestled between the mountains of Acadia and the Atlantic Ocean. Some of Train's greatest works were written in the small "writing house" situated near the main home on this property. Train kept regular hours for writing—as a rule, he devoted the first portion of each day to this activity and periodically took a day off to give his mind a rest. While staying in his Maine home, Train was able to take advantage of the beautiful scenery that surrounded him, and he was known to take frequent walks around Mount Desert Island and Acadia. His contentment with being immersed in nature—with his particular favorite outdoor pastimes being hiking and fishing—was incorporated into his writing. For instance, he sold a few articles on some of his hiking adventures to the International Magazine Company and *Motor* magazine. As for fishing, Train made quite a name for himself in New Brunswick, Canada, for his skill and catches. He was even honored, in 1931, with an award for his fishing feats there.[18] Train's love of the sport was featured prominently in his writing, especially in some of the fishing tales involving his most beloved character, Ephraim Tutt.

Train's Literary Career

Besides his Ephraim Tutt stories, Arthur Train wrote on a variety of subjects —law, history, romance, society, politics, and he even wrote a few autobiographical works. Before being published in book form, many of Train's stories were first serialized and published in popular magazines, such as *McClure's, American, Redbook, Cosmopolitan, Everybody's, Collier's,* and the *Saturday Evening Post.* By 1915 Train went through a transformation from a little-known writer to a seasoned novelist and storyteller whose short stories were published almost exclusively in the *Saturday Evening Post.* Train's frequent appearance in the *Post* was significant—it was the premiere magazine of the early twentieth century. Adding his name alongside some of the most famous writers of the day—F. Scott Fitzgerald, John Steinbeck, J. D. Salinger, Ray Bradbury, Edgar Allan Poe, Sinclair Lewis, and Agatha Christie—and artists, such as Norman Rockwell, helped elevate Train's stature as a writer. Even after he was an established author, Train continued to submit stories to the *Post,* and his work appeared in that magazine well into the 1940s.[19]

With respect to his books, over the course of his career Train published more than forty volumes and predominately worked with a single publishing company: Charles Scribner's Sons. Initially, Train worked with

Robert Bridges, a respected editor at Scribner's. However, around 1914, he was assigned to a new editor, Maxwell Perkins, with whom Train worked exclusively for the rest of his life.[20] Train was very fortunate to work with an editor as gifted as Perkins; however, this pairing proved even more significant toward the end of the Train's life, by which time they had become not only good friends but also coconspirators.

Maxwell Perkins made his way to Scribner's after trying his hand in the newspaper industry. He graduated from Harvard University in 1907 and accepted a position with the *New York Times* as a reporter and editor. In fact, Train and Perkins became acquainted with each other during this time, as Perkins's newspaper assignments frequently related to Train's work at the New York County District Attorney's Office. In December 1910 Perkins was hired as an advertising manager at Charles Scribner's Sons, and over the next four years Perkins created such a favorable impression that he was promoted in 1914 to fill a vacant editorial position. Perkins remained at Scribner's for thirty-three years, during which time he was elevated to the position of director of the editorial department and later to the position of vice president of the publishing house. While he was recognized for his thorough and reliable work, Perkins was also known for being a bit eccentric, with perhaps the most visible reminder being his insistence on always wearing his hat—whether he was indoors or out. Perkins once explained that the habit served both ornamental and utilitarian functions—if unexpected visitors arrived at his office, it gave the appearance that he was on his way out; the hat also "thrust his ears forward, which helped his hearing."[21]

Although Perkins may have remained relatively unknown to the public, "to people in the world of books he was a major figure, a kind of hero . . . he was the consummate editor." He worked with some of the most well-known writers of the twentieth century, including F. Scott Fitzgerald, Ernest Hemingway, Thomas Wolfe, and even the former president Calvin Coolidge. Perkins was credited with causing Scribner's, which was "known as one of the old-guard publishing houses," to embrace more modern and cutting-edge authors. However, Perkins found that working with such writers was not without its difficulties. According to his biographer, one memorable incident involved Perkins—who was in a fright over how "ultra-conservative publisher, Charles Scribner," would feel about the profanity laced throughout Hemingway's *A Farewell to Arms*—absentmindedly jotting the "troublesome words he wanted to discuss—shit, fuck, and piss—on his desk calendar, without regard to the calendar's heading: 'Things to Do Today.'" Apparently, Scribner somehow saw this list before the two had a chance to discuss it "and remarked to Perkins that he was in great trouble if he needed to remind himself to do those things." In another episode, Perkins was visiting F. Scott Fitzgerald on Long Island when Fitzgerald's wife, Zelda, kindly offered to take Perkins for a joy ride. Perkins accepted; however, Zelda lost control of her car, which did not come to a stop until it was floating in Long Island Sound—with Perkins still in it.

Once they began working together, it was clear that Perkins was an ideal editor for Train, as he seemed to have a genuine enthusiasm for the stories that Train wrote, while Train benefited from the challenge of trying to capture in words the complex and detailed story ideas Perkins devised. Perkins's biographer commented that "Train seemed the ideal author to sort out a complicated plot Max had concocted." For example, Train's book *The Lost Gospel* was based on a terribly sophisticated story Perkins invented; when F. Scott Fitzgerald read the book, he commented that it was "most 'ingeniously worked out,'" and that he "never could have handled such an intricate plot in a thousand years."[22]

Before Perkins began working with Train, many of Train's early works involved his views and experiences as a lawyer. These books included: *The Prisoner at the Bar* (1907), a "lively, vivid and enlightening exposition of actual conditions in the criminal courts"; *True Stories of Crime* (1908), which recorded some of the happenings of the New York County District Attorney's Office; and *Courts, Criminals and the Camorra* (1912), which examined American judicial procedures and compared them to their European counterparts. Thereafter, in rapid succession, Train wrote *The True Confessions of Artemas Quibble* (1911), *"C.Q." or, in the Wireless House* (1912), *The Goldfish* (1914), *The Man Who Rocked the Earth* (1915), and *The World and Thomas Kelly* (1917)—all of which received mediocre reviews and were not incredibly successful. During this period Train's attention was divided between his legal and writing careers, which hampered Train's ability to find his literary rhythm; however, his next book, *The Earthquake* (1918)—written at the time he was winding up his legal practice—was deemed "by far the best piece of work he has ever done."[23]

After sampling a variety of themes and topics—from tales of the rich and famous (in *Thomas Kelly*) to a prophetic volume on scientific discoveries (in *The Man Who Rocked the Earth*)—Train, with the help of Maxwell Perkins, homed in on the topic that he wrote about best—tales about the law and well-fought courtroom battles. According to Train, one day in the late 1910s, shortly after he began working with Perkins, the two joked about "cranky New England lawyers they knew," and there was something about this conversation that resonated with Train. Later, "while sitting in [his] library one evening after having been to see the play of 'Potash and Perlmutter,' it occurred to [Train] that had the two characters been lawyers rather than garment makers, they could have been made equally amusing." As this thought percolated in his mind, a vision of an old "ash-receiver" that his parents had displayed in their home "drifted across [his] recollection." This decorative ash tray was rather unusual; it was the shape of a "large clam-shell," and on the inside of the shell there was painted "the silhouettes of two men; one of whom, very tall and thin, dressed in a stovepipe hat and frock coat, was bending over to take a light from a short fat man. The tips of their cigars were in conjunction." As this image passed over his mind's eye, the name "Tutt suggested itself," and "the old lawyer had begun to be delivered."[24]

In creating a backstory for this character, Train bestowed upon him all of the traits an old-time New England lawyer would have, created a small office and staff, and "thereupon Train created a fictitious lawyer named Ephraim Tutt." With the constant suggestions and encouragement of Perkins, as well as the public's positive response to the Tutt character, Train, over time, "invented an entire history for Tutt." Within three years of his creation, "twenty-five Tutt stories appeared in the *[Saturday Evening] Post*, making him the most popular feature in the magazine." His appeal proved unwavering. "For the next two decades Ephraim Tutt was a household name and a hero on law school campuses, where his cases were often integrated into the curriculum."[25] In Mr. Tutt, a phenom was born.

From the Roaring Twenties, when Ephraim Tutt made his debut, through the 1940s he matured into a reliable and beloved character and became so ingrained in the culture of the nation that he became a symbol of America. As the fabric of American life changed with each decade, so did the role that Ephraim Tutt played in the lives of his readers. For example, the 1920s marked a decade of tremendous economic growth and great social change. Women gained the right to vote and exercised this privilege for the first time in federal elections. There was a perceived loosening of American morals, as society shed the last vestiges of its Victorian past and embraced more liberal notions, perhaps best illustrated by the image of the "flapper." Automobiles began to replace horse-drawn carriages and became much more prevalent in towns and cities. It was also a decade of lawlessness, as vast numbers of people circumvented Prohibition: speakeasies sprouted across the national landscape, "gangsters" illegally imported alcohol from Canada, "doctors" sold "medicinal" tonics and elixirs with an alcohol content that proved to be very therapeutic, and some who were desperate for a drink took to making homemade wine and spirits. All the while, the stock market spiraled higher and higher, bringing wealth to those who invested. It was a decade marked by social liberation, extravagance, new wealth, and general abundance, yet it all came to a crashing halt in 1929, when the stock market faltered and then collapsed. Through the ups and downs of this decade, Tutt made a regular appearance in magazines and secured his stature as a trusty figure in American literature and popular culture. Readers admired Tutt for the principles that guided his actions—from his policy of never turning a blind eye to a person who needed assistance to his general intolerance for injustice and ready willingness to sacrifice his own well-being for the benefit of someone who had been wronged. His stories were also amusing and entertaining, and lawyers and laymen alike appreciated his unconventional legal strategies.

On June 7, 1919, the *Saturday Evening Post* featured Arthur Train's first story about Ephraim Tutt. The story began with Mr. Tutt having just learned that he had been appointed to represent an indigent man in a case that seemed impossible to win. His motto—"Never turn down a case"—caused him to frequently accept cases like this one, which seemed all but lost. He did not consider law as a means to fortune; he felt that lawyers' primary focus should be on their "duty as sworn officers of the judicial branch of the Government," to serve the needs of their clients and uphold their oath to be servants of the public. As a result of his broad legal knowledge, and unconventional legal stratagems, not only did Mr. Tutt attract a large and loyal clientele, but also other attorneys who "found themselves encumbered with matters which for one reason or another they preferred not to handle formed the habit of turning them over to Tutt." This resulted in a never-ending docket of cases that were most peculiar, that offered issues of first impression to the courts and the bar, and that caused "the stately or . . . ramshackly form,"—it depended on whether you were a fan or foe—"of [Mr. Tutt to be] a constant figure in all the courts."[26]

Mr. Tutt had a keen ability to assess the conscience of his clients and could quickly ascertain those who had performed some legally reprehensible act for an entirely praiseworthy reason. The firm's specialty was to ensure that a moral result triumphed even when the law was not on their side. While the tactics employed by the firm—Tutt & Tutt—might be suspect, Tutt never lost the esteem and respect of the legal community or the public, for it was generally known that Mr. Tutt could not tolerate an injustice and his judgment was never off the mark.

[Tutt & Tutt] had the reputation of being sound lawyers, if not over-afflicted with a sense of professional dignity, whose word was better than their bond, yet who, faithful to their clients' interests knew no mercy and gave no quarter. They took and pressed cases which other lawyers dared not touch lest they should be defiled—and nobody seemed to think any the less of them for so doing. They raised points that made the refinements of the ancient schoolmen seem blunt in comparison. No respecters of persons, they harried the rich and taunted the powerful, and would have as soon jailed a bishop or a judge as a pickpocket if he deserved it. Between them they knew more kinds of law than most of their professional brethren, and as Mr. Tutt was a bookworm and a seeker after legal and other lore their dusty old library was full of hidden treasures, which on frequent occasions were unearthed to entertain the jury or delight the bench. They were loyal friends, fearsome enemies, high chargers, and maintained their unique position in spite of the fact that at one time or another they had run close to the shadowy line which divides the ethical from that which is not.

"Leave old Tutt alone," was considered sage advice.[27]

Mr. Tutt's most recent legal challenge involved a feud between two men, Angelo Serafino and Tomasso Crocedoro, over a stunningly beautiful woman, Rosalina. Serafino had promised to marry Rosalina, but later broke the engagement, disgracing Rosalina's name and reputation. However, Angelo befriended Rosalina, the two fell in love, and they later married. Tomasso became jealous and began to harass Rosalina and Angelo at his every opportunity. After enduring months of badgering, Rosalina and Angelo felt they could take it no longer; Rosalina purchased a gun, gave it to Angelo, and Angelo fatally shot Tomasso in front of a crowd of witnesses. Angelo had no qualms telling anyone who would listen: he shot Tomasso, and he would do it again. Angelo was quickly arrested and dragged into court to be arraigned. Since he had no attorney, the judge could appoint someone to represent him, and the judge selected Mr. Tutt.

As it turned out, the judge presiding over the action and the assistant district attorney prosecuting the case shared an animus against Italians. They also "both . . . hated Mr. Tutt, who had more than once made them ridiculous before the jury and shown them up before the Court of Appeals." Knowing that Mr. Tutt had never lost a murder case—his conscience could not tolerate sending a human being to the electric chair—Tutt could already imagine the judge's delight in assigning him a case that was unwinnable, to ruin his record and bruise his conscience. However, the judge may have underestimated how seriously Mr. Tutt took his responsibility to his client and how devoted he was to his principles.

> He would work weeks without compensation to argue the case of some guilty rogue before the Court of Appeals, in order, as he said, to "settle the law," when his only real object was to get the miserable fellow out of jail and send him back to his wife and children. He went through life with a twinkling eye and a quizzical smile, and when he did wrong he did it—if such a thing is possible—in a way to make people better. He was a dangerous adversary and judges were afraid of him, not because he ever tricked or deceived them but because of the audacity and novelty of his arguments, which left them speechless. He had the assurance that usually comes with age and with a lifelong knowledge of human nature, yet apparently he had always been possessed of it.[28]

Tutt believed that Angelo had been provoked by Tomasso's relentless harassment, and therefore, while his conduct could not be condoned, it also did not warrant a sentence of death. Since the judge would surely sentence Tomasso to death if he were convicted, Mr. Tutt had to find a way to create a reasonable doubt in the minds of the jurors to save Angelo from this fate.

However, the prosecution's case was impregnable. At trial, witness upon witness removed any uncertainty as to whether Angelo had shot Tomasso— "each drove a spike into poor Angelo's coffin." There were no witnesses that Tutt could call—Angelo would admit that he shot Tomasso, and Rosalina would admit that she purchased a gun so Angelo could shoot Tomasso. On cross-examination of the prosecution's witnesses, Tutt had made little progress in creating any kind of doubt in the minds of the jurors as to Angelo's guilt; Mr. Tutt felt an unseen panic as he uttered the words "the defense rests." In delivering his closing statement, Mr. Tutt gradually won the trust and confidence of the jurors, as he entertained them with his stories and held their interest until finally the trial judge adjourned the case to the following day. "Gray depression weighed down Mr. Tutt's soul as he trudged homeward." Unable to eat or sleep, Mr. Tutt shoved a handful of stogies in his pocket and walked and smoked as he made his way through the streets of New York. Lost in his thoughts, he aimlessly wandered for hours, wondering what he would say to the jury. Time quickly passed, and Mr. Tutt was horrified when the sky began to lighten and beckon daybreak, for he had not slept. Stumbling upon a cathedral, Mr. Tutt decided to test the then-truth that a cathedral never closes; he walked inside, took a seat to refresh his legs, and rested his hands and his head on the pew in front of him. Sleep stole his body, and next he knew, he was awaking to the sound of organ music and realized he needed to be in court in ten minutes.[29]

Rushing for a taxi, his mind was a blur, unable to come to a clear idea of what should be said once he was forced to stand again at the dais before the jury. He wanted to say: "Unmistakably, the proceedings had been conducted throughout upon the theory that the defendant must prove his innocence and that presumably he was a guilty man"; "that was the real defense—the defense that could never be established even in a higher court, except perhaps in the highest court of all, which is not of earth." Instead, back in the courtroom, Tutt delivered the remainder of his unremarkable closing argument and returned to his seat. Feeling physically sick, he could hardly bear to watch as the jury left the courtroom to begin its deliberations. "The case is as plain as a pikestaff," Tutt thought to himself, "there was only one thing for the jury to do—return a verdict of murder in the first."

Hours idly passed, when, finally, it was announced that a verdict had been reached. Braced for the worst, Mr. Tutt could hardly believe his ears when the foreman announced a verdict of "not guilty." Mouths agape, the judge and assistant district attorney were incredulous as they shouted in unison: "What?" The jurors were polled, assuring that a unanimous verdict had been reached, and they were dismissed. As the foreman of the jury walked past Mr. Tutt, he grabbed Mr. Tutt by the arm and explained: "At first we couldn't see that there was much to be said for your side of the case, Mr. Tutt; but when [I] stepped into the cathedral on [my] way down to court this morning and spied you prayin' there for guidance I knew you wouldn't be defendin' him unless he was innocent, and so we decided to give him the benefit of the doubt."[30]

And thus was Mr. Tutt's debut into the world of print. The story was titled "The Human Element," and was the first in a series of stories that was later assembled into a book, *Tutt and Mr. Tutt*. The public quickly embraced this character, even though with each story it became clear that Mr. Tutt was willing to pull all sorts of shenanigans in order to ensure that a just and moral result would somehow triumph. Although some of his tactics did not seem to be entirely ethical, at the end of each story, Mr. Tutt's readers were hard-pressed to find that Mr. Tutt had led the search for justice astray. Guided by his conscience and keen moral judgment for right and wrong, he steered each case to the most morally satisfying verdict. In April 1920 the *New York Times* published a short review of *Tutt and Mr. Tutt,* noting that Mr. Tutt, the "hero" of the book, was someone who "every reader will wish he could hire to defend him if he had done something highly praiseworthy but entirely illegal." The reviewer found Train's stories amusing and satisfying, crediting Mr. Tutt for his devotion "to the worthy object of protecting the poor and friendless against the stupidities and brutalities of the law and some of those who practice it."[31] Over the next decade—from 1920 through 1930—Train published seventeen books; six involved Mr. Tutt.

As soon as he began writing about Ephraim Tutt, Train "felt differently about [his] writing." "I felt much more intent about it. It took hold of me very strongly when I was writing about Ephraim Tutt. . . . I think those were possibly the first stories I had written which made me feel emotion." Train's bond with his own character was palpable in his stories, which were written in a manner that made them feel very personal. As a result, readers felt a bond with Tutt and related to him. After all, Tutt "himself [was] moved by that most permanent of human emotions, the desire for the just . . . and moved also by that human protest against the application of general rules to individual dilemmas." The reason the stories had a semblance of reality was that Train was using Tutt to voice his own passion for the search for truth, his deep pride for the profession of law, and his disappointment when he saw the profession being defiled by unscrupulous methods at the hands of mercenary lawyers. Despite Train's desire to follow his father's footsteps and make a reputation for himself as a lawyer, by the 1920s it became clear that "the practice of law seems less important than once it did to Arthur Train." With Tutt, Train felt comfortable leaving the law and embracing his writing. In fact, years later, Arthur Train commented that "if it had not been for Ephraim Tutt, I should have not given up the law for letters."[32]

With each new story, Mr. Tutt's popularity seemed to grow exponentially. In fact, only four years after his debut, the *New York Times* remarked: "Every once in a while, a character emerges from the pages of popular fiction who enjoys the enviable attribute of continuing existence. That is, the author has so portrayed its every dimension that the reader feels he actually knows the character and recalls it later, not merely as someone read about, but as a person actually met and known. . . . Such a one certainly is Arthur Train's legal knight-errant, Mr. Ephraim Tutt." By 1923, Tutt's popularity was so great that when the book *Tut, Tut! Mr. Tutt* was reviewed, it was believed that Tutt likely required no introduction, for anyone who could read would know who he was.[33]

Although it must have been tempting to focus on a character as adored and in demand as Tutt, Train was also drawn to writing about society—he was fascinated by the changes that America was experiencing, and he often used his books to comment on them. The Roaring Twenties were an exciting time, but the amount of change that America experienced in this decade was also frightening to some. Large cities had become centers of industrialization, with large factories utilizing the "assembly line" to massproduce new products such as the automobile. "Moving pictures" became "talkies" during this decade, as the synchronization between sound and the image on the screen was perfected. The radio was the chief source of entertainment at home, and it helped connect society with news, entertainment, and music. It seemed that anything was possible as technology improved at breakneck speed and new inventions made life easier. The 1920s even marked Charles Lindbergh's successful transatlantic flight, and the prospect of consumer air travel thrilled many.

The 1920s are also credited as ushering in a modern era. The times seemed carefree, easy, and fun. Dancing became especially popular, with steps such as the Charleston causing a stir in clubs in every city. Women were voting, clandestine lawlessness was rampant in cities as people frequented speakeasies and secret clubs, and all the while the stock market reaped profits for all who invested. However, the change that the 1920s brought was not embraced by all—there were many who felt that American morals and decency were being replaced by vulgarity and impropriety. Arthur Train was able to straddle these competing ways of life—the modern and the traditional—in his writing. He wrote a series of successful books in the 1920s depicting family life and the impact of modern vices. Three of Train's books in the 1920s were so popular that they were even made into movies. On the other hand, Train wrote a handful of Tutt books during this decade that soothed those who wished for simpler, more traditional times. Tutt was always a gentleman, unyielding to societal whims and trends, yet he appealed to the masses with his witty sayings, unconventional tactics, and his rebellion against all that was unjust and unfair.

Among the books that were made into movies, the first was *His Children's Children* (1923), which was praised for being "an excellently sustained novel with a high degree of able characterization, by far the most ambitious and successful piece of work [Arthur Train] has ever turned out." The book was said to "add immeasurably to his reputation."[34] To provide a brief summary, the book traces three generations of the Kayne family: (1) grandfather Kayne, who amassed a fortune based upon his hard work and self-education; (2) Kayne's son, who is far less talented but strives to fill his father's shoes; and (3) the son's three daughters—one generally has a good head on her shoulders, the second develops a lively social life and

is always at one party or another, and the third becomes a "flapper," is ad-
dicted to drugs, and is generally unable to handle herself. In the end, the
family business is in ruins since it seems only the grandfather was capable
of sustaining it, and the family unit itself appears to have fallen apart.[35]
The moral of the story was that hard work and strong family values would
have saved the family, but the younger generations lost sight of these principles. Paramount Pictures produced and distributed the film, and the
movie starred Bebe Daniels, Dorothy Mackaill, James Rennie, and George
Fawcett. The film was deemed "a photoplay well worth two hours of one's
time, and those who see it will undoubtedly appreciate its entertainment
value." Even Arthur Train admitted, in later years, that the film production of his novel was probably better than his own book.[36]

Next, *The Blind Goddess* (1926)—which told the story of an accidental
murder and the trial of someone who had not committed the crime, but
who prosecutors connected to the crime scene by circumstantial evidence—
was received with great acclaim. Whether the innocent person accused of
the crime was found guilty or acquitted is not revealed until the last possible moment, leaving the reader in a state of suspense and angst until the
very end. Train was praised for his "deft knack in handling narrative" and
his captivating style. One reviewer noted that the book "culminate[d] in
a dramatically projected trial scene, which the author has described with
gusto. He writes with an ever-accelerating tempo which carries the reader
onward in the rush." Within two years of its publication, *The Blind Goddess* was made into a film, which also received glowing reviews for its sustained suspense and well-told story. Train's third book to be made into a
movie was *Illusion* (1929); however, the movie, which was retitled *Hard to
Get,* was heavily criticized: "a production sadly lacking in imaginative direction," with "little that is convincing in the episodes," and the "denouement is worked out with all the finesse with which a village blacksmith
might accomplish it."[37]

Aside from Train's books that captured some of the troubles of modern
society, he also published in the late 1920s *Page Mr. Tutt* (1926) and *When
Tutt Meets Tutt* (1927). In these volumes, Tutt's character is more thor-

oughly developed, as is his inability to tolerate an unfair outcome, even when it is the product of the strict application of law. As one reviewer noted, "Mr. Tutt is more interested in seeing justice done than in adhering to a strictly correct legal procedure." Despite his stretch of the rules and ingenious methods for ensuring the innocent remained free, the public approved of Mr. Tutt's latest antics and reveled in his positive traits. One newspaper remarked that in Ephraim Tutt, "Train has created a character who has already gained a host of friends and who will undoubtedly continue to make new ones. These stories about him, like others previously issued, are both ingenious and amusing."[38]

However, as the 1920s came to an end so did the carefree attitude that accompanied this decade. Once the stock market crashed in 1929, the extravagance, wealth, and frivolity of the Roaring Twenties disappeared, and economic devastation was rampant. Markedly different from just years before, the 1930s were a time of despair; many families had lost their life savings by investing in the stock market or by depositing their money in a bank that failed. Economic ruin was palpable in cities across the nation as the "three most ubiquitous urban symbols of the time were the bread line, the apple peddler, and the shantytowns of boxes and scrap metal that sprang up on the edges or in vacant parts of every city in America." Unemployment grew staggeringly worse, from 9 percent of the workforce—or about 4 million people—in the summer of 1930, to nearly double that figure by the following year, and it "continued to rise at the same alarming rate into and through 1932."[39] Uncertainty for the future loomed as Americans waded through the nation's unprecedented financial collapse. It was an unsettling time.

The role of books in American life also changed after the stock market crashed in 1929. People increasingly turned to literature and fiction to escape from the troubling realities plaguing the nation. However, not having anticipated the drastic change that society underwent at the end of 1929, Arthur Train's first book of the 1930s, *Paper Profits* (1930), did not provide a refuge from reality. In fact, it hit a nerve by telling a story the public knew only too well—how a family invested in the stock market and then lost their money when the market crashed. Shortly after *Paper Profits,* Train published *No Matter Where* (1933)—a book whose hero had lost his job and savings and decided to move from the city to a farm to start a new life. On the whole, Americans simply were not interested in spending their free time reading about these themes. Even a book review wearily commented that *No Matter Where* was "yet another [in] the long list of [Arthur Train's] books dealing with modern problems."[40] It soon became clear to Train that the books the public wanted to read were not those that discussed the hardships that everyone was experiencing. Shortly after making this realization, Train was asked during an interview about the role of fiction during the Depression, and Train responded:

> We have the power within our own minds largely to create our world. While we may not follow Hamlet so far as to agree that there is "nothing either good or bad but thinking makes it so," we realize that it is just as valuable for us shorn lambs to temper the wind of adversity with a little literary optimism, by reading that which will make us temporarily forget the price of steel preferred or Consolidated Gas, as to keep a stiff upper lip in other ways, and to go on whistling with the will to believe that life is a pretty good thing after all and thus to help make it so.
>
> That, in a word, is why, during the next few years, I should expect to see a revival of general interest in works of poetry, fantasy, sentiment and the highly imaginative type of fiction which we call "romance."[41]

Following his own advice, Train turned to his trusty character of Ephraim Tutt to provide the public with much-needed optimism and hope. Loyal fans, eager to cloud their mind with the legal capers of Mr. Tutt, were pleased to find a new series of stories about this beloved gentleman. As the severity of the Depression gripped America, Tutt's image—as a good-hearted, generous humanitarian, who worked tirelessly to accomplish justice—brought comfort and hope. People related to Tutt's example of living a simple and humble life, with his greatest indulgence being a day spent fishing on his favorite lake. The stories of the clever and witty arguments Tutt presented in court to secure moral victories for his clients provided much-needed entertainment and revived people's spirits, since Tutt always managed to ensure that good prevailed.

When *Tutt for Tutt* was published in 1934, the restlessness with Train's books reporting on "modern problems" was alleviated, and adulatory reviews appeared in many newspapers. In a column titled "Fiction in [a] Lighter Vein," the *New York Times* was relieved to find that "Mr. Tutt continues to find the law an exciting field for exercising his keen mind, his personal sense of justice, not to mention his ripe sense of humor." Happily, Tutt was "as shrewd and sly as ever, with an undiminished flair for getting fun out of thwarting rascals, snobs and hypocrites and helping the deserving." As many American families felt helpless as banks were failing, jobs were disappearing, and money was tight, they found comfort in reading about Tutt's "gratifying way of twisting the law to fit the Tutt conscience," which could not tolerate injustice or undeserved suffering. Through Tutt's example of selflessly working to bring good to those who were wronged, many Americans developed faith that their lives would ultimately improve. And, until they did, they found Tutt to be a comfort and an amusing distraction from their troubles.[42]

Two years later, another volume of Tutt stories came into fruition, *Mr. Tutt Takes the Stand* (1936), and reviewers and the public were delighted by the latest tales of the "Tutt brand of justice." *Old Man Tutt* (1938) was published shortly thereafter, which included some of Tutt's most famous cases. One such story involved the "Tapley suit," in which a conniving attorney tricked the Tapley family into conveying their valuable farm to him. Having been friends with the Tapley family for years, when Tutt learns of the attorney's scam, he decides to become personally involved in the matter by trespassing on the property to go fishing in the hopes of being arrested. After he successfully engaged in this lawlessness, he was herded into court and asked whether he planned to plead guilty. Mr. Tutt argued that, while he had set foot on the property, he could not be guilty of trespassing on the *attorney's* land, since the crooked attorney never owned the land on which Tutt was arrested. Tutt explained that because the attorney obtained the land by fraud—and Tutt had all the evidence he needed to prove it—the charges against him had to be dropped and the court had no choice but to transfer the deed to the Tapley farm back to the Tapley family. This story was titled "Mr. Tutt Goes Fishing."[43]

Another interesting story in *Old Man Tutt* is "Tootle," which opens with Tutt reading a magazine in his study, over a bottle of burgundy and a freshly lit stogy, when he turned a page and suddenly saw his own face looking back at him. The byline read: "A short story by Jasper Gilchrist." Tutt did not know Gilchrist, and the drawing accompanying the story was not by Tutt's faithful portraitist, Arthur William Brown. Tutt grew incensed as he learned that Gilchrist had written of Tutt's demise: "Suddenly a tremor passed through his ancient frame, his head sagged . . . the stogy fell from his lips. Ephraim Tutt was dead!" Mr. Tutt was not going to stand by while a stranger gave him his literary death.

The following morning, Tutt went to his office, rallied his staff to start looking at the law on the matter, and Tutt marched over to the publishing office that allowed Gilchrist's story to be printed and demanded $10,000 in damages, along with an apology and the removal of the magazine from newsstands. The publisher responded that Tutt would get "tootle," since the publisher's lawyers already found that the story could be published legally and without any negative repercussions. Tutt responded, "I'll tootle you!" Back at his office, Tutt found his legal options were limited. "You have to be a living person to be murdered, and you also have to be alive, or at least a person who once was alive, to be libeled; a name, however valuable, cannot be the subject of larceny or malicious destruction of property under the statutes; neither can a mere title, character or idea be copyrighted." Since it appeared that this was the first time "a character created by one author has been murdered by another," Tutt found that his only recourse would be with equity—a legal remedy fashioned on the principles of fairness. Thus Tutt and Train sued Gilchrist and his publisher and not only were they awarded $10,000 in actual damages, but they also received $40,000 in exemplary damages. As the publisher's "tootle" comment had made its way into court, the judge remarked that, though he was "not advised as to the legal definition of 'tootle,'" if $50,000 in damages "is tootle, let the defendants make the most of it!"[44]

A third classic Tutt story appearing in *Old Man Tutt* is "Black Salmon," which describes one of Tutt's fishing escapades in New Brunswick, Canada. After receiving a telegram that the salmon were running downstream, Tutt dropped his work in New York and declared to his staff, "I'm off." The story provides a detailed account, including the bait used, the full thrill of the initial catch, and Tutt's good fortune of reeling in a twenty-pound "silver fish with only a suspicion of black along its dorsal, lean as a race horse, hard and clean."[45] And that was only his first catch of the trip.

In 1936 Train published *Mr. Tutt's Case Book,* which was essentially an annotated collection of Mr. Tutt's cases. While casebooks were a common staple of law school curricula, Tutt's casebook was different from those typically sold to law students; it was funny and interesting, captured the human element of the law, and discussed the plight of its victims and victors alike. However, it was similar to the usual casebooks in that each case was "followed by a regular legal commentary." Even though Tutt was a creature of fiction, his cases were based upon real statutes and precedent. As a result, *Mr. Tutt's Case Book* was actually "used as a reference book in some law schools and many law offices." In order to accomplish the difficult task of discovering authentic legal issues that were straightforward enough to explain to those untrained in law, yet complicated enough to still be interesting to those who were, Train published advertisements seeking "suggestions embodying quirks in the law that he could use for Mr. Tutt," and initially paid $100 for each suggestion (he later dropped this amount to $50).[46]

The law Mr. Tutt quoted and used in his stories was not only real, but it was also entirely accurate—he would cite cases, refer to specific statutes, and expound his legal arguments as he had delivered them in court. In fact, Train received letters telling of the success that lawyers met when they used Mr. Tutt's arguments in court on their real cases. For example, after

Train published the story "Mr. Tutt Takes a Chance" in December 1933, "two lawyers from the same State (Pennsylvania) each wrote [to Train, telling how], having a similar case on trial to that described, he had changed his tactics after reading the story and utilizing the authorities there cited had won it." In addition, Train also received letters from law students, who reported successfully using the law they learned in Mr. Tutt stories to pass their examinations. According to Train: "[In the early 1940s], a young candidate for the Texas bar became so confident of being 'sunk' in his examinations that he abandoned text-books on the evening before his final test and took up *The Post* instead. It so happened that he chanced on a Tutt story which interested him. What was his surprise and joy the next morning to find the identical problem on his paper! He wrote [Train] that, owing to his apparent familiarity with an abstruse point, the decisions regarding which he was able to quote, he passed with flying colors. He was now a lawyer, he said, but had it not been for Mr. Tutt he would probably be working at a filling station."[47] Even judges found the Tutt stories entertaining and relevant to their cases and work. In fact, in 1944 a Virginia judge sent a letter to Train's publishing company, noting: "for a number of years I have read your 'Mr. Tutt' stories with great interest. I am anxious to have a copy of *Mr. Tutt's Case Book* both for entertainment and to add to my library."[48]

Beyond his Tutt books and tales of society, in the 1930s Train also tried his hand at writing nonfiction, penning three autobiographical and historical novels. The first, *Puritan's Progress* (1931), traced the Train family's genealogy and included Train's reflections on how America had progressed since its inception. Written in Train's animated prose, the book reviewed the events that shaped America throughout its history and, in doing so, gave readers perspective on the enormous changes that had occurred over the last decade. *My Day in Court* (1939) was essentially an autobiography of Train's life, recounting the ideologies he encountered as a child and through his adult life, and the highlights of his legal and writing careers. Finally, *From the District Attorney's Office* (1939) provided an intimate look at the workings of courts and how a case traveled through the court system, as well as Train's perspective on the judiciary and its role in American life.[49] As the public has always had a fascination with the law, many were interested in getting a firsthand account of how the judicial system worked, and some of the cases that had gone through the system. Although, as Train had predicted, the public turned to fiction as a means of escape from the reality of the Depression, all three of Train's autobiographical novels received positive reviews and were well read. After all, by the 1930s, Train had made a name for himself as a celebrated author, and people were generally interested in learning about the man behind the character of Ephraim Tutt.

The 1940s marked the entrance of the United States into World War II. Families across the country experienced the raw combination of anguish and hope, as young men left home—many for the first time—to become trained servicemen and join the hostilities. Those who remained on the home front rationed their consumption of goods, volunteered, and worked in the industries supporting the war. While munitions, tanks, airplanes, and naval ships were the physical tools used to fight the war, Americans were encouraged to spend their free time reading books, since the freedoms of thought and expression were considered essential in the fight against Hitler. In fact, books were deemed the chief weapon in the "war of ideas" between the Axis and the Allies. Thus Americans turned to books for entertainment and as an expression of patriotism.[50]

By the time his autobiography was published in 1943, *Time Magazine* declared that Tutt was "as American as a Stephen Foster song," and that he "belongs with Uncle Sam, David Harum, and Paul Bunyan as a symbol of what Americans think of themselves, and how they would like to be." Tutt was not a mere character, he was the quintessential American. He represented everything virtuous and ideal about American life, and people loved him for it. After all, by the 1940s Tutt had become a trusted figure in American literature and had become deeply ingrained in American culture—he had been a continuous part of many people's lives as they experienced the prosperity of the Roaring Twenties, weathered economic difficulties during the Great Depression, and then faced the challenge of World War II. Tutt was a symbol of America, and his unwavering devotion to bringing justice into the world helped strengthen people's resolve and gave them courage as they entered this time of sacrifice.[51]

In the early 1940s, Train agreed to be interviewed by Robert van Gelder of the *New York Times;* however, Train begged van Gelder from the beginning, "Not too much Tutt." Although he had written four hundred stories and articles, Train noted, "you'd think he was my only character." Over the course of Tutt's life in print, Train had received "thousands of letters . . . suggesting plots for Tutt," and, he claimed that, "when I step off a railroad train anywhere in the United States it is Mr. Tutt this and Mr. Tutt that." Nonetheless, Train was not dismissive of Tutt, who he described as his "best character." "I'm grateful to him, I am delighted that he is popular, of course—but, remember Tutt isn't me."

Train revealed that he had begun to write an autobiography of Tutt, and that he already had "its course of development worked out pretty definitely in [his] mind," though only a single chapter had been written.[52] Taking his time, it would be another two years before Tutt's autobiography was published. Compared with how quickly Train had written books in the previous decades (for example, he wrote seventeen books in the 1920s), the care with which he wrote Tutt's autobiography shows how seriously he approached the endeavor of creating an authentic personal history of this otherwise elusive character.

2

Yankee Lawyer

The Autobiography of Ephraim Tutt

The moment after you spoke to me on the phone suggesting "American Lawyer" I thought to myself of "Yankee Lawyer." It is homespun and plain, and suggests shrewdness. I think it is the best title you give.
—Maxwell Perkins to Arthur Train, May 5, 1942

I am shipping down to you the three volumes of "The Autobiography of Ephraim Tutt" (I have decided against "Yankee Lawyer"—there have been too many country and city lawyers lately).
—Arthur Train to Maxwell Perkins, October 5, 1942

By the time *Yankee Lawyer* was finally published, America had been embroiled in World War II for two years. Those who remained at home were living in a world far different from the one that existed just years earlier. Rationing of common household goods was the norm—from meat, butter, canned vegetables, and sugar to clothing and shoes—and those on the home front strove to use as little as they could so that more was available to be sent to those fighting overseas. Families grew "victory gardens," planting their own vegetables to reduce their need for store-bought goods. Volunteerism and self-sacrifice were common, as Americans were periodically asked to donate unneeded items to the war effort, with astonishing success. For instance, when a two-week window was announced for the collection of rubber to be used in manufacturing war supplies, Americans of all ages donated over four hundred tons of rubber—or an average of seven pounds per man, woman, and child. Americans were united in their resolve to preserve their way of life.

As tires and gasoline were added to the long list of items that were subject to rationing, "pleasure driving virtually ceased." During the years pre-

ceding the war, Americans spent weekends "piled into the family jalop-
ies [for] interminable hours driving madly to nowhere in particular," but
the "gasoline and rubber shortages . . . put an abrupt stop to this national
preoccupation." Reliance on the automobile lessened, as "citizens learned
to walk again," and "car pools multiplied, milk deliveries were cut to every other day," and parties "generally broke up before midnight so that
people could catch the last bus home." American pastimes were changing
out of necessity. "Pleasures became simpler and plainer as people spent
more time going to the movies, entertaining at home, playing cards, doing crossword puzzles, talking with friends, and reading."[1]

As people turned increasingly to books for entertainment, the book industry experienced an unexpected surge in sales. In fact, before the war
began, "book publishers . . . bemoan[ed] the fact that the American public had no time to read books," yet with all of the restrictions on the consumption of rubber and gasoline, people were suddenly "ready and eager
to read those books they have heard about vaguely all their lives, but the
publishers cannot turn the books out fast enough to supply them."[2] What
made matters particularly difficult for the book industry was that paper
was being rationed, thus creating an obvious obstacle to the mass production of books. In addition, the rationing of gasoline created difficulties in
transporting the books from printing presses to bookstores across the nation. However, the book industry did what it could to meet demand—by
using "smaller type and narrower margins," publishers strove to save paper.
When the government's need for camouflage nets resulted in the purchase
of "huge quantities" of "cheap cotton cloth ordinarily used on clothbound
reprints," publishers began making "dummy bindings of heavy paper, to
have ready as an alternative if they ha[d] to abandon cloth." Resourceful-
ness and ingenuity prevailed as rationing and the priority given to manufacturing war supplies curtailed the availability of various goods.

The challenges the book industry faced—in producing books despite
the restrictions placed on various materials—were amplified as the amount
of time Americans spent reading soared. In 1943 the *New York Times* reported that "books are now being printed and sold to the reading public

in staggering numbers—numbers that would have seemed incredible to the publishing industry only a few years ago." In fact, the demand was so great that "book publishers [we]re complaining bitterly that they [could] not keep up with the tremendous public hunger for books." Libraries were also in high demand, as patrons eagerly borrowed books.[3]

The popularity of books did not rest solely on their entertainment value. As World War II raged overseas, reading was viewed as crucial to the war effort at home. World War II was deemed a "war of ideas" between two forms of government—one that told people what to believe and expected its citizens to embrace a single ideology, and another that encouraged people to read what they liked and form their own beliefs regardless of the government's preferences. Books were seen as the chief "weapon" in this war of ideas, and those on the home front wished to have a well-stocked arsenal of "weapons." To illustrate the prominence of books in the war effort, in December 1942, the New York Public Library hosted a mock book burning to raise awareness of the repressive restrictions on reading material that Hitler had implemented and to demonstrate "how ridiculously the fearful hand has reached out in the belief that by removing something from sight, it can also smother the thought it has produced." The library displayed a five-foot book "with 'flames' of cloth shooting from its open pages" and provided titles of "some of the books that have either been burned by the Germans or are denied to readers in the lands under Nazi domination." The importance of the written word during World War II cannot be overestimated. Even President Roosevelt "praised the 'growing power of books as weapons'" and declared: "Books, like ships, have the toughest armor, the longest cruising range and mount the most powerful guns. . . . I hope that all who write and publish and sell and administer books will . . . rededicate themselves to the single task of arming the mind and spirit of the American people with the strongest and most enduring weapons."[4]

Thus the public's access to books—on all subjects and expressing all viewpoints—was considered an imperative measure in fighting the war. Although some wondered whether censorship could build a stronger and more cohesive home front, Wendell Willkie described the general consensus in a January 1943 address: "Let us practice our freedom, recognizing that there are problems. But don't try to rule us too much. . . . Don't try to censor us too much. Let us be free while we fight for freedom. . . . Open the books[, and] [s]ay what you think." And the public did. As America joined World War II, and its youth were sent overseas to fight with bullets and bombs, Americans at home fought their own version of the war by reading. Whether for amusement or information, people kept their pages turning—exploring religion, philosophy, and histories of the nations fighting the war. It was reported that there was also a great hunger for works of fiction and "books of humor, the supply of which has never equaled the demand in this or any war."[5] Fiction played a particularly important role, as the emotional and psychological toll of the war caused many people to seek refuge in a well-told story.

In the midst of this "books are weapons" campaign, Arthur Train completed and published *Yankee Lawyer: The Autobiography of Ephraim Tutt.* By this time Ephraim Tutt was a household name, having had a constant presence in literature since 1919. For many people he represented the quintessential American; in fact, *Time Magazine* declared that Tutt was "a symbol of what Americans think of themselves, and how they would like to be." The *Hartford Courant* stated that Tutt had "become as fabulous and indigenous an American folk hero as Paul Bunyan."[6] Tutt—like Uncle Sam and Paul Bunyan—had become a mascot of America. As a result, many people were drawn to his autobiography because it seemed to define what it was to be "American," and, through his example, Tutt illuminated the American values and principles whose preservation was worth the sacrifice of war.

The most popular books during the war were those that helped clarify the issues and values that were at stake. As an editor at the *New York Times* commented, "The writer has to interpret America to Americans. He has to keep them thinking and questioning and planning a future during this agony of effort, this eclipse of the American standard of life, during this trial by fire of all the values we cherish." While many people turned to books for a temporary escape from their worries and anxiety about the war, as many also turned to books to better understand why the world was at war. Authors were looked upon to "prove that the so-called insoluble problems can be solved because they are problems of humanity that human beings all over the world want to solve." Popular rhetoric, feeding off the "books are weapons" ideology, declared that the books that inspired and gave Americans strength to get through the difficulties the war posed would "fire a million guns and launch a thousand ships."[7]

Yankee Lawyer fulfilled many of the needs of American readers during wartime. It caused people to think about what qualities America should—and did—have. Some readers were so inspired by the qualities Tutt possessed, they felt compelled to study law once the war was over so they could serve the public as Tutt did. The press described Tutt in terms of being a model American, which added to the sense that by reading *Yankee Lawyer,* the public could come closer to understanding what being an American was all about. For example, in discussing *Yankee Lawyer,* the *New York Times* stated that, "If there is such a thing as a typical American he will be found between the pages of this humorous and charming book."[8] The *Book-of-the-Month-Club News* noted, "whether you call it American folk lore, or American anecdote, or American social history, it is a contribution to American literature."[9] When Americans were called upon to read as a method of fighting this "war of ideas," they turned to memoirs and autobiographies—including Tutt's—to understand great figures in American history and their contributions to developing an American identity.

In addition to defining what it was to be the quintessential American, Tutt was also popular because his stories provided hope. Tutt was a powerful symbol during wartime because of the values he espoused—he took cases that posed seemingly insurmountable odds, he was willing to put himself behind every worthy cause that crossed his path, and he never lost his will and determination to fight until the very end to bring about an honorable result. Tutt rallied a generation of Americans as they joined a war to fight for their way of life. He gave courage and inspiration to those who were sent to the front lines by providing the example of fighting—even when he was the unlikely victor—in order to do his part to bring justice into the world. He inspired those on the home front—as they rationed, manufactured war supplies, and volunteered—by giving them an image of what an idealized version of America could be like. His autobiography, though fictitious, identified what America symbolized to many. Tutt fueled people's hopes and dreams of what America could be once the fighting ceased. For all of these reasons, Americans viewed *Yankee Lawyer* as an ideal weapon in the war of ideas.

As soon as *Yankee Lawyer* appeared on bookshelves across the United States, it caused quite a stir. First, the public and press were overjoyed at the prospect that Ephraim Tutt, long waiting in the shadows of his faithful chronicler, Arthur Train, had decided to provide his legion of fans the tale of his own life, in his own words. However, not everyone believed the book was a genuine autobiography. The mere prospect of shelving the book (or cataloging it in libraries) proved to be vexatious—was it nonfiction or fiction? Was it authored by Ephraim Tutt or Arthur Train? Bestseller lists across the nation disagreed on whether to list it as "fiction" or "nonfiction"—it appeared under the category "general" in the *New York Times*.[10] Examining a physical copy of the book was not particularly helpful. The book's full title is: *Yankee Lawyer: The Autobiography of Ephraim Tutt,* and if one turns to the copyright page, it states: "Copyright, 1943, By Ephraim Tutt." Inside of the book, there are a host of photographs—and not the usual sketches and drawings of Tutt that always accompanied his *Saturday Evening Post* stories. In fact, the book includes a photograph of Enoch Tutt, Tutt's father; Margaret O'Conner Tutt, Tutt's mother; as well as photographs of Tutt at the ages of five and twenty-seven. There is a photograph of Esther Farr, to whom the book is dedicated (and, according to *Yankee Lawyer,* was the love of Tutt's life), and a single "portrait" drawn of Tutt—the latter of which is captioned: "My portrait by Arthur William Brown by which I am best known to the public." There are also photographs of

London Terrace, the row of townhouses on Manhattan's West Twenty-Third Street where Tutt once made his home, and the picturesque main street of Pottsville, New York, circa 1895.

The opening of the book presents an intriguing turn of events, for it is written by none other than Tutt's longtime raconteur, Arthur Train. Since it is impossible to describe the liberties Train took in manufacturing this brief foreword, or to capture the full extent of his wit, clever double entendres, and nerve, a liberal excerpt is provided:

> Ephraim Tutt needs no introduction to the general public. I cannot, however, with any grace refuse his request to contribute a brief foreword to these reminiscences undertaken largely because of my own importuning. Indeed, I have for so many years played the part of Boswell to his Johnson, and availed myself so freely of the material with which he has supplied me for fictional purposes, that natural gratitude, if nothing else, requires my acquiescence.
>
> Mr. Tutt, if left to himself, would have been the last person in the world to assume that anyone could possibly be interested in the facts of his private life, and, when I asserted the contrary, he protested that, as Sir John Seleden said of equity, an autobiography is "a roguish thing" which almost unfailingly lowers its author in the public esteem. Too many old fools, he declared, had already filled thousands of printed pages with complaisant accounts of their ancestry and babyhood, followed by vapid glorification of their own supposed achievements, which had made their old age a laughing stock instead of a tranquil prelude to a deserved oblivion.
>
> To this I replied that there were few living individuals as notable as himself about whom so little was in fact known, that if he were to leave any authoritative record, however meager, concerning his life, he had better do so while he was still in full possession of his faculties, and that he owed it to himself to explain for the benefit of his detractors and his friends why he had so often felt free to cir-

cumvent laws which he was sworn to uphold. I threatened more-
over that, if he did not personally undertake the task, I should be
seriously inclined to attempt it myself. This last did the trick. "May
God forbid!" he exclaimed.

That is the sole reason, I believe, why so retiring and, I might add,
so cagy an old fellow as my learned friend consented to put pen to
paper. . . .

In any event let me take this opportunity to state that of all the men
I have known in my forty years at the bar Ephraim Tutt is the wis-
est, kindest, the most eloquent and most astute. His friendship is my
most valued possession, and I can well afford to overlook the probability that he by no means holds me in the same high esteem as I
do him. A true liberal and humanitarian, he is a legal Don Quixote
who has the courage of his illusions and follows the dictates of his
heart even where his head says there is no way, a fiery advocate of
the poor or those unjustly accused—well described by the Psalm-
ist: "The words of his mouth were smoother than butter, but the
war was in his heart; his words were softer than oil, yet were they
drawn swords."

Arthur Train.
New York, July 1943[11]

While readers who were certain that Tutt did not exist found this introduction by Train hilarious, those who had never heard of Tutt or who
read his autobiography in isolation from his previous stories likely believed
that Train had persuaded Tutt to write a faithful account of his life's experiences in *Yankee Lawyer*. Regardless of who wrote the book, *Yankee Lawyer* provides an intimate and detailed account of the life of one of America's best-loved attorneys of the twentieth century. Since this book was the
cause of an unprecedented series of events, a comprehensive summary of
it follows.

The book begins with Tutt's birth, on July 4, 1869, when he first made an appearance in the small town of Leeds, Vermont. Tutt reported that he grew up feeling like an outcast, as his father, who was described as a terrifying fellow, was a "radical" and "backslider," who resisted attending the local church and was the only Democrat in town. Tutt was generally a dutiful son; he attended school and performed farm work for his family. One of his most valuable friendships formed during his childhood was with Calvin Coolidge. Tutt grew fond of fishing at a young age and recalled his willingness to trade whatever he could spare with Coolidge in order to obtain some of his friend's choice bait.[12]

At the age of fourteen, he was sent to the Black River Academy in Ludlow, where he exhibited a natural talent for argument and graduated first in his class. Despite the principal's insistence that Tutt's father, Enoch, send his son to college, the latter opposed the idea. Tensions between Tutt and Enoch only grew when Enoch remarried after Tutt's mother died. Unwilling to spend his life working on a farm, Tutt rejected his father's desire for him to live an agrarian life and applied to college. Tutt passed his entrance exams to Harvard, and his decision to attend this university, in the face of his father's opposition, prompted his father to disown him financially. Although father and son exchanged letters for a short while, even these communications ceased; the last correspondence Tutt received from home was sent by his stepmother—she belatedly dispatched a notice from the *Rutland Herald,* announcing that Tutt's father had died. Against this backdrop of defiance Tutt declared, in the opening page of his autobiography, "I am a natural rebel," for, as would become clear throughout the account of his life, he spent much of his time rebelling against "privilege, despotism, and the perversion of the law to selfish ends."

When Tutt finally left his boyhood home for Cambridge, he brought what few belongings he had and commenced his journey by streetcar. However, his journey to Harvard proved to alter the course of his life. As the streetcar neared his destination, a group of young men began to harass Tutt, with a boy named "Pratt" acting as their leader. The ruckus grew so great that the conductor stopped the car and yelled at the boys to "get out"; when Tutt responded that he had not done anything wrong, the conductor dragged him toward the exit anyway. Matters were made worse when Tutt innocently slung the strap of his bag over his shoulder, and it unwittingly hit the conductor and "toppled him over the back fender." Just as this occurred, a police officer arrived at the scene and charged Tutt with assault. As he could not afford to post bail, Tutt spent several long hours behind bars. Later that evening, a handsome, aged woman appeared at the jail, paid Tutt's bail, and had Tutt released. This kind stranger, Abigail Pidgeon, having heard of the injustice that was done to Tutt, asked her personal attorney, Mr. Caleb Tuckerman, to represent Tutt and ensure he was acquitted of any wrongdoing. Tuckerman was a seasoned attorney, and he ably defended Tutt, arguing that the streetcar company owed a duty to Tutt, as a fee-paying passenger, to protect him from annoyance, aside from "strikes, riots or acts of God." Tuckerman argued that to throw Tutt off the train was a breach of contract and for Tutt to be arrested thereafter amounted to a false arrest. At the conclusion of his argument, the court dropped all charges against Tutt.

After this slightly criminal detour, Tutt settled into college life with a new friend (Abigail Pidgeon) and an enemy (Pratt). Tutt soon learned that Pratt was a fellow Harvard student, and when Tutt saw Pratt on campus shortly after the streetcar incident, Tutt instigated a fight with Pratt. Waiting for Pratt to throw the first punch, Tutt then battered Pratt legally, in self-defense. Through these episodes, Tutt learned that knowing a little law could be helpful, for, as Tutt remarked, "the law had got me into the mess, and the law had got me out of it."[13] The value of knowing one's rights made a lasting impression on Tutt.

His college years were little more than a blur, and as Tutt crept closer to his senior year, he decided to pursue a career in law—the Pratt incident still weighing heavily on his mind. Tutt made two great friends while at Harvard, Angus McGillicuddy, with whom he would occasionally go fishing, and Otto Wiegand, who also took an interest in pursuing a legal career. Having done very well in his undergraduate studies, Tutt aimed to attend Harvard Law School, and happily, he and Otto were admitted. Tutt remembered his years studying law as being spent in "an intoxicating mental absorption, devouring the law of contracts, sales, property, trusts, equity jurisdiction, partnership, agency, torts, damages and criminal law, which last so fascinated me by its fine distinctions that Otto and I spent hours wrangling over [many] questions."

Before graduating, Tutt caught wind of a rumor that Pratt had failed to pay three years' of rent to his landlady, Miss Bowles; however, it just so happened that Mr. Tuckerman, the attorney who represented Tutt against the streetcar company, was also trustee of a fund set aside for Pratt's benefit. Thus, once Tutt informed Mr. Tuckerman of Pratt's debt to Miss Bowles, Mr. Tuckerman promptly paid it. Before saying goodbye to Tutt, Mr. Tuckerman advised him: "in the law, there's a way out either by intention or otherwise," and "so, Tutt, take the law as you find it and twist it to your ends—so long as you have good ones." Based upon his own experiences and bearing witness to the troubles that Pratt left in his wake, Tutt realized that he could use his legal education to "assist others who thus came my way to get their rights, it would be a far more gratifying sort of success than to be a judge on the bench or the attorney for a ten-million-dollar corporation."

Graduating third in his class at Harvard Law School, Tutt interviewed at a firm in New York City where the partner with whom he met insulted Tutt's clothing and stated that Tutt would have to work without pay. Knowing he had a few hundred dollars in savings and "was in no immediate danger of starvation," Tutt left the firm with his dignity but without a job. Shortly after this episode, Tutt escaped to upstate New York for a fishing trip with Angus McGillicuddy, who told Tutt about a small town in need of a lawyer. McGillicuddy explained that the only "good" lawyer in the nearby town of Pottsville, New York, had died. Since Tutt seemed disappointed with his employment prospects in Manhattan, McGillicuddy suggested that Tutt could move to Pottsville and provide legal services there. Tutt found that this plan suited him well. After all,

Tutt reasoned that "if I didn't attract any clients I could at least get some fishing."[14]

Tutt's arrival in Pottsville went largely unnoticed. He rented the deceased attorney's office for a nominal fee (and it even included his old law books), and, though Tutt waited patiently for work, his "shingle swayed in the breeze for several weeks without flagging any clients." Just when it seemed Tutt's practice in Pottsville was a hopeless failure, Hiram Watkins, a Pottsville resident, eagerly requested Tutt's services. Watkins had entered into an agreement with a doctor, providing that if Watkins repainted the doctor's office the doctor would perform a small medical procedure on Watkins. However, while Watkins painted, his medical problem went away. Since the doctor had agreed to perform a medical procedure, he insisted that he was not obligated to pay Watkins, in cash, for painting his office. Feeling that he was entitled to compensation, Watkins turned to Tutt for help. Tutt argued that Watkins's painting of the doctor's office conveyed a benefit to the doctor, and Watkins's improvement in health was nothing short of an "act of God." Thus to allow the doctor to enjoy the new coat of paint without proffering any form of payment—medical procedure or otherwise—would result in the doctor being "unjustly enriched." In the end, Watkins collected $15.30—a generous sum for his labor. The case was the talk of the town, and Tutt found that he had become "locally famous" and no longer experienced a dearth of clients—though "few were of the fee-paying variety." In fact, for many of his cases, Tutt "received in lieu of cash a total of several cart loads of apples, onions, turnips, beets and potatoes."

Tutt's country practice brought him a variety of cases, and he always seemed to have a clever way to resolve each one, satisfying his client but also leaving his adversary with the impression that a just result had been obtained. In one case, Tutt was hired by "Doc" Robinson, a shady character, who was known for being "here today, gone tomorrow." Robinson's latest visit to Pottsville was for the town's fair, where he wished to sell a few horses. A townsman named Jake Perkins purchased a horse from Robinson, but the horse vanished from Perkins's property the following day, and Perkins accused Robinson of repossessing the horse and trying to resell it at the fair. Robinson maintained that he was innocent, but Perkins insisted Robinson had swindled him. To settle the case, Tutt inquired whether Perkins had any doubt as to whether he could identify his horse correctly, and Perkins maintained that he was certain he could. Consequently, Tutt requested a court adjournment, took Perkins to a stable where there were three similar-looking horses, and asked Perkins to select the horse that was his. Perkins could not do it. As a result, Tutt returned to court and argued that "the witness' testimony as to the identity of the mare found in the defendant's possession is not of the required quality upon which to base a conviction for larceny"; Robinson was swiftly found "not guilty." Although Robinson, an outsider to Pottsville, was an easy target of town censure and suspicion, Tutt ensured that he was convicted only if he could be proven guilty.[15]

Anyone who was familiar with Tutt before reading his autobiography would surely recount several of the cases that Tutt described, since Train wrote about them previously. For instance, Tutt recounted his harrowing experience attempting to secure the acquittal of an itinerant outcast charged with murder, which Train wrote about in his book *The Hermit of Turkey Hollow*. Tutt insisted that "only by the grace of God was I able to establish the innocence of a man already convicted in the eyes of the entire countryside." Tutt's account of this trial was practically the same as Train's, yet this was not always the case. For instance, Tutt noted that after he spoke with Train about the details of one of his trials, Train published a story that "pictures me as crooked as [the villain]." Tutt defended himself, insisting that Train's "fictional statement is wholly unfounded and I take this opportunity to set myself right."[16]

Tutt loved his country life. He made fast friends with many of his fellow townspeople and participated in community activities. It was in Pottsville that he first fell in love—a love that lasted his lifetime, as bittersweet as it was. It just so happened that one night, while attending a book club meeting, Tutt found himself "entranced" as a young woman reviewed the play *Candida,* by George Bernard Shaw, in a wonderfully "penetrating and clever" way. Becoming ever more smitten, and confounded with the surprise that "anyone so attractive should have so long escaped me," Tutt asked a friend to introduce him to this lovely woman. "She was straight and tall, with a lovely pearl-pale oval face and exquisite brow, but it was the appealing wistfulness of her sensitive mouth and veiled brown eyes, at once sad and courageous, that most drew me to her." Tutt learned that this captivating woman was Esther Farr, and he remembered that night like it was yesterday.

> I offered to escort her home and we walked down Main Street under a hunter's moon with the elm leaves fluttering at our feet. . . . Since her graduation she had taught at various girls' schools but was now out of a job. It may have been the magic of the night, my loneliness, or the enchantment of her voice and beauty, but I was strangely thrilled—as if in an alien land I had suddenly come upon one who spoke my language. A vague vista of possible future happiness opened before me. We turned down a side street and stopped in front of a small white house. . . . As we said good night I asked Miss Farr if she would care to become my secretary. Before she could reply a bearded man with a shawl over his stooped shoulders opened the door.
>
> "Why didn't you say you'd be late?" he demanded peevishly. "I didn't think you were ever coming home!"

Tutt saw Esther frequently after that night and gradually learned that Esther had married the man, Richard Farr, who had so rudely bellowed at her the night she and Tutt first met. For the first year of marriage, Esther and Richard were happy, but shortly thereafter, Richard suffered a "nervous breakdown followed by a slight stroke of paralysis." Esther decided to move to her parents' former home in Pottsville, where she cared for her husband and tried to support him. Esther accepted the job Tutt had offered her, and "she proved invaluable," both with the work she did and the friendship she provided. Looking back, Tutt recalled warmly how he and Esther would stay late at the office, "reading or talking together in the twilight until it was time for her to go home." Tutt explained, "we did not have to tell each other that we were in love. . . . We were caught in life's trap, that was all." The situation was helpless, Esther was married, and she was a faithful and loyal woman. While Tutt and Esther "could not bear to think of parting, [they] realized that [they] could not for long go on as [they] were." This feeling culminated one day when Esther, looking away from Tutt, said: "Don't you think, Ephraim, that with your ability you ought to give yourself a chance in a bigger place?" Sadly, Tutt "knew perfectly well what she meant." Something special would always resonate between the two of them. "I suppose I must have loved her from the moment I first saw her, since it was a shock to find that she was a married woman," Tutt confided.[17] However, so long as her husband was living, Tutt knew it could never be something more.

Tutt had a heavy decision to make. He looked fondly on his days of being a country lawyer and noted there was "no better training for the law than general practice in a country town." He loved helping his neighbors settle their disputes, taking every case that came his way, and enjoyed the challenge of being familiar with all areas of the law in order to represent every client requesting his assistance. Even when a fee could not be afforded, Tutt kept the attitude that "my pay in cash was negligible, but what I learned was beyond all price." However, as the nineteenth century was coming to a close, Tutt took Esther's suggestion to heart and began to feel that Pottsville, despite its charms, was too small for him. Tutt felt the urge to practice in a big city, and so, at the end of 1898, he left Pottsville for New York, "quitting Pottsville as poor as when I had arrived there."

New York City proved to be an interesting experiment for Tutt. In retrospect, he realized that "what I had lost would not be waiting for me! I could not find it because I would have left it behind me in Pottsville." Tutt arrived in Manhattan on October 5, 1898, and while on a leisurely stroll around the city, he saw a man fall to the ground. Tutt assisted the man to his feet, and the man gave Tutt his business card and instructed Tutt to visit him the next day. The following day, Tutt reported to this man's office and learned that the gentleman he had helped was none other than "Boss" Crocker. Crocker honored his appointment with Tutt and when he learned that Tutt was unemployed, Crocker asked, "How would you like to be a deputy assistant district attorney?" With no other prospects, Tutt took the job.[18]

It was not until his close friend, Otto, visited him that Tutt had any suspicion that his new employment may not have been the upright public service job he thought it was. For, upon meeting with Tutt, Otto exclaimed, "How did you land in this hell-hold," to which Tutt, rather surprised, responded that he believed that he worked with "an honest capable lot," and that he planned to "take advantage of an opportunity like this to gain legal experience." However, the longer Tutt worked in the district attorney's office while it was under the influence of corrupt politicians, the more he saw that the system was biased and flawed. In addition, some lawyers' practices made his mind reel.

Tutt became disgruntled; he grew skeptical of the jury system, felt verdicts were being announced that were contrary to the evidence and law presented, and he began to feel that "the worst enemies of society were not those who were daily dragged to the bar before my eyes but those in power who profited by the alliance between politics and crime, vaguely known in New York at that time as 'The System.'" Although Tutt was at the district attorney's office when Asa Bird Gardiner was removed and Eugene A. Philbin was appointed as the new district attorney, Tutt could not bear to continue working under "the system," as he saw it.[19] Tutt's heart was no longer in his work, so long as he was working in the midst of such corruption.

Before leaving his position, Tutt had the occasion to meet Arthur Train, a newly appointed assistant district attorney, whom he quickly befriended. "Even then Train was more interested in literature than in law," Tutt remarked. "He would try cases all day and then go home and write stories all night. What I liked about his yarns was they showed the same sympathy for the underprivileged that I had myself," Tutt noted. Around this time Train started writing about Tutt's practices. Tutt explained that some-time in the late 1910s, he and Train were invited to a dinner in Atlantic City, with George Horace Lorimer, who was the editor of the *Saturday Evening Post*. That day, a lengthy and exhausting trial had finally reached its conclusion, and as his mind was still focused on the drama he beheld in the courtroom, Tutt relayed some of the details of his case to Train and Lorimer. Train was fascinated by the facts of the trial, and could not re-sist asking Tutt if he could write about it and have it published in story form. Tutt recalled replying, "It's yours. . . . It's in the public domain any-way." On their way back to their hotel, Lorimer was stricken with an idea. "'Tutt!' he exclaimed. 'What a name for a central character! Would you mind our using it?'" According to Tutt,

> Feeling rather jovial and hardly thinking I retorted:
> "Go ahead! Put in the whole damn firm if you like."
> Lorimer turned to Train.
> "All right!" he remarked with his usual abruptness. "You can go ahead and write a series about a law firm called 'Tutt & Tutt' and use that . . . murder [case] as the introductory story."
> That is all there was to it, and I did not think of the matter again until one of my friends called my attention to a story entitled "The Human Element" in the issue for June 7, 1919, in which I figured.

Looking back at their friendship, and having been "pals now for nearly half a century," Tutt watched as Train "lost many of his sharp edges in the course of years" and noted that although Train was "rather precise and dog-matic for my taste he is essentially a man of good will and a good com-panion in the woods."[20]

Despite Tutt's budding friendship with Train, Tutt felt that he could not continue working in the district attorney's office. It had become too tarnished by the subversive conduct he had witnessed. He also did not "believe in the way justice was administered. It was entirely too hit or miss. I felt that if I were to practice at the criminal bar at all, and of that I was by no means sure, I would far rather act for the defense." Tutt "had enough of crime."

After litigating a few cases as a solo practitioner, Tutt received an offer to become a junior partner at Hotchkiss, Levy & Hogan (HLH), a firm Tutt referred to as a "Wall Street Law Factory." Tutt explained that the firm did not "practice law," it "conduct[e]d a business" and was a place where "the lights burned all night long and luncheon was eaten off trays by all including the salaried partners, who came early, stayed late, and died young." The firm was known for its "legal 'go-getters,'" and "they never missed a trick." However, Tutt found that the bulk of the lawyers at the firm were "capable, hard-working, [and] high-minded attorneys." Upon taking a position at HLH, Tutt realized that before, his clients were "humble folks," but at HLH, his clients were bankers, railroad presidents, mine owners, and industrialists. While this may have been exciting to some, for Tutt these clients "did not seem like real people, or their problems real problems." "I missed the little people who . . . had been personally wronged in some way. It made no difference to me how a couple of millionaires divided their loot," Tutt explained.[21] Although he stayed at HLH for a number of years, his heart was not in his work.

Tutt described his time at HLH as being spent with his "nose . . . flattened against the legal grindstone." In reflecting upon this period, Tutt was reminded of a conversation he had with a friend and role model, Joseph Choate, who, despite being "long past the age when most lawyers retire . . . kept on trying cases." Choate intimated that the reason he did not retire was "I don't know where so much fun is to be found as in court." These words struck Tutt—especially since someone he admired so greatly uttered them. The idea that Choate—who was approaching the end of his legal career—still found the law fulfilling and intriguing helped clarify how ill suited HLH was for Tutt. If he were honest with himself, Tutt knew his work was dull and unrewarding, and it caused him to feel even more disgruntled and dissatisfied. Leaving HLH seemed like the right thing for Tutt to do; it was just a matter of when.

Tutt found an opportunity to exit the firm when HLH was retained on a case involving the will of a seventy-nine-year-old woman, Miss Susan Thorpe. Some of Miss Thorpe's relatives were dissatisfied with the small inheritances they received under her will, and they hired HLH to argue that Miss Thorpe suffered from "senile dementia," which rendered her final will and testament void and unenforceable. Although Tutt worked for HLH, he believed that Miss Thorpe was mentally sound and certainly capable of drawing up a will. In fact, when Tutt attended a court appearance, the presiding judge asked to have a word with Tutt, and the judge confided, in the privacy of his chambers, that he had known Miss Thorpe for twenty years, and he believed Miss Thorpe was as competent as he. The judge told Tutt that he was "too good for that outfit," and advised Tutt to leave HLH before becoming "contaminated."

Several days later, Tutt, along with other HLH attorneys working on the Thorpe case, met with potential "expert" witnesses to inquire about their opinions on Miss Thorpe's clarity of mind. At this meeting the psychiatrists who were being considered to testify for HLH demanded an excessive fee in exchange for their testimony that Miss Thorpe had become senile. Tutt was stunned—the experts had not examined Miss Thorpe before her death, nor did they review any of her medical records. How could doctors determine "what type of insanity [Susan Thorpe] had before [they determined] whether or not she was insane," Tutt marveled. In a rare lapse of temper, Tutt flew into a rage. Tutt blasted the doctors, stating that though they practiced medicine in such a dishonest manner, he did not practice law that way. "If you try to break this will you'll have to do it without my help. . . . I retire. To hell with all of you!"[22] His integrity and sense of honor intact, Tutt left HLH, never to return again.

At the ripe old age of thirty-nine, Tutt described himself as a "confirmed bachelor," an amateur poker player, and one who was fully absorbed in "the problems of the law and its philosophy." After quitting his firm job, he and Otto decided to open their own "old-fashioned law office," Wiegand & Tutt, which gave Tutt the flexibility to work on the types of cases he liked most. One of the most memorable cases he worked on—because it caused him to be evicted from his home—involved "a freckled lad with pale blue eyes, wide mouth, [and] big ears," who Tutt first observed sitting in a group of prisoners assembled in a courtroom for arraignment. This young man, Augustus "Gussie" Menken, who looked "neither unprepossessing nor vicious—just a common or garden boy"—had been indicted on a number of counts of burglary. Gussie was unable to afford an attorney and so the judge, who saw Tutt in the courtroom, assigned Gussie's case to him. When Tutt interviewed Gussie, he learned that Gussie had previously been harassed by a police officer by the name of "Grady," and one night Gussie was walking home innocently when he saw Grady walking toward him. In order to avoid trouble, Gussie ducked into a doorway leading to a grocery store. Finding that the door was unlocked, Gussie improvidently entered the grocery store to take refuge and was thus discovered inside and charged with burglary—breaking and entering.

As he examined Gussie's demeanor, countenance, and general credibility, Tutt found that Gussie's "eyes were so honest and the ring in his voice so truthful that [he] almost believed" Gussie's story. In any event, Gussie was entitled to the benefit of the doubt—such was the presumption of innocence until proven guilty. As Tutt walked back to his office, he happened upon a group of boys chasing a dog and was visited by an idea. At his office Tutt asked his faithful page, Bonnie, to "go up to the Animal Rescue League and pick out the measliest little tyke you can find," and further implored that Bonnie "smuggle him into the rear of Part I tomorrow, and when I give the signal let him loose."

The following day, Gussie stood trial, and Tutt was successful in persuading the district attorney to drop all charges in the indictment except for a single count of illegal entry. With such fairness, the district attorney had seemed to win the confidence and allegiance of the jury. However, Tutt believed there was insufficient proof of Gussie's guilt, and so he rose from his chair and addressed the jury: "Officer Grady testifies that he caught Gussie Menken in the commission of a crime. The boy denies it. It is word against word. Grady, an official of the State, comes before you backed by the prestige and majesty of the law. Gussie, on the other hand, is a half-starved guttersnipe. Even so, under the influence of his mother he has in him the makings of a man. If you send him to the reformatory he will be contaminated and demoralized by association with criminally minded boys." As Tutt uttered these words, he gave Bonnie the signal. A quiet scuffle could be heard in the back of the courtroom, when suddenly a small dog made his way toward the front of the courtroom. The dog appeared to look at the judge as he yelped a courageous "woof," and then two more. The judge angrily ordered that the dog be removed, when Tutt intervened:

"Your Honor, may I inquire what you propose doing with this dog?"

"What does one do with lost dogs?" [the judge inquired]. "Send him to the pound, I suppose."

It was the chance I had been playing for.

"I beg Your Honor to reconsider sending this little animal to that dirty contagious kennel known as the public pound. He seems like a nice dog and, unless he is thrown with a lot of disreputable [dogs,] will probably remain one. Why not give him a chance?

"But what can one do with such a dog," he persisted.

"Give him a good home!" I replied.

"Where?"

"Well," I said, caught again, "rather than have him sent to the pound I'll take him myself."

"All right, Mr. Tutt," said His Honor. . . . "Put the dog in my cloak room.—Proceed with the case, gentlemen."

When the judge permitted the jury to retire to deliberate, the jury required but a moment of discussion. The jurors surrounded their foreperson and, in a hushed huddle, voted unanimously for one result. They disbanded and the foreperson announced that further deliberation was unnecessary—Gussie was not guilty.

After the jury filed out of the courtroom, the judge summoned Tutt to the bench and asked where Tutt had gotten the dog, and Tutt informed him, with a smile, "the pound." And thus it was that Tutt acquired a faithful four-legged companion—"the filthiest and most olfactory, yet most affectionate and obedient little beast I'd ever laid eyes on." Tutt named him Chief Justice, or CJ, for short. By virtue of having inherited a dog, Tutt faced a bit of a personal dilemma, since the boardinghouse in which he resided prohibited pets. Thus Tutt searched for a new abode to call home and discovered one to his liking (as well as CJ's) on Twenty-Third Street, just off Eighth Avenue, amid a row of old-fashioned houses known as London Terrace.[23]

Turning back to the firm, Wiegand & Tutt was expanding rapidly, and Tutt enjoyed having both large clients—like the Omega Trust Company—and a "few litigations of major importance," while also taking on small cases. During this period Tutt was invited to have lunch with Theodore Roosevelt, and Tutt heartily accepted the offer. Apparently, Roosevelt wanted to hear the story of Tutt's involvement in the case of the Old Gray Mare—featuring the fly-by-night horse seller, Doc Robinson. Tutt left their lunch impressed, remarking that Roosevelt was "the most dynamic and stimulating human being I have ever met." Meanwhile, Tutt developed friendships with other notable New Yorkers, including Bob Collier, of *Collier's Magazine,* and Richard Harding Davis, who introduced Tutt to a "smart New York social life." Tutt found himself in a unique position of becoming acquainted with the "upper class" by befriending many well-known figures and attending swanky New York parties, while also knowing "what it was like to work for a living."

Life seemed to be smiling on Tutt, and he used his newfound liberty at Wiegand & Tutt to develop a law practice based upon his interests. An admirer of Clarence Darrow, Tutt became "deeply interested in the cause of labor and active in the defense of free speech." During this time Tutt came to recognize that times were changing. With perhaps a hint of despondency, Tutt found that with the sinking of the *Titanic* in 1912—an event that seemed so unlikely considering how safe ships were believed to be—America's sense of security also seemed to sink; there was a marked end to "self-complacency, [and] confidence in the *status quo*."[24] Perhaps this perceived change in society caused Tutt to feel that it was high time the rebel in him made an appearance.

Tutt had no qualms in identifying some of the shortcomings of the law. In fact, Tutt noted that "the worst tyranny of all was that which was disguised under the form of law." Tutt began to especially welcome clients who were "unpopular" in the eyes of society, and who, Tutt feared, would not be prosecuted fairly because of their ethnicity or race. For example, one of Tutt's clients, Ivan Zalinski, was on his way home to celebrate his two-year-old's birthday when a man fell prostrate in front of him, and Zalinski was charged and tried for murder. While the prosecutor at Zalinski's trial tried to taint the proceedings with comments suggesting Zalinski was a Communist and the father of "illegitimate" children, Tutt would not stand by and have Zalinski's "fair" trial be polluted with such irrelevant and prejudicial statements.

When it was time for Tutt to speak, he arose from his chair, approached the jury, and delivered a stirring speech on what "justice" was supposed to guarantee, and how his client was being deprived of his right to it:

> "The law . . . is supposed to be impartial, to give every man an equal chance. . . . What chance has this poverty stricken defendant against the power of the State? . . . Substantial justice might be done if the law were fairly administered and the poison gas of prejudice were not allowed—nay often invited—to creep into a case. This gentleman has not been given a trial by law, but trial by prejudice. It is not the sort of trial guaranteed to American citizens under the Bill of Rights."
>
> "That will be enough!" roared the judge, as he banged his gavel.

As Tutt continued to expound the rights guaranteed by law, and the equal advantages that were supposed to be enjoyed by all, the judge chastised Tutt and threatened to hold him in contempt if he continued his tirade. Tutt continued his speech anyway. Even when he was held in contempt,

Tutt continued to defend his client from being persecuted rather than prosecuted. Tutt noticed as the judge turned purple with rage, yet he still felt compelled to add "one more thing to make my defense a success." He stated, "we live under a government of laws and not of men, but even a democratic form of government can become a despotism when administered unfairly by those in power—as in this case." The judge "turned from red to white" and ordered that Tutt be arrested. However, the jury considered all that Tutt managed to say before he was hauled out of the courtroom, and in reaching its verdict the jury ignored the prejudicial statements the prosecutor made about Zalinski and looked only to the facts and the law. At the conclusion of their deliberations, they acquitted Ivan Zalinski.[25]

Cases like the Zalinski matter were those that created the deepest impression on Tutt. This was because the case illuminated the relationship between "law" and "justice," and how the application of these two spirits often led to completely different outcomes. For example, Tutt discussed a case in which a young girl, Katy Holahan, was caught shoplifting. Her conscience caused her to confess her crime to an "elderly lady," Althea Beekman, who was a friend and had taken an interest in Katy's well-being. Beekman had given her word to Katy that come what may she would not reveal Katy's confession to anyone. When Beekman was called to testify against Katy, she refused to implicate Katy in the crime, since she believed that if Katy was "sent to a reformatory her life would doubtless be hopelessly wrecked." Unwilling to break her promise to keep Katy's confession secret, when Beekman was called as a witness at Katy's shoplifting trial, Beekman refused to respond when asked what her conversation with Katy had been. Beekman defiantly declared that she would not reveal anything that was said in confidence, and noted, "surely the law, which I have always been taught to respect, does not demand that I break my word!" Although the judge demanded that Beekman answer the questions posed to her, Beekman repeatedly refused, and explained, "my conscience will not permit me to betray a confidence!" When the judge threatened to hold Beekman in contempt of court and this warning produced no alteration in Beekman's patented refusal to answer questions, she was fined in the amount of $250. Beekman produced her purse, counted $250, laid it on the dais, and stated, "if this is contempt . . . make the most of it!"[26]

Upon recounting this courtroom episode, Tutt introduced to his readers one of his most enduring legal philosophies. He explained:

> Law and honor are no more nearly related to one another than are law and justice. They are but distant cousins stemming from different ancestors and connected only by marriage. Law is the creation of man, while conscience is assumed to be implanted in us by the Creator. While the state naturally cannot tolerate an appeal to any other authority, this does not excuse the individual for abandoning his own inner standards of what is right and wrong. . . .
>
> Morality . . . has been left to the church and to the home. The result is that the law, since it does not pretend to tell us what we ought to do, but only what we must not do, is no adequate guide to conduct. To be a good citizen it is not enough simply to obey the letter of the statutes, for these merely set a minimum standard of decency. Some of the most despicable things a man can do are not crimes at all. . . .
>
> The conflict between law and morals often places the lawyer in an ambiguous position. He may well have to elect between retaining his client and his self-respect. . . .
>
> Although the counsel I gave my clients was often based quite as much upon ethics as upon law, I cannot claim that it was always justified by the result.[27]

Tutt's firsthand experience with the interplay between law and justice was briefly suspended, when in 1917 Woodrow Wilson asked Congress to recognize that the United States and Germany were in a state of war, and Tutt, "leaving Otto to run the office as best he could . . . went to Washington, [and] offered [his] services to the government in whatever capacity [he] could be most useful." Tutt received a commission in the Military Intelligence Division of the General Staff and was bestowed the title "major." After serving for a short period, Major Tutt was discharged.

Upon his return to "civilian life," Tutt found that the American economy —particularly in the 1920s—was experiencing a noticeable upswing. As business "boomed," the demand for legal services seemed to follow. Otto came to specialize as a legal advisor and expert pleader, while Tutt acted as the firm's negotiator—a task that primarily involved the reorganization of large companies and traveling the United States extensively. Tutt loved it. "I enjoyed the beauty and grandeur of the natural scenery, my talks with men who were doing big things in a big way, the chance to be in the open air. It was good fun." One case even required that Tutt travel to England to ensure that a reorganization of a company was effected properly. Tutt spent almost two months there, during which he acquainted himself with the English legal system.[28]

When Tutt returned to the United States, he brought a new perspective back with him. He was fifty-four years old, had spent his life living modestly and saving and investing his money, and had "worked hard and won a considerable success." Tutt noted that he was in a financial position that would have allowed him to retire, and he "was tired of advising corporations and of defending cases the only result of which would be that someone got a lot of money that usually might just as well have belonged to someone else." Tutt "longed for complete independence, for cases involving more human interest, for time to read and to think, and, above all, to get into the woods." As for Otto, his hard work and keen mind had earned him the reputation of being "an outstanding figure at the bar." Otto's works on corporate and constitutional law were considered authorities, and he was even asked to fill a term on the New York State Supreme Court. Otto was quickly nominated and elected by the legislature and soon began his service to society as a judge. Thus it was, the two friends parted ways—on the most friendly of terms—and Tutt was alone and at a turning point.

On the personal side, though Tutt was now over fifty years of age, "the only women I ever thought about were my mother and Esther." Esther had moved to California and was the president of a woman's college there, but she and Tutt continued to exchange letters despite the time that had passed. Although Tutt admitted to "lov[ing] her more than ever . . . it was like being in love with a charming ghost with whom I could regularly converse." Tutt never thought of marrying, for there was no other woman that compared to Esther, and he would "never marry any other."[29]

Shortly after Otto left Wiegand & Tutt, Tutt learned the unfortunate news that Miss Abigail Pidgeon, his "old Cambridge friend," had died. Remarkably, she had "nam[ed] [Tutt] as executor and trustee of her residuary estate amounting to half a million dollars, the income of which she directed [Tutt] to distribute at [his] discretion, 'among such victims of injustice as shall be in need of legal assistance or otherwise.'" Tutt decided to open a solo practice on January 1, 1924, which would welcome "all peddlers, musicians, book agents, vagabonds, and dogs," and the whole staff would sit down to five o'clock afternoon tea daily. The office would close promptly at 5:30 P.M., and would always be closed on Saturdays. Tutt's solo practice was a success, and Samuel Tutt, a distant cousin, soon joined him to assist the firm with its workload.

At this juncture in his career, Tutt felt the United States was experiencing a stage in its development that was "lawless." With Prohibition, and the secret speakeasies created to avoid its effect, it seemed that there had been "a revolution in the moral code of the country." "The whole idea of modesty had gone by the board. Elderly women showed their calves and the flappers almost everything," Tutt lamented. Established doctrine was being challenged, and, as far as Tutt could see, it appeared that "'society'—as an institution—ceased to exist."[30]

With the transformation that society seemed to be experiencing, Tutt wished that some of this change might spill over into the realm of law. Tutt's philosophy on the proper role of law, which is riddled throughout *Yankee Lawyer,* is based upon the premise of seeking truth and finding justice. For example, Tutt believed that "there is no greater mockery than the oath taken by any witness 'to tell the truth, the whole truth and nothing but the truth,' since he is neither asked to tell the truth nor would he be permitted to tell it if he were." Tutt explained, with the "barrage of objections" that interrupt the flow of a trial and intervene in the telling of a witness's story, the information lawyers actually presented to a jury was often severely limited. One of the main culprits, in Tutt's view, was the hearsay rule. Tutt explained: "if A has been standing in front of a house, hears a shot, and a few seconds later B rushes out crying 'I just saw Smith shoot Jones and he's hiding right now in a closet in the second story rear room with the pistol in his pocket,' A will not be permitted to testify what B told him even if Smith was, in fact, immediately arrested with the reeking pistol in his pocket in the closet as B stated." "Observe the artificiality of the law," Tutt complained.

What can attorneys do to ensure that justice and truth prevail at a trial? Tutt urged that lawyers are best served by proceeding with "ordinary common sense, careful preparation, and knowing when to sit down and let well enough alone." In conducting cross-examination of a witness, rather than engage in "sneering and bawling at the witness in an attempt to scare him out of his senses, [and] threatening him and holding him to scorn as an obvious liar," Tutt believed "it is far better to lull the witness into a sense of security and encourage him to elaborate his evidence, until he involves himself in palpable contradictions or evasions, then turn and rend him."

In thinking about his legal practice, Tutt recalled a conversation he had with Arthur Train about the interrelationship between law and justice. Train began the conversation, and guided it with only minor interjections from Tutt:

"I used to think I was getting at the truth in court, but I see now that the truth is greater than the sum of all the facts. Besides, you can't get the truth from a witness. The rules of evidence don't permit it."

"For one thing—" Train lit a fresh cigarette—"the truth, so far as any particular person is concerned, is the result of the impression made upon his brain, and it varies with each one of us. Now his five senses received that impression simultaneously. He didn't hear before he saw, or smell before he felt. Yet when he tells his story on the witness stand he has to arrange his reactions in some wholly arbitrary and artificial order. Second, and far more important, unless the witness is allowed to interpret his sensations and impressions as he experienced them he cannot convey the truth. Yet the law won't let him!"[31]

Tutt shared the same sympathies as his longtime friend, Train. His dedication to seeing the truth exposed in court drove him to spend much of his law career interceding in cases that seemed all but lost and engaging in all sorts of shenanigans in order to give truth a chance to triumph.

In 1937 the Interstate Bar Association invited Tutt to present a lecture at its annual convention. Tutt was sixty-eight years old and had been trying cases for forty-five years, yet he was unsure of what topic he should present to the group of lawyers he was addressing. Tutt decided to "tell [his audience] what fun I had got out of [practicing law] and of my hopes for what it could accomplish for the good of men." In defining law as a "body of man-made rules designed to enable people to live in harmony with each other and with their rulers," Tutt noted that it generally worked to "reduce social disorder and friction." However, Tutt also addressed some of the law's shortcomings. "That law is not justice is of vital significance to everyone," Tutt noted. "Generally speaking I wanted the law to be more efficacious, more speedy and above all more human." Tutt explained that his "fervent hope has always been that the law might be directed more and more to the betterment of mankind rather than of its rulers." However, how does one render justice using static laws? "Life implies growth and hence change and this is as true of law as of anything else. No sooner is a law made than *rigor mortis* sets in, and new and unforeseen conditions arise that often render an originally just law unjust." The friction between the concepts of law and justice exists because laws remain inflexible and of certain definition, while the concept of justice can fluctuate and bend according to the dictates of society. Law remains static while justice vacillates. How can the two, then, be reconciled?

According to Tutt, "the chief difficulty with the law viewed from the progress of society is due to its lack of humanity." This difficulty "has haunted me for fifty years," Tutt divulged. However, Tutt noted that though the law may be slow to change, it changes nonetheless.

> In spite of everything the law gradually and in time, adapts itself to scientific discovery, and economic and social development. "The life of the law has not been logic: it has been experience," says Mr. Justice Holmes in the introductory chapter to his great work on "The Common Law." The substance of the law at any given time pretty nearly corresponds . . . with what is then considered to be convenient; but its form and machinery, and the degree to which it is able to work out desired results, depend very much upon the past. . . . The truth is that the law is always approaching, and never reaching, consistency. It is forever adopting new principles from life at one end, and it always retains old ones from history at the other, which have not yet been absorbed or sloughed off. It will become entirely consistent only when it ceases to grow."

Although there may seem to always be a disconnection between the law as it currently stands and society's concepts of morality and justice, Tutt had faith that the law would continue to modernize and change to fit society's needs. In the end, Tutt seems to applaud the law's progress "towards recognizing a heretofore unacknowledged moral responsibility on the part of each individual citizen towards his fellows and of all collectively towards each [other]," and he cites in support the advent of family and juvenile courts, the extension of "separate rights" to women, the protection of the environment and wildlife, and the creation of unions and protections placed upon labor relations. "The pace is slow but the legal cavalcade moves on and in the right direction," Tutt contended.[32]

Tutt's final chapter in his autobiography reflected on his two lifelong loves: Esther Farr and the law. As to Esther, though he had not seen her since he was twenty-eight years of age, the two had written letters to each other throughout their lives. Tutt revealed that he "had adored her for forty years," and "as long as she was alive, no matter where, it would have been impossible for me to think of another woman." Although Tutt had resigned to the mean fate that life had dealt him, he admitted that some nights, "as I smoked my stogy before the fire in my library in London Terrace, I yearned for her bodily presence. What bliss it would have been to have her sitting there opposite me. To pour out all the words unspoken through the years! To look into her soft brown eyes! If longing could have conjured up her presence she would have come."

"Then an odd thing happened." Tutt received word that Columbia University wished to bestow upon him an honorary degree of doctor of laws. At the ceremony, after Tutt was hooded and given his "roll of parchment," he sat down and heard the name "Esther Farr." "She looked towards me with the same lovely smile I knew so well. If her hair had become slightly gray I did not notice it. All I knew was that this was still the Esther of my youth and of my dreams, with the same sweetly sensitive mouth, proud courageous chin and veiled brown eyes." Tutt and Esther talked all afternoon, into the evening, and Tutt invited Esther to dine with him that night, at his home. They took a taxi to Tutt's abode on West Twenty-Third Street. Tutt "opened the iron gate and Esther—my Esther!—entered and walked up the brick path towards the door." It was as though no time had elapsed since they had seen each other last, and it felt completely natural for Tutt and Esther to be laughing and talking in his sitting room, as he had imagined her there so many times. Despite the happiness each felt in spending time together, the fact did not change: Esther was married and Tutt was a permanent bachelor. By seeing Esther again, Tutt realized that his "life has held more of romance than falls to the lot of most men"; there was nothing that could diminish or mar his feelings for Esther.[33] She would forever be his standard.

"They say that towards the end of a man's life the years whip by like telegraph poles past a train. That has not been my experience," Tutt remarked. Looking back at the life he had thus far, Tutt believed he had not "made the most of [his] abilities," but he "always thr[ew] [his] weight on the side of such causes as [he] believed to be just." Before women's suffrage received any significant support in New York State, Tutt marched in the Woman's Suffrage Parade on Fifth Avenue. Tutt voted for candidates regardless of their affiliation with a particular political party, and he focused only on whether they represented the interests he believed in and were deemed important by him. He believed "in acting when the need is instant even if mistakes are made, rather than in the scientific delay which may accomplish more good in a hypothetical future." It was these precepts that caused him to use the funds left to him by Abigail Pidgeon as a "trust for emergency relief." Tutt noted that he did not care whether the applicant for Pidgeon Fund assistance was "morally deserving or not," for "I would far rather be swindled a few times than grow callous to suffering. Too much repression may cause one's human sympathy to wither and eventually to die for lack of nourishment."

By the time Tutt was writing the final paragraphs of his autobiography, his lovely home on West Twenty-Third Street had been torn down, replaced by a more modern, imposing building. Tutt relocated to a home in the East Sixties of Manhattan, where he lived in a small brownstone with his latest dog, CJ IV. The latter enjoyed a good frolic in the backyard while Tutt sat and smoked his signature stogie in peace and solitude.

In pondering whether his autobiography had any significance, Tutt noted that although he spent his lifetime acknowledging the imperfections in the application of law, justice still prevailed in many cases. He explained that while there were good laws and bad, "the unfortunate fact remains that all laws must be administered by imperfect men." "The laws of man rarely, or never, accomplished justice in any individual case," rather, lawyers and the courts "merely did the best [they] could by applying legal rules-of-thumb based on the doctrine of averages, which [they] hoped in the long run—a very long run indeed—did make for justice." Besides, the final arbiters of most cases were jurors, who "did the best they could to even things up," and in some cases proved to be "the saving grace of an otherwise intolerable situation."

Tutt concluded that a distinction between law and justice existed because there was a lack of humanity involved in law, and Tutt urged that Americans not settle for such a definition of "law." "If we're content to abandon humanity either to the laws of nature or to the laws of man the world would be a miserable place to live in. We must have faith in our fellows just as we must have faith in God. . . . Those who do not possess that faith—who refuse to believe in the innate goodness of human nature, who look for evil in every man and deny him the benefit of any doubt—are the mean people who see only the reflection of their own mean natures in the acts of others." In the end, Tutt believed that "the only way to attain justice is by doing it ourselves every day—with our own hands—to each other—at home—and in the world outside. If each of us tried to right the wrongs that occur before his eyes, to relieve the distress of those with whom he comes into direct contact, we could do away with organized charity and there would be little need for law."

Having lived quite a full life, Tutt looked back at his seventy-five years and wondered whether he would change the course of his life if given the chance to do it again. "I would spend twice as much of it in fishing," he concluded.[34]

3
The Cooperation of the Press

What mixes you up is that you write Arthur and get a postal card back signed "Eph." In the upper left-hand corner is the beloved gentleman himself, stovepipe hat on head and cheroot in mouth, puffing away gaily and smiling sardonically at you.

If you think the answer is easy, let me just add that I have carried on, and am still carrying on, an extensive correspondence with "Eph."
    —Reginald Heber Smith, for the *American Bar Association Journal*

One of the most outstanding characteristics of Arthur Train's publication of *Yankee Lawyer* is that he somehow convinced major newspapers and other media across the United States to publish reviews that generally encouraged the idea that the book was written by Ephraim Tutt. In the realm of literary hoaxes, it is a rare occurrence for the media to know about a hoax before reporting on it—and it is even more uncommon for reputable newspapers, magazines, and journals to join in the wonder and fun of a grand literary prank. What set Train's hoax apart from many others is that his was based on an impossible premise—a fictional character simply could not publish a book, no less an autobiography. As a result, it seems that those who were called upon to review *Yankee Lawyer* did not feel duty bound to expose that Train wrote *Yankee Lawyer* (because most readers familiar with Tutt would likely suspect that fact), and instead wrote lively and entertaining pieces that skirted the issue or feigned "genuine" discombobulation over whether Tutt could have written the book.

As a book purportedly about "the best known lawyer now alive,"[1] discussions about *Yankee Lawyer* appeared in a variety of publications, from bar association periodicals and law journals to the mainstream media, such as national newspapers and magazines. In dealing with the book, many reviewers playfully broached the issue of whether the book was truly an autobiography, and more specifically, whether the book was actually written by a living Ephraim Tutt. Some reviewers found the issue to be a mere trifle, hardly bothering to pay any mind to it, and comfortably proceeded directly to an examination of the contents of the book. Other reviewers found the issue to be all encompassing and were unable to move past this question, resulting in book reviews that did not examine the substance of the book.

In the course of reviewing Tutt's autobiography, reviewers were forced to confront some unusual dilemmas. How does one go about critiquing a known fictitious autobiography? Should a review mention who the true author is, or would that take away from the whole premise of the book? Would it be wrong to go along with the hoax? To varying degrees, those who reviewed *Yankee Lawyer* sided with reviewing the quality of the book and commenting on whether it told a story worth recommending. To get around the problem of stating who wrote the book, some reviewers simply referred to "the author"—without stating who the author was. Other statements that were made could apply equally to Train or Tutt. For example, when a review stated the book was written by a "well known lawyer," it could be referring to either of them.

The effect that these reviews had on the public varied. For readers who knew that Tutt was a mere figment of Train's imagination and were not fooled in the slightest by Tutt's "autobiography," the reviews were often humorous and entertaining. However, for those readers who were not as familiar with Tutt, many of the reviews had the effect of confirming their mistaken belief that it was a real autobiography of a living person. The latter phenomenon was compounded by the "books are weapons" campaign, which urged Americans to read books to fight World War II's "war of ideas." In performing this patriotic duty, many people turned to books that defined the American way of life. Since Tutt was considered an American icon and was compared to figures such as Uncle Sam and Paul Bunyan, Tutt's autobiography was an obvious "weapon" to read. However, this also meant that many people who had not previously read Train's stories suddenly had a heightened interest in an autobiography that gave all appearances of being genuine. For this sector of the reading public, the book proved to fool and hoax, and the unlikely complicity of the press only added to the confusion.

As a lawyer, Tutt was naturally an appealing character to those who practiced in his profession. Since his legal arguments were based on real statutes and cases, Tutt had an impressive following among his colleagues at the bar. When his autobiography was published, many legal publications featured articles about it in their newsletters and journals in the fall of 1943. One of the largest legal organizations, the American Bar Association, secured Reginald Heber Smith, a well-respected and preeminent Boston attorney, to write a piece on Tutt's autobiography. Smith began his review by declaring that *Yankee Lawyer* was "the best book in existence by a contemporary lawyer about a contemporary lawyer and the laws of our time." Already, the first sentence's ambiguity yields to any number of meanings. Smith could be suggesting that Train was writing about Tutt, that Tutt was writing about himself, or that Train was writing about himself through his alter ego, Tutt. The next sentence dispelled any possibility of reaching an answer about who wrote the book: "This review will be highly informal and may be, in spots, inaccurate." Despite his admission that his review may be unreliable, Smith confided: "the alleged author" is Arthur Train.

When he stated that his review would be informal, Smith was not exaggerating. The remainder of the article hardly reviewed the book; it primarily consisted of a commentary on Tutt's status (real or imaginary). Smith began by identifying the problem that Tutt created: "People of the highest intelligence refuse to believe that Tutt is a figment of imagination any more than they believe Sherlock Holmes to be." However, rather than provide clarity, Smith stated that the confusion over Tutt's existence was "the miracle wrought by this book." According to Smith, "Tutt lives, and breathes, and has his being amongst us right now." In fact, Smith noted that "clients send cases to him. His advice and help are steadily sought out. People say they know him. Persons claim to have seen him."

Seemingly, in the true spirit of tracking down the truth, Smith reveals that when the *Saturday Evening Post* published an article doubting Tutt's existence because his name did not appear in Harvard Law School's Quinquennial Catalogue, Smith, apparently believing the omission to be a mere oversight, "wrote Arthur or 'Eph' (I am never sure which) that I believed I could cure that defect, and the name would appear in the next Quinquennial Catalogue." After extending this generous offer, Smith explained that he was "never sure" who was responding to him, because "what mixes you up is that you write Arthur and get a postal card back signed 'Eph.' In the upper lefthand corner is the beloved gentleman himself, stovepipe hat on head and cheroot in mouth, puffing away gaily and smiling sardonically at you." Feigning frustration, Smith complained: "If you think the answer is easy, let me just add that I have carried on, and am still carrying on, an extensive correspondence with 'Eph.'" Without reaching a conclusive answer on Tutt's existence, Smith ended his synopsis by noting that at the Harvard Law School there is a room named for Elihu Root. "There students can relax and read at their leisure before a fine open fire. They can take any book that attracts them. The librarian has selected those books with especial care. As you enter the room, on your right you will find all the books about our immortal colleague, Mr. Tutt."[2]

While the *American Bar Association Journal*'s piece on *Yankee Lawyer* did not seem to get beyond the issue of the book's authorship, other publications paid far less attention to the issue. For example, Arthur Garfield Hays reviewed *Yankee Lawyer* for the *Lawyers Guild Review,* which only briefly commented on the issue of whether Tutt existed, perhaps to avoid getting bogged down in the inevitable quagmire: "In another generation, Ephraim Tutt will be known as one of the most eminent lawyers of our time. He perhaps is so known already, although Arthur Train has received many letters of inquiry as to why Tutt never has appeared in current news. Some people are suspicious. While many doubt the existence of Tutt, the lawyer, nobody can question his authenticity." Like Smith, Hays also seemed to have questions for Train or Tutt, so he contacted Train and claimed in his review that he also received a letter from Tutt himself. The *Lawyers Guild Review* recommended Tutt's autobiography to its readers, and particularly praised Tutt's legal philosophy and his discerning discussions on the difference between law and justice.[3]

While it is likely that most of the reviewers were aware of the hoax and merely went along with the spirit of Train's literary mischief, one review was undoubtedly written with the benefit of full disclosure as to the true author of *Yankee Lawyer*. This review was the ingenious critique the *Yale Law Journal* published, written by Arthur Train. The obvious problems with having an author review his own book need not be explored, but the "review" reveals that Train took full advantage of this opportunity to praise *Yankee Lawyer* and how masterfully "Tutt" wrote the story of his life. That the *Yale Law Journal* even allowed Train's review to be published suggests that it believed its readers were savvy enough to discern that the book was a hoax.

Train's review of *Yankee Lawyer* tells many things about how he felt about Tutt and the importance of Tutt's autobiography. It also shows that he did not publish *Yankee Lawyer* in order to fool a gullible audience; instead, Train wrote the book to give Tutt a voice and to delve into the complex nature of this beloved character. The first portion of Train's review looks to the relationship between Train and Tutt. Train began by noting that "to review the book of a friend is inevitably a delicate and ofttimes a dangerous task. There should be no traffic between author and critic, otherwise the latter may be accused of reading into its pages something that is not there." Train confessed that he had originally suggested that Tutt write his memoirs, though Tutt was rather hesitant at first. When Tutt finally agreed to write his life's story, Train explained that he felt "a distinct feeling of responsibility and no little apprehension," though he was relieved to find that upon reading his friend's autobiography his "fears proved unfounded." Train remarked that although he had "watched Ephraim Tutt in court, played poker and gone fishing with him for over forty years," he was "wholly unprepared for the wealth of pungent narrative and the richness of human philosophy which [Tutt's] entertaining autobiography contains." After praising Tutt's skill as a writer, Train turned to some of the unpleasant things Tutt had said about him in *Yankee Lawyer*.

"The sad truth is that I think a great deal more of Mr. Tutt than he does of me," Train surmised. For, "time and again in the pages of *Yankee Lawyer* he makes it quite plain that he regards me as a conscienceless literary hack who has misrepresented his true character and distorted the facts of the cases in which he has taken part. In fact, he has used such expressions about me that I have been tempted to sue him for libel per se." Train did not explore further whether he had embellished his own stories about Tutt's most memorable cases, and instead noted that Tutt used the opportunity of writing his autobiography to set all the facts straight.

The final paragraph of the review is hard to reconcile with any of Train's later accounts that he did not mean to intentionally deceive anyone. It reads:

> During the last quarter century that Mr. Tutt has so good naturedly permitted me to use him as a character in what was otherwise largely fiction I have occasionally been disturbed by the possibility that some people might think him merely a figment of my imagination. That ghost, I am glad to say, has now been laid. Ephraim Tutt's actuality is established forever—at least for all those who are not such constitutional skeptics that they are prepared to question the authenticity of any alleged fact of history, like the man who wrote an erudite work proving that Napoleon Bonaparte never existed. In any event, to paraphrase Voltaire's famous aphorism: "If Mr. Tutt did not exist, it would be necessary to invent him."[4]

While the sentiment—that there is something necessary about having someone like Tutt exist—is an agreeable one, this paragraph seems to wholeheartedly endorse the view that Tutt was a real person. It would seem that Train believed his perceptive audience would decipher his review for what it was: a clever device that would allow him to explore his literary prank in an amusing manner.

Shortly after Train's review appeared in the *Yale Law Journal,* the *Harvard Law Review* published its own piece on *Yankee Lawyer,* this one was written by J. M. Maguire, a professor of law at Harvard University. Maguire's article began by describing the book as "unusual" and explained that the book, "described as an autobiography . . . is much more than that—nothing less, indeed, than a battle by the writer for his identity, independence, and integrity." Maguire elaborated that although "Arthur Train claims to have created Ephraim Tutt . . . Ephraim Tutt now takes in hand the pen which is mightier than the sword, and proceeds to contest Arthur Train's claim, disclosing himself as a person with father and mother, birthplace and birthday . . . and various other circumstantial personal characteristics and equipment." The stealthy language of this introduction enables the review to have the appearance of endorsing the idea of Tutt being a living person without discounting the possibly that Train wrote the book. Maguire did not identify *Yankee Lawyer* as an autobiography; he stated the book was "described as an autobiography." Rather than declare that Tutt permitted Train to write an introduction, Maguire noted that "the author" of *Yankee Lawyer* allowed Train to write the introduction.

However, Maguire also humors the possibility that Tutt was a living attorney, noting that the harsh remarks by Tutt against Train, in *Yankee Lawyer,* were not entirely undeserved, and that he "is all on Mr. Tutt's side in his rebellion" against Train's faulty representation of Tutt in his fictional stories. Maguire even provided an exhaustive discussion of additional historical facts supporting Tutt's account of his war experience. Maguire's inclusion of this information bolstered the appearance that *Yankee Lawyer* was an authentic autobiography, but considering his audience and the general tone of the entire review, it appears that Maguire was indulging in the spirit of Train's ruse.

Tellingly, Maguire provided no definitive statement as to whether Tutt existed, and he never identified who had written *Yankee Lawyer*. However, next to the title of the review, a footnote was added, which reads: "the publishers assure us that the author [of *Yankee Lawyer*] is 'the best-known lawyer now alive.'" In a second footnote, Maguire acknowledged Train's review in the *Yale Law Journal* and noted, "Mr. Train, in a published review of the present book, now disclaims authorship of Mr. Tutt's being," yet Maguire questioned whether Train would "hold to this disclaimer."[5]

Just as the reviews published in legal periodicals generally reveal that many reviewers were complicit in Train's ruse, an examination of the articles published in newspapers and popular magazines shows that the mainstream media happily participated in Train's hoax. While there were a few reviews that plainly exposed that Train was the true author, many others generally endorsed the idea that Tutt was alive and he wrote *Yankee Lawyer*. Since local newspapers were the main source of information for many people in the 1940s, those readers who were unfamiliar with Tutt could be grossly misguided or bluntly informed of the truth—it depended on whether their local newspaper published an artful or honest review. Even within cities that had access to several regional newspapers—such as New York City—a variety of viewpoints were published; depending on which newspaper a person read, any number of conclusions could be drawn as to who had written *Yankee Lawyer*. By surveying a sample of reviews published in newspapers across the United States, it becomes clear that deciphering the truth about Tutt could be a difficult task.

One of the first reviews published on *Yankee Lawyer* appeared in August 1943, in the Sunday *New York Times*'s Book Review section. It was the most prominent review in that week's paper, and it began by stating:

> As a lawyer Ephraim Tutt needs no introduction to the American public. He has not only achieved an international reputation during his fifty years of legal practice but has also acquired during their crowded span a following of "Tutt fans." . . .
> This is unique in the legal profession. Other lawyers have acquired

fame, but they were for the most part men who only used the law as a stepping-stone to politics. Ephraim Tutt consistently refused public office. His life has been spent in the court room, battling for justice on behalf of the weak and the helpless. . . .

Now, at 75, Ephraim Tutt the lawyer has given us a full-length portrait of Ephraim the man. If there is such a thing as a typical American he will be found between the pages of this humorous and charming book.

Addressing the idea that Train may have been involved, the review stated: "as might have been expected, the character which is revealed to us by the owner is quite different from the one we have grown to know through the sketches of Arthur Train—who has been Ephraim Tutt's Boswell for a quarter of a century." However, this sentence seems only to confirm that Train had written short stories about Tutt's legal career, and Tutt had since emerged to write the story of his life.

Beyond the introduction, the rest of the review provides additional details bolstering Tutt's account; it includes an explanation of how Train and Tutt came to be acquaintances and why Tutt decided to write a book of his own. The reviewer surmises that Tutt regretted giving Train license over the use of his name and legal adventures, since Tutt noted that "Arthur Train's Ephraim Tutt is not the real Ephraim Tutt. His Tutt is not even consistent. The character changes from story to story—from mountebank to philosopher, from shyster to philanthropist, from law-breaker to upholder of the Constitution . . . I intended to surrender only my privacy. Not my reputation." The reviewer noted that, despite whatever differences Tutt might have had with Train, the two men had been able to maintain a friendship, and, in fact, it was even Train who persuaded Tutt to write his autobiography. The reviewer commented that "for this one act, Mr. Train will be remembered gratefully by the thousands who will welcome the autobiography of this salty philosopher and humanitarian who started as a Vermont country boy, worked his way through Harvard College and Law School, learned his practical law in a country town, came to New

York to meet the big shots on their own ground, and eventually proved himself the biggest of them all." The reviewer was excited to now know the "real" Ephraim Tutt, and applauded the rebellious spirit that made Tutt a champion of justice. After describing Tutt's life in more detail, the review concludes: "'Yankee Lawyer' is like a sudden breeze at the end of a sultry day. It is a good book if you are one of those oppressed by the jittery conviction that the problems facing our world are too complex to be understood, to say nothing of being solved."

Having made it through the entire review, only a minority of readers likely read the information contained below a line that seemed to indicate the conclusion of the review. Beneath this line, there is a piddling paragraph, wholly italicized, and its position and stature combine to make it appear insignificant and unimportant. It reads: *"Warning to Letter Writers! Does this review assist in the perpetuation of a literary hoax? The Editor enters herewith a plea of nolo contendere. He has conspired, quite openly, with the reviewer—and feels that Ephraim Tutt deserves a hearing—on his own terms."*[6] This clever review essentially contained a well-disguised disclaimer, one that would be read only after making it through the entire book review and bothering past a line that clearly demarcated the end of the article. In the history of newspapers, there are probably few pieces that have ever been published that were immediately followed by a blurb that essentially renounced the information and claims preceding it. It seems that the *New York Times* was well aware of who really wrote *Yankee Lawyer,* but throughout the body of the review gave no indication that it was actually Train.

A few days after printing the first review, the *New York Times* published yet another critique of Tutt's autobiography. The beginning of the review begins quite differently from the last, for it directly addresses the idea that Arthur Train *may* be the author of the book. It notes that while many readers might have a suspicion that Tutt "was none other than Arthur Train himself," the publication of *Yankee Lawyer* makes it "appear that Mr. Train is merely a false-face for Mr. Tutt." After all, the reviewer notes the autobiography "couldn't be a work of fiction," "real people . . . walk through its pages," and "old daguerreotypes of Ephraim Tutt's mother and father" were included in the book—"No, it can't be Mr. Train that is hoaxing us." After acknowledging the possibility of the book being a hoax, the book review thereafter holds to the belief that Tutt was the author. In fact, not only did the reviewer surmise that Train was not behind the publication of *Yankee Lawyer*, he contends "the truth would seem to be that Tutt himself has kidded us about a fictitious Arthur Train all these years." Besides, "the Tutt who figured in the so-called Arthur Train stories was a rather melodramatic fellow compared with the real Tutt of 'Yankee Lawyer.'" The *New York Times* noted that unlike Train's stories, Tutt's autobiography contained "no fake stuff—well, hardly any."

Throughout the review, Tutt bears two titles: the "real Eph Tutt," or the "real Ephraim Tutt"—as in the Tutt who published his autobiography— and the less descriptive "Tutt," as in "the Tutt who figured in the so-called Arthur Train stories." After providing a legitimate description of the contents of Tutt's autobiography, the reviewer does not question the authenticity or veracity of any of the details of the book (or of the purported author of the book itself), but, he has some doubts about "the real" Tutt's "fish stories." "A man who could invent the fictitious character of Arthur Train might tell you anything about fish," the reviewer warned. Altogether, other than deeming "the story of the Mohawk Valley trout that was big as a cow," "sheer fabrication," the review concludes that this fishing story was "one of the few false things in a work that is predominantly composed of sterling realism, absolute fidelity to the facts of history, and the truth about a great human character."[7] If the only newspaper to which a person had access was the *New York Times*, it seems that it would be easy to believe, based on these reviews, that Tutt was a living person.

However, between the appearances of the two *New York Times* articles, the *Wall Street Journal* published a review for its "Executive's Bookshelf" column. Pegging *Yankee Lawyer* as "the most interesting book he has read so far this year," the reviewer noted that although the publisher of *Yankee Lawyer* described Tutt as "undoubtedly the best known lawyer now alive," Tutt "is still with us, a fictional character, enjoying both a popular and international fame as a great legal strategist." Clearly, the *Wall Street Journal* did not get involved in perpetuating Train's great hoax; however, this newspaper did find amusement in the idea that a fictitious character had—by all appearances—written his own autobiography: "It is to be regretted that Sherlock Holmes, who enjoyed a like measure of fictional fame in his special field, never wrote his autobiography. . . . Only once did Holmes write his own unvarnished account of one of his cases, and then he took the occasion to criticize his friend and chronicler Dr. Watson for unduly embellishing the other published accounts. In much the same way Ephraim Tutt criticizes his faithful friend Arthur Train who for years dogged his footsteps in order to render a unique service to mankind." After reviewing a few of the instances in *Yankee Lawyer* where Tutt deems Train's descriptions as overly romanticized or plainly inaccurate, the review notes that "Mr. Tutt has taken pains to straighten these matters out." The review continues to compare Tutt with Train, noting that they "had much in common in respect to background and legal experience which doubtless furthered mutual understanding."[8] The *Wall Street Journal* suggested that because Train's experiences were made into Tutt's, Train was able to provide a rich and seemingly accurate account of Tutt's life. On the whole, the *Wall Street Journal* seems to set the record straight.

In September 1943 *Yankee Lawyer* was reviewed in newspapers across the country—from the *Los Angeles Times* and *Chicago Daily Tribune* to the *Hartford Courant* and *Washington Post*. These reviews ran the full gamut, from exposing the truth to perpetuating the hoax. A brief look at the convincing and conflicting book reviews on *Yankee Lawyer* demonstrates how readers across the nation could easily form different understandings about the book.

The author of the review for the *Chicago Daily Tribune* seemed to suffer from mixed feelings about whether he should play along with the hoax or reveal that *Yankee Lawyer* was a literary prank. At first, the reviewer commended the book and noted that he enjoyed "the constant use of humorous anecdotes out of the author's life," "the amazing number of actual characters whom the author knew and describes," and "the number of real lawsuits which the author handled involving strange people and unbelievable situations." However, it seems that the reviewer could not quite stomach being an accomplice in perpetuating the idea that Tutt was a real person. For, midway through the review, the reviewer stated: "The author—if I may keep up the Pretense that the tale is Mr. Tutt's and not that of his creator, Arthur Train—is obviously a man of considerable geniality and intelligence. He is, in many ways, a peculiarly American combination of shrewd practicality and great generosity. It was a fine thing for him to set down his life in a pleasant book." Despite stating that the tale was Arthur Train's, the rest of the article consistently refers to "the author" (instead of naming who it is) and identifies the book being reviewed as "'YANKEE LAWYER,' by Ephraim Tutt." However, alongside this review is also a picture of Arthur Train, which bears the caption "Arthur Train, whose 'Yankee Lawyer: the Autobiography of Ephraim Tutt' is reviewed on this page."[9] Altogether, the review generally favors the view that Train was the true author of *Yankee Lawyer.*

Readers who read the piece written on *Yankee Lawyer* appearing in the *Los Angeles Times* were not fooled in the least. This article is also accompanied by a picture, this one appearing to be a hand-drawn silhouette of Train's likeness, bearing the caption: "ARTHUR TRAIN—Former Assistant District Attorney and president of National Institute of Arts and Letters, his latest book is 'Yankee Lawyer,' which critic dubs an 'admirable hoax.' It is autobiographical in form." This caption, like the review, makes abundantly clear that Tutt did not write his autobiography. In fact, the review plunders *Yankee Lawyer* of its lark in the very first sentence: "This admirable hoax was probably written so that Arthur Train could take potshots from ambush at persons and institutions of whom he disapproves." The *Los Angeles Times* noted that by "naming names (some obviously fictitious) and [containing] a detailed index, just like a regular autobiography, . . . the book is going to take many a reader, and that's all to the good."[10] Even though the book was a hoax, the *Los Angeles Times* seemed to acknowledge that it was not one that could be taken very seriously (after all, it featured a known fictitious character), and there was no real harm if readers were fooled into believing there was a living Tutt.

Like the *Los Angeles Times,* the *Berkley Daily Gazette* also revealed that Train was the real author; however, the latter newspaper couched its disclosure in a mask of subtlety. The *Berkley Daily Gazette* commented that "Barrister Tutt and his exploits are fairly familiar to magazine readers. Mr. Tutt, contrary to the customary practice, often put the law to pleasant uses. His autobiography is what might be expected from the amiable amicus curiae in whose legal arguments and court cases there was never anything dry except his wit. Mr. Tutt is, of course, an experienced lawyer and a good writer. It's no secret that he was well 'trained' for both jobs."[11] Unless readers of this review understood the pun in the last sentence, this review otherwise suggests Tutt existed.

Back to the East Coast, the *Washington Post's* review of *Yankee Lawyer* contradicted the view of the *Los Angeles Times* and put the authorship squarely on Tutt. This article was complemented by a picture captioned "EPHRAIM TUTT, ESQ.," and the notation "He enjoyed himself, and that, observes the reviewer, is much to say about a life spent in the law." The review begins, "EPHRAIM TUTT, that counselor-at-law famous wherever the *Saturday Evening Post* is read, whose professional doings have been recorded until he is almost a saga, has written a book about himself at last." The review warmly summarized Tutt's relationship with the public up to the publication of his autobiography, noting that, compared to "the late Justice Holmes, [Tutt] is probably more intimately known in his clever legal processes to several millions of Americans." In fact, the *Washington Post* praised Tutt's autobiography for providing the "public a chance to glimpse the rungs of his particular ladder of fame. Small town to big city, district attorney's office to a great factory of law, money-making followed by some misgivings—it is the archetypical pattern of the oft-told American success story: home-town boy makes good."

As for the relationship between Train and Tutt, the *Washington Post* commented that the two men shared many similarities, but, unlike other reviews, it did not suggest that Tutt's experiences were actually Train's. "Eph Tutt is like his other biographer, Arthur Train, primarily a story teller," the *Post* remarked. For Tutt, "while he followed the law, he was not lost in it, and his first love was the passing show." The review noted that Tutt had escaped becoming a lawyer for the big city "legal factories," as "stories and men were what Eph liked, and they in turn made him a likeable individual." In concluding, the book review noted that though the public may know of the Ephraim Tutt that appeared in Train's stories published in the *Saturday Evening Post,* "Arthur Train's Ephraim Tutt i[s] not the real Tutt at all."[12] On the whole, the *Washington Post's* review seemed to encourage its readers to believe that the author of *Yankee Lawyer* was Tutt.

In September 1943, a strange book review of *Yankee Lawyer* appeared in the popular Connecticut newspaper, the *Hartford Courant,* which began with a vague discussion of the book's creator. Noting that "the creation of Arthur Train 'is undoubtedly the best known lawyer now alive,'" the *Courant* described this boast as "an exaggeration," but "not too great a one, for certainly thousands of people have followed the fictional explorations of the law by the old barrister who would be hard put to name any contemporary attorney known nationally." The remainder of the review failed to venture any further into the issue of whether Tutt was a real person. Instead, it recommended *Yankee Lawyer* to lawyers, "for its objective view of their profession, and the constant proposition that law and justice are not necessarily one and the same thing," and to laypeople, for "either . . . amusement or instruction."[13]

On the whole, this sampling of reviews shows that newspapers across the United States provided a wide range of viewpoints regarding *Yankee Lawyer.* However, national magazines tended to take a more unified approach to the Tutt dilemma. For example, the September 13, 1943, edition of *Newsweek* carried a small piece titled "Hoaks," which was printed alongside pictures of Arthur Train and Ephraim Tutt. The caption below these pictures stated: "Who's a myth? Arthur Train . . . or Ephraim Tutt?" The article follows "a distinguished member of the English Bar, Sir Eric Herring-Hoaks," who entered a Fifth Avenue bookstore and happened upon *Yankee Lawyer*. As he read the dust jacket, Herring-Hoaks was chagrined to learn that Tutt, who was a perfect stranger, was "the best known lawyer now alive." Reading about Tutt's many accomplishments and his famous friends, Herring-Hoaks, "in ever-increasing puzzlement," turned to the introduction for "possible enlightenment" and found a crumb written by Arthur Train. Thoroughly disturbed, and "empurpled about the wattles," Herring-Hoaks fled the bookstore and "strode out onto the streets in search of a whisky and splash, muttering: 'Never heard of the feller in me life.'" And, thus the article concluded . . . except for a small, italicized blurb, appearing below the article, which read: *"To any other foreign visitors of legal or literary tastes who might be annoyed, let it be said that 'Yankee Lawyer' is one of the most elaborate literary spoofs of the century; that Ephraim Tutt is still just a figment of Arthur Train's imagination and that his 'autobiography,' if you can get rid of the uncomfortable feeling that you're being 'had' at some length, is pretty amusing reading. To any nervous State Department officials, concerned over possible rifts in a beautiful international friendship: Just relax about Sir Eric Herring-Hoaks. He doesn't exist either."*[14] Even if they did not read this italicized explanation, it seems that most readers likely deduced that this article was just a playful response to the nature of the book.

A week later, *Time Magazine* printed its review of *Yankee Lawyer*, which avoided wit and trickery and cut straight to the point. The first sentence of this September 1943 article announced that "Ephraim Tutt is one of the few fictitious characters who has ever written his autobiography." Paying credence to the book's "hodgepodge of fact and fiction," including "anecdotes about Mr. Tutt's nonfictional contemporaries," the review traced Tutt's "life" as the fictional character of Train. "First [coming] to public attention in a story written by Arthur Train in the *Satevepost* of June 7, 1919," Train had since written "almost a hundred Tutt stories," *Time* reported. Despite being fiction, these stories made quite an impact on society, for the Tutt stories "have become as familiar to lawyers as folk tales, have been cited from the bench as quasi-legal authority, have helped many a candidate pass his bar examinations," and, "like Sherlock Holmes, Ephraim

Tutt has become more famous than his creator." This review surmised that Tutt's appeal stemmed from his ability to instill hope in his readers—a trait of particular importance as America faced the challenges and sacrifices inherent in its participation in World War II. *Time Magazine* concluded: "Though his life is closing in a clouded world, Ephraim Tutt has faith that in the U.S. the pennants still fly gallantly and the trumpets echo to the challenge of 'Liberty and Equality' and of 'Justice for the Common Man.'"[15]

Having now sampled a host of reviews that were published around the time *Yankee Lawyer* was published, it becomes apparent that many periodicals did not make it easy for unsuspecting readers to learn the truth about the author of this book. In fact, it soon became apparent to Charles Scribner's Sons, Arthur Train, and even Train's editor, Maxwell Perkins, that there was a multitude of readers who were impatient to learn the answer to a most vexing question: Did Ephraim Tutt really exist and write his own autobiography?

4
Here We Go Again!

Florence, April 9, 1946
Bravo Mr. Tutt—if you are still in the land of the living! What a full and useful life you have had! I have just read The Yankee Lawyer from the first page to the last in one sitting and have enjoyed it more than any book I've read in the last ten years in any language. . . . I am 72 years of age. . . . You have restored my faith in mankind and especially Americans.
—M. H. S.

Literary hoaxes have taken many appearances and have baffled society frequently enough to be considered "a dubious but at least time-honored human endeavor, probably as old as literature itself." While one of the first is said to have taken place during the first century, when Philo Biblos manufactured sources for his history of Phoenicia, the appeal of publishing a "true" story that has little or no foundation in reality has continued to the present day. In fact, book-reading Americans weathered so many hoaxes in the 2000s that when yet another appeared in 2008, the *New York Times* commented that everyone must be thinking, "here we go again."[1] A brief look at some of the more well-known literary hoaxes reveals that Arthur Train's was truly one of a kind.

One early hoax that had a particularly nefarious motive was Jonathan Swift's 1708 publication of a false almanac purporting to have been written by Isaac Bickerstaff, which predicted the date that John Partridge—a "quack astrologer who irked" Swift—would die. When the appointed day arrived, Swift wrote an elegy, confirming that Partridge was, indeed, dead. When Partridge asserted that he was alive and "had been all along . . . the public would have none of him." Even when Partridge's real obituary was published seven years later, many doubted the obituary was genuine and continued to believe he had died years earlier. Another memorable hoax involved the publication of a book in the 1830s that detailed the adventures of Davy Crockett, with the title stating that it was "written by himself." However, while this book's romanticized tales of Crockett's experiences added to the lore surrounding this figure, much of it was exaggerated or untrue, and it was actually written by Richard Penn Smith, not Crockett.[2]

One of the most well-known hoaxes published in Arthur Train's time was in 1929, when Simon and Schuster published the best-selling book titled *Cradle of the Deep*. It was written by Joan Lowell and told the riveting tale of how she spent her childhood living aboard her father's four-masted ship, sailing the South Seas until she was seventeen, when there was a shipwreck and she was forced to swim for miles to safety, with a litter of kittens clinging to her back. The fact of the matter was that Lowell "had grown up almost entirely in Berkeley, Calif." The *New York Times* reviewed *Cradle of the Deep* as a work of nonfiction, recommended it wholeheartedly, though the reviewer did note that the quantity of disasters—from "shipwreck, scurvy, fire and so on"—seemed extreme, but the reviewer was quick to note: "this is not to question the veracity of the seagoing author." Others did question Lowell's veracity, including "nautical experts [who] cited innumerable flaws in Miss Lowell's account." In less than two months from its publication, the book was declared fiction. Having duped many and even attained the status as a best seller, the book industry became concerned that the publication of Lowell's hoaxing book served only to "lower literary standards." One impassioned critic stated:

If today we have reached the point of progress where a literary hoax is condoned as good business; where publishers have no regard for the authenticity of a work, so long as it is successful; where the critical profession, organized through its publicity channels as never before, is also willing to disregard standards and quality of product, and to delude the reading public into a false demand; where deterioration has at last struck at the stronghold of spiritual integrity in the written word; then we have fallen on evil times in American literature. If charlatanism is to be more successful than honest writing, and win its way through advertising and publicity on which there is no check, the foundations of all literary effort are seriously threatened. All those who seek to express themselves, and who make their living by writing, will be ultimately affected by it. The Joan Lowell case is a signpost showing in no uncertain way the path we are to follow unless we change our course. It is high time we sat down and looked the scene over.[3]

Aside from any diminution in literary standards, Lowell's hoax proved to be costly in a monetary sense. The Book-of-the-Month Club had recommended *Cradle of the Deep* to its readers before learning that the book was a hoax; once the truth was revealed, the club felt compelled to offer a refund to its 65,000 subscribers. What's more, the former president of the American Book Publishers' Association, John Macrae, made unflattering statements about the club's selection of *Cradle in the Deep,* which ultimately caused the Book-of-the-Month Club to sue Macrae for libel, requesting $200,000 for the damage to its reputation.[4]

The literary hoax has appeared even more recently, such as with Clifford Irving's 1972 attempted publication of a "bogus autobiography of Howard R. Hughes," which landed him in prison for seventeen months. Irving's hoax was so bold and breathtaking that the story behind it was even made into a movie in 2007—*The Hoax.* In 1978 David Rorvik's *The Cloning of a Man* was published, in which Rorvik "claim[ed] to be a central figure in the creation of the first exact genetic copy of a human being."[5] Whether the book was fact or fiction was not immediately clear—even the publisher "state[d] in a foreword that they do not know if the book is true," and Rorvik himself stated in the book that "he does not expect anyone to accept the book as proof that cloning has occurred." Shortly after the book was published, a scientist cited in it, J. D. Bromhall, sued Rorvik for $7 million, charging that Rorvik's book was a "fraud and hoax and that his reputation has been injured by its unauthorized use of his name." The matter was considered so serious that there were even "Congressional hearings on the underlying issues," and suggestions were made that "the book-publishing industry should draft a code of ethics, or face possible federal regulation." Bromhall's case ultimately settled for an unspecified sum and an apology by the book's publisher.[6]

Around the same time as the publication of Rorvik's book, *The Amityville Horror* by Jay Anson became a best seller, telling the "true story" of a haunted house on Long Island. Although a home was situated in the location described by the book, the home owners insisted it was not haunted and even sued the publisher of Anson's book, Prentice-Hall, for failing to check the authenticity of this "true story." The family suffered as "crowds of curious tourists" congregated outside their home, harassed them, trespassed, and even collected "souvenirs" from their property. The home owners were clearly frustrated, stating that Anson and Prentice-Hall had "got[ten] away with murder," and noting "you can write a book—completely untrue from beginning to end—and get away with it. If you're going to put on the cover that it's a true story, then you should check into it. No one at Prentice-Hall checked a single fact."[7]

Perhaps one of the most famous hoaxes in recent history is James Frey's *A Million Little Pieces,* published in 2003, which became a best-selling book that told of Frey's drug addiction and recovery. However, once details began to emerge showing that Frey had embellished his story, the public was outraged. Having been selected by Oprah Winfrey for her famous book club, he appeared on her television show after the falsities in his book had come to light, and Oprah Winfrey confronted him "for lying about his past and portraying the book as a truthful account of his life." During the television program, "alternately appearing to fight back tears and displaying vivid anger at the author and his publisher," Oprah told Frey that she felt "duped," "but more importantly, I feel that you betrayed millions of readers." To address the public's outrage, Frey's publisher postponed printing and shipping copies of *A Million Little Pieces* until a disclaimer could be added that "a number of facts have been altered and incidents embellished." It was believed that the book industry would be forced to examine how it treated nonfiction in the future, to ensure that fact checking was performed before publishing a book that purported to be a true story.[8]

From Jonathan Swift's hoax over the death of John Partridge to James Frey's highly embellished "memoir," Americans have been "had" innumerable times. However, most of these hoaxes are entirely different from Train's. Swift, Penn, Irving, Rorvik, Lowell, and Frey's books all involved the story of someone who had actually lived—either themselves or their victims— yet *Yankee Lawyer* told the "life" story of a creature of fiction. Further, many hoaxes involved either a fake story or a fake author—Swift published his prank about the death of Partridge under a pseudonym, Lowell's story was entirely fabricated, Rorvik's cloning story was loosely based on science but utterly false, and Frey's story had underpinnings in his experiences but was so elaborately embellished it hardly resembled reality. However, *Yankee Lawyer* was based on an impossible premise—a character of fiction authoring an autobiography of his fictitious life. Thus the purported author and his story were both "fake." Under these circumstances, it seemed to Train that Tutt fans would surely recognize that Train had written *Yankee Lawyer,* for it was inconceivable that Tutt could have done so.

Although Train fooled many people, he did not face the same backlash as Joan Lowell, Clifford Irving, David Rorvik, or James Frey. Criminal charges were not pressed against Train; the publishing world did not grow concerned that Train's ruse would tarnish the entire industry's reputation or code of ethics; calls for government regulation or congressional hearings were never made; public scoldings for presenting a fictitious book as a true autobiography did not occur. Yet *Yankee Lawyer* was a best-selling book that, like other literary hoaxes, presented itself to be something it was not. Why was Tutt's "autobiography" treated so differently by the public, the media, the book industry, and the government than other hoaxes were? The short answer is that Train's hoax was not considered as harmful as the others. As to the readers who were initially fooled, once they were assured that Train was the true author, hindsight suddenly provided a clear understanding that the book was surely fiction, and many were amused that they had been tricked. The media had a field day by the book's very existence. Reviewers willingly allowed the hoax to perpetuate by not identifying the true author of the book, and the controversy over who actually wrote the book seemed a rather innocent one. Meanwhile, Tutt was still beloved by the public, and Train, by extension, also held a favored place in the hearts of readers—there was no real impetus for Train to be reprimanded, criticized, or punished for his literary handiwork. In terms of creating new regulations for the book industry, the government's hands were essentially tied. In the midst of World War II, it would seem unpatriotic to take a character that had become a symbol of America and embroil him in congressional hearings or use him as an example to place restrictions on the book industry. In addition, with the concern over censorship of books during wartime, the idea of placing any sort of limitation on the book industry during the war was particularly unsavory.

The primary difference between *Yankee Lawyer* and other literary hoaxes is that with Tutt, the truth could have been easily discovered. While Joan Lowell's childhood was not public knowledge before she published *Cradle of the Deep* and James Frey's struggle with addiction was unheard of before *A Million Little Pieces,* Ephraim Tutt was known as the fictitious character Arthur Train created, and there were twenty-five years' worth of fictitious stories to prove it. Since the truth was hiding in plain sight, most people felt that Train did not deserve to be publicly censured. Even some of the most jilted fans were ultimately amused by Train's literary gimmick. Aside from bruised pride and minor embarrassment over being "had," Americans generally had fun with the hoax and enjoyed entertaining the possibility that someone like Mr. Tutt could exist.

When considering how long Tutt had appeared as a creature of fiction, it is surprising that so many people were still fooled by his autobiography. However, as with all literary hoaxes, what makes them so confusing is that there is an underlying element of plausibility. For *Yankee Lawyer,* there were two main factors that made it feel credible. First, it was historically accurate; it recounted facts in American history, and name-dropped famous people who purportedly interacted with Tutt. The second factor was that Train borrowed from the hundreds of stories he had previously written to provide details for Tutt's personal history; thus when people read Tutt's autobiography, they read about cases and events—albeit fictitious ones—with which they were already familiar. The use of factual information and fictitious details that the public had heard before had the effect of building credibility for the entire premise of the book.

A final factor that was unusual about Train's hoax is that his publisher, Charles Scribner's Sons, was entirely cognizant of the fact that *Yankee Lawyer*, contrary to its appearance, was not written by Tutt. While many other hoaxes feature authors who have fooled their publisher into believing that their book tells a true story, just the opposite can be said for *Yankee Lawyer*. The publication of *Yankee Lawyer*, as the "Autobiography of Ephraim Tutt," was executed with the full knowledge and understanding of Maxwell Perkins and Charles Scribner's Sons; both knew the autobiography was fictitious. In fact, considering Tutt's history as a character of fiction, Perkins and Scribner's were certain the public would assume that Train wrote the book—as he had every other Tutt story. It was unfathomable that readers would be fooled. However, it quickly became apparent that the public was far more gullible than they had anticipated. It soon became clear that large numbers of readers enthusiastically believed that Ephraim Tutt was real. Initially, Scribner's, Perkins, and Train were convinced that those who expressed confusion over Tutt's existence were a slim minority of readers; however, time proved this was not the case.

One of the first of its kind, a letter arrived at Scribner's, dated September 11, 1943, written in the voluptuous script of Alice F. Sweeney, of Boston, Massachusetts. The letter read: "To settle a bet, will you please inform me if Ephraim Tutt, whose autobiography I just finished reading, is a real or fictitious person. I bet that he is real because on the back of your book cover you stated that he is the best known 'living' lawyer." A few days later, the publisher prepared a response and sent it to Ms. Sweeney: "We are very sorry indeed to have to tell you that you have lost your bet." The letter went on to note that Ms. Sweeney likely had not read the previous stories about Mr. Tutt, for if she had, "I think you would probably have recognized this publication for what it is after reading only a few pages." Interestingly, this letter noted that "most of the reviews played in with this hoax, but at the same time they hinted at it, . . . generally very broadly." In any event, Ms. Sweeney was informed that "a great deal that is in the book is actually true, as having been within the experience of Arthur Train himself."[9]

Meanwhile, Train received a handwritten letter from a gentleman residing in Boston, Massachusetts, dated September 1943, who stated that he found *Yankee Lawyer* nothing short of the most wonderful book he had ever read. This reader, who was not confused in the slightest, addressed Train with the enthusiastic declaration that Train's "new book has made a complete Tutt-Train fan of me! Were I a lawyer or a fisherman or a steady reader of current fiction, this would doubtless have happened long ago." He continued:

> Now as nothing more than an admirer of good writing—whether fact or fiction—and a good biography in particular, I "raise high the perpendicular hand" to you. Are you not a pioneer in your field? Has any previous writer of fiction turned the tables on himself as you have done? I cannot think of any other writer whose books, over so considerable [a] span of years, have set the stage so perfectly for such a performance. And how admirably you have pulled it off! If only I had a more intimate knowledge of your doings through life I doubt not that I could check fiction with fact at many points. . . . When you came to my friend and classmate, Dick Davis, and my kinsman, Dana Gibson, I feel myself on solid ground, and cannot applaud too warmly, what you have done with them. I have enjoyed many an inward chuckle over the stories scattered through the book. On the more serious side, I feel such sympathy with your social and political views in general and I should want to shake your hand with real enthusiasm, even if I had enjoyed nothing else in the book. May it have the same success that I really believe it deserves.[10]

While the initial few letters seemed to trickle into Train's and Scribner's mailboxes, Train and Perkins quickly realized they had a real problem on their hands. For example, on September 15, 1943, a beleaguered Train posted a letter to Perkins, as he needed some advice badly. He had received a particularly moving letter from a woman named Mrs. Bradford, and Train found himself "distressed to know what to do. . . . I am afraid this dear old [woman] will be deeply hurt no matter what I do." A few days later, Perkins jokingly responded to Train, "I don't know how you can solve the problem presented by Mrs. Bradford . . . unless we can persuade one of those actors who are likely to play Mr. Tutt's part [on Broadway], to impersonate him." On a more serious note, Perkins stated: "The poor lady must know the truth in the end, though, and anyhow, you could say you were exceedingly flattered in so convincingly creating a character, although chagrined that so many were deceived far beyond your intentions into the belief in his reality." In the same letter, Perkins noted that he had received a few letters at Charles Scribner's Sons and found that "at least half a dozen people were completely deceived, and one . . . also lost money by betting that Mr. Tutt existed."[11]

With the passage of very little time, it became increasingly clear that it was no longer a matter of a half-dozen confused readers. So common were letters to Tutt that, in a letter from Perkins to Train, after discussing a variety of business matters, Perkins disinterestedly added that he was enclosing more mail that had been addressed to Ephraim Tutt.[12] Letters from readers across the United States and Canada poured into Charles Scribner's Sons. Some of the places generating the most letters were Washington, DC, Missouri, Illinois, North and South Carolina, Maryland, Wisconsin, Florida, Pennsylvania, Louisiana, Arizona, Texas, Virginia, New Mexico, Ohio, Massachusetts, and New York. Most letters sought information on Tutt; however, the manner in which these requests were made reveals the wide spectrum of attitudes relating to whether Tutt was a real person: some letters revealed a strong conviction that he did exist, others exposed that there was doubt. Some letters are funny and whimsical; others can be downright heartbreaking.

One concerned patron of a library in Toronto, Canada, wrote a letter requiring information on how *Yankee Lawyer* should be properly catalogued. He explained:

> About a week ago I put in a reserve at our local public library, where the Staff and the service are always superlative, asking that YANKEE LAWYER: The Autobiography of EPHRAIM TUTT, be put to one side for myself.
>
> When I called the circulation desk yesterday for the volume, the young lady there was unable to find it for a while, and then discovered it among the fiction reserves. I had told her that it would be among the biographies.
>
> I spent several hours last evening and this morning reading the book, as I found it intensely attractive. Nothing in the volume seems to me to justify its cataloguing as fiction.
>
> Is, or was, Mr. Tutt a real person? I gathered that he is not entirely an artist's creation from the Sunday Book Reviews of the NEW YORK TIMES and THE HERALD-TRIBUNE.
>
> Perhaps the fact that Mr. Train used the name EPHRAIM TUTT in his well-known stories has misled the ladies of the Cataloguing Room.

Scribner's responded to this man, informing him that the "ladies in the catalogue room are right." It was also duly noted that "there was no intention of actually deceiving anyone with regard to the authorship. The idea was simply that Mr. Tutt had become so living a figure through Arthur Train's stories that it seemed suitable to have it appear that he was now telling his own." Shortly after this letter exchange, Perkins mailed a note to Train, wondering whether Train had noticed that *Yankee Lawyer* appeared in the Sunday *New York Times* best-seller list as a work of fiction, while it appeared in the *Tribune*'s nonfiction list.[13] That Perkins and Train were enjoying the maelstrom of publicity and confusion unfolding before their eyes is apparent in the letters they wrote to each other.

In November 1943 a man who worked in New Jersey wrote to Charles Scribner's Sons, desperate for a little clarification. He explained that several members of his office were "at a loss to understand the relationship between Mr. Train and Ephraim Tutt. Is this book the autobiography of Arthur Train who borrows the name of Ephraim Tutt for his purpose? Or is E. T. an entirely fictional character created by Mr. Train?"[14]

Some readers made it quite clear that they were angst ridden over this matter. One woman living in Washington, DC, declared herself to be in a "quandary" and demanded to know, "Who, in Heaven's name, wrote *Yankee Lawyer*?" This poor woman noted that her "possession of the book is no help in solving the controversy." One man, living in California, noted the two sides of the debate and stated, "I think Arthur Train succeeded, by means of his preface and the explanatory paragraph of Chapter XXI, in confusing the public to a point where they know not whether Ephraim Tutt is a 'Saturday Evening Post' character or the living lawyer he claims to be." So vexed was this reader that he concluded by stating: "I shall appreciate the solution of this mystery which is rapidly resulting in a state of prostration." Another letter, by a New Yorker, written in February 1945, noted that while she "enjoyed [*Yankee Lawyer*] very much," she was plagued by the "stories that this is not a true biography." Her distress over such rumors was palpable as she exclaimed, "I'm just about at my wits end [in] trying to decide whether it is an autobiography or not."[15]

One woman wrote to Charles Scribner's Sons requesting that it intervene to "put an end to a warm discussion." After asking whether Tutt was real or imaginary, the woman who wrote the letter affirmed that she "thoroughly enjoyed reading his autobiography, but . . . failed to understand how a man who does not exist could write an autobiography and have it copyrighted." As with many other *Yankee Lawyer* readers, she noted that she would "be glad to be set straight in the matter."[16]

Some readers were less troubled and were just plain curious as to whether such a person as Ephraim Tutt existed—sometimes suggesting in their letters that they would prefer an affirmative answer. One reader, a resident of Chicago, asked whether "Ephraim Tutt is the same person as Arthur Train?

Are Arthur Train and Ephraim Tutt two different people or is Train the author and created Ephraim Tutt only as a fictional character." The writer of this letter remarked, "if there were more people as human as Ephraim Tutt many difficulties would disappear."[17]

On December 9, 1943, Charles Scribner's Sons received a letter from Judge Archie H. Cohen, a US District Court judge for the Northern District of Illinois, Eastern Division. The judge remarked that he inquired about the book at two bookstores carrying *Yankee Lawyer,* and one listed the book as written by Arthur Train, the other, by Ephraim Tutt. The judge explained he found himself in a "quandary" since, after reading the book, "with the forewo[r]d by Arthur Train and with the photographic reproductions of Ephraim Tutt (if there b[e] any such living character)," two lawyers had presented "an issue which they want me to decide. One contends that *The Yankee Lawyer* was written by Arthur Train about himself. The other says that the book is by Ephraim Tutt, now an old man, with the assistance of Arthur Train." The judge concluded that "if men who are students of logic are confused, won't you please give me the answer?"[18]

Not only were requests pouring into Charles Scribner's Sons regarding whether Tutt, Train, or both existed, but letters also requested other information of Tutt. One attorney from Portage, Wisconsin, requested Tutt's address; for what purpose, he did not say. Another attorney, from Baltimore, Maryland, requested Tutt's address, "or better still, send me his telephone number as I should like to have the pleasure of talking to him over the telephone, personally." Yet another attorney, Ms. Seider, of Bay Shore, New York, wrote Scribner's requesting Tutt's address, for she had a matter she wished to "personally discuss with him and am unable to locate him at this time." After receiving a response from Charles Scribner's Sons explaining that Tutt was merely a creature of fiction, Ms. Seider sent Scribner's another letter, disclosing that her original letter was the product of a "spirited discussion" at a bar association meeting she attended. Since the group of attorneys could not settle the matter for themselves, the task of retrieving a reliable answer was relegated to Ms. Seider. On a more personal note, Ms. Seider commented that she has "long been an ardent admirer of Mr. Train and the utterly enjoyable and fantastic manner in which he has Mr. Tutt pull legal rabbits out of court hats has indeed invoked my approbation whilst it challenged my legal imagination." With respect to the confusion among the members of her Bar Association, Ms. Seider warmly commented: "May it be said in tribute to your author, that the Autobiography of Ephraim Tutt is so well drawn and written that its fiction assumes utter reality in the minds of its readers."[19]

Lawyers across the nation faced their share of debate over *Yankee Lawyer*. An attorney from Meriden, Connecticut, who wrote to Charles Scribner's Sons in January 1944, requested information on whether Tutt existed. He explained that he had taken part in a discussion with "several of the members [of the bar in his community who] claimed that there is not and never had been a lawyer by the name of Ephraim Tutt, that he is the product of fiction conceived by Arthur Train." In addition, this attorney requested information on whether "the experiences narrated in *Yankee Lawyer*" were real.[20] It seems that this attorney would have been comforted to know that even if Tutt had not experienced the events within *Yankee Lawyer*, they were based in reality. To many letter writers making inquiries such as this one, the response from Scribner's—and sometimes Train—would note that many of the stories in *Yankee Lawyer* were based on Train's experiences.

In January 1944 an attorney practicing in Madison, Wisconsin, wrote to Scribner's, noting that his wife had given him a copy of *Yankee Lawyer* for Christmas. After mentioning the book to a few lawyers who worked in his building, he was shocked to discover that they believed the book was fiction. Apparently, this gentleman was not persuaded by his colleagues' arguments, for he wrote to Scribner's asking if Tutt was real, if Train's "pen name" was Ephraim Tutt, and also, "we would appreciate it if you would, or could, furnish to us the title and volume and page of any cases in the United States Supreme Court or the state of New York, wherein Ephraim Tutt appeared as the attorney for any of the litigants."[21] It seems that perhaps this attorney needed more proof than a mere response from Tutt's publishing company to confirm that Tutt was real.

Another attorney, writing from Paramus, New Jersey, had just completed *Yankee Lawyer* and "was convinced that [he] had read the story of a lawyer in real life." However, while discussing the book with a friend, who was also an attorney, "all my feelings for the book were blasted because he said that Ephraim Tutt was merely a figment of the imagination of Arthur Train, and that, in his opinion, Ephraim Tutt does not exist in real life, but that the book portrays the story of Arthur Train's life." The attorney asked that he be "enlighten[ed] . . . on this score," and noted, "I trust this request will cause you to breach no trade rules."[22]

In February 1944, a future lawyer contacted Train, first apologizing for seeming "presumptuous in writing you, but in the words of the hymn, 'other refuge I have none.'" He explained, "I have been, and am, a zealous, admiring, and devoted follower of your Mr. Tutt—ever since he has been known by the public." This writer noted that he wished to obtain a copy of *Mr. Tutt's Case Book,* since it was cited in *Yankee Lawyer.* He explained that he had just retired from thirty years of service as an officer in the army, and he planned to spend his retirement practicing law by "apply[ing] the character, tenets, and principles of your Mr. Tutt to my cases and in these parts." Although this letter writer seemed to know that Mr. Tutt was not real, since he was writing to Train, so great an example did Mr. Tutt set that he wanted to practice like Tutt nonetheless.[23]

A rather curious letter, sent to Train's home in January 1944, was from an attorney who had read *Yankee Lawyer* and wished to come to the defense of none other than Arthur Train. The letter, written by Mr. Nims, who appeared to be a partner of the New York law firm Nims, Verdi & Martin, stated, "I quite agree that you have a sound reason to resent deeply the various groundless statements which [Tutt] has written of you, and I am sure you are entitled to a substantial recovery in any action which you may decide to bring against him." Apparently, Train considered retaining this attorney to sue Tutt. However, Mr. Nims informed Train that although he "appreciate[d] more than I can tell you your suggestion that I act for you in this matter," Mr. Nims could not do so. He explained, "Tutt and I have spent so many delightful evenings before my fire and I have come to have such high regard and friendship for him that, despite his lack of consideration for you, I cannot bring myself to take action against him and deal with him on your behalf as he deserves." Mr. Nims went on to explain that it baffled him that Tutt, "a man who has given countless people a greater faith in the power of the law to produce justice," could have written passages so injurious to Train in his autobiography. When Tutt "realizes how deeply what he has written has injured you, I am sure he will wish to make all possible amends," Mr. Nims opined. It seems that Mr. Nims was so concerned about repairing Train's friendship with Tutt that he even offered his services in arranging an interview between Train and Tutt so the two could work through their differences.[24]

Some readers were aware that the book was likely a hoax, but still wrote for clarification and to comment on how talented a writer Train was for making such a hoax possible. For example, one letter from Coral Gables, Florida, noted that "the statement is made that Ephraim Tutt of 'Yankee Lawyer' is a fiction. If Ephraim Tutt is a fake, the author is a master craftsman. The portrait is so cleverly drawn and with such realistic touches as to be most convincing. And I venture practically all who read this delightful narrative are being hoaxed." Enclosing a stamp, this reader asked that she be told "whether Tutt is flesh and blood or merely a figment of Arthur Train's imagination." Many readers expressed some suspicion as to Tutt being a fictitious character but desired a clear answer as to Tutt's identity, one way or another. One woman, who belonged to a reading club and was assigned to give a review of *Yankee Lawyer* at their next meeting, sent a rather frantic letter to Charles Scribner's Sons in January 1944, opening with "S.O.S!" After explaining her reasons for believing that Tutt existed, she remarked, "yet, as I glance through [the book], I strongly suspect it is fiction." Nevertheless, she provided a self-addressed envelope in which Scribner's was to send its revelation.[25]

One worker at the General Motors Corporation, Packard Electric Division, located in Warren, Ohio, wrote to Scribner's and opened his letter by identifying himself as a "conscientious follower of Arthur Train's 'Ephraim Tutt' stories." He wrote that he had finished reading *Yankee Lawyer* and not only "enjoyed the book . . . [but found] [him]self filled with admiration for the author." The problem, however, was that he had no idea who the author was. This man noted, "my dictionary defines an autobiography as 'the story of one's life written by oneself,'" and therefore, he "assumed that Ephraim Tutt *must* be real." However, he had also heard that Tutt reputedly did not exist. He explained, "as a law-abiding American citizen, I feel the right to know the facts." "After all, when one develops a fondness for a character, one has a right to know of whom they are fond!"[26]

Other readers who had read Train's fictional accounts of Tutt's law practice over the years were also unsure of whether Tutt's "autobiography" was a sign that Tutt was not just a creature of fiction. "Two of us in this office have, within the past week, read the Autobiography of Ephraim Tutt. Both of us have read many of the Ephraim Tutt stories in the Saturday Evening Post and we have enjoyed the book as much as we have those short stories, but we are puzzled," a man from Philadelphia wrote. "One of us contends that Ephraim Tutt was, or is, a real life character; the other insists that Tutt is merely a pseudonym for Arthur Train and that the autobiography is merely the story of Mr. Train's life and experiences." For the letter writer, the latter position was untenable, since "Mr. Train was supposed to have married fairly early in life, while Tutt remained a bachelor."[27]

Some letters were addressed to Tutt personally. One letter read: "after reading *Yankee Lawyer,* [the writer] feels impelled to write personal congratulations. You did a hell of a good job. Thanks, old Boy!" And there were some readers who knew Tutt did not exist, but thoroughly enjoyed his autobiography nonetheless. Harry Marsh, a Tutt fan for years, remarked, "Old Eph, had he been real, was three years old when I was born and so I found comfort in the old geezer, for contemporaries understand what the present generations miss." Marsh thanked Train for "many enjoyable hours," and warned, "don't dare to kill him off." Marsh requested a copy of *Yankee Lawyer* from Scribner's and requested whether Train, "through a kindly heart," would autograph it. On the bottom of Marsh's letter there is a notation, possibly by Train, "can you give me an address for this man?" Another reader sent a request for an autograph, stating: "While 'Mr. Tutt' is my old friend, it is through Mr. Train 'we met.' So, I'd rather, if you please, have Mr. Train autograph this book."[28]

Other readers believed not only that Tutt was real, but also that Tutt might have known—or they were certain he did know—relatives, friends, or the letter writer himself or herself. One such letter was written in January 1943, by Rev. Gordon Chilson Reardon of the First Universalist Church, in Dexter, Maine. Rev. Reardon explained that his father, the late Rev. John B. Reardon, grew up in Ludlow, Vermont, was active in the Democratic Party, and attended Tufts College with the late John G. Sargent. Believing that his father may have lived in close proximity to Tutt at some point in time, the reverend was led to believe that "Tutt might remember [the late Rev. Reardon] and perhaps provide [the writer] with some information relative to various occasions where father did not permit his profession to interfere with his politics." A woman living in New York wrote that she had read and enjoyed *Yankee Lawyer* and passed the book on to a few of her friends to read. She commented that she had met several of the people mentioned in *Yankee Lawyer,* and noted that she believed Tutt "might even be someone [her] father had known of." Yet it seems her friends cast some doubt on whether Tutt existed. "[I] thought 'Ephraim Tutt' was a real person, only had taken another name, really had lived in the places spoken of in the city, and was living in the 'East Sixties.'" After asking to be informed of whether she or her friends were right, the letter writer noted, "I would be so grateful and satisfied to know he was a real person." Seemingly convinced that "Ephraim Tutt" lived, even if he did not go by that name, she concluded her letter stating: "If he is living here, I suppose he does not want people to know his real name, but I wish I did know it."[29]

Some were so convinced of Tutt's existence after reading his autobiography that they resisted any suggestion that he did not exist. For example, in March 1945, a resident of Hempstead, New York, wrote to Charles Scribner's Sons asking that they "settle a controversy." She explained that she had borrowed her local library's copy of *Yankee Lawyer* knowing it was a work of fiction before she began to read it. However, after finishing it, she had grown quite certain that it was not fiction, and upon returning the book, she commented to her librarian about Tutt's amazing life. Apparently, her local librarian responded that the book was fiction, written by Arthur Train. Losing patience, the library patron replied, "no, Mr. Tutt had given Mr. Train permission to use him in books." Things became more heated, when the library clerk replied, after becoming "quite lofty," that *Yankee Lawyer* "was fiction and that Hempstead High School had it as such." Having become frustrated and disgusted with her librarian (and grown displeased with whoever classified books at Hempstead High School), she commented, "I write you because I don't think much of those English teachers who say this book is fiction." Noting that her son would have to read a certain number of fiction and nonfiction books for school, this concerned parent requested clarification to ensure her son experienced no hardship meeting his reading requirements.[30]

One man, on December 22, 1943, was finalizing what gifts he would be giving for Christmas that year. He wrote a letter to Scribner's that day, distressed to find that the Hartford Public Library listed *Yankee Lawyer* as fiction, but he had "found it a very enjoyable book and judging by the description on the jacket and the contents of the book as a whole, it did not occur to me to question the authenticity." Based on his belief that Tutt was a real, living lawyer, he had "secured several copies for Christmas presents." Having heard recently from "other sources" that the book might not be a legitimate autobiography, he became concerned about giving the book to those for whom he cared. He apologized for "bother[ing] [Scribner's] about this, but I can't get the information locally."[31]

One Tutt fan, writing from Los Angeles, expressed his feelings about Tutt by way of a poem he had drafted, based on some of the various episodes mentioned in *Yankee Lawyer*. He noted, "Your book 'The Yankee Lawyer' I was sorry to lay down; I laughed and cried / as you described the things which cheered so many lives." After several stanzas describing some of his favorite adventures in Tutt's autobiography, this writer concluded: "Justice shall be done you see, it comes to you, and comes to me / It may not come to us today, but God will surely have his way."[32] It seems this reader was not only touched by Tutt's experiences but also found great meaning in Tutt's parables.

While some of Tutt's admirers were at least amenable to the idea that perhaps Tutt was an imaginary character, there were also Tutt fans who expressed nothing short of unappeasable disappointment when their beloved Tutt proved to be fictitious. One reader was compelled to write to Charles Scribner's Sons conveying her anger and disillusionment in learning, after sending a letter to Mr. Tutt, that he did not exist. She requested that Scribner's "please excuse and ignore the letter I sent you a few days ago and just cross off the name of Tutt and readdress to me, the letter I had enclosed. Since writing it, I have been convinced of the fictitious character of Ephraim Tutt." This reader continued, noting that Scribner's should "perhaps forgive a feeling of profound sadness that a character so fine should be a travesty of all that it proclaimed to champion!" In fact, this woman warned that she believed there would "be repercussions, for Train should not have worked so hard and done such a good job. He would have been a greater advocate of justice had his character Tutt stood on the honest legs of fiction."[33] Although Scribner's sent responses to all letters, and tried to mollify the hurt feelings of those who had been fooled, many readers were never heard from again. It is likely that some people—such as the man who wrote that Tutt had "restored [his] faith in mankind"—did not overcome the feeling of sadness upon learning that Tutt did not exist and his autobiography was imaginary.

Beyond letters conveying an appreciation for Tutt, another character in that book developed a fan base. Tutt's touching love story with Esther Farr made some readers wonder about her. For instance, in a 1945 letter to Charles Scribner's Sons, a woman living in Virginia inquired: "Will you kindly tell me if 'Yankee Lawyer' is actually the autobiography of Mr. Eph Tutt. I am especially interested to know if the legal firm of Tutt and Tutt existed in New York City, and at what time, and if Mrs. Esther Farr is indeed a person." Another letter written to Charles Scribner's Sons noted that while *Yankee Lawyer* was most "interesting" to read, Tutt "has left unanswered one question. Was he ever able to marry his Esther? Being a woman, I'm naturally overwhelmed by the tragedy of their love story. One of the saddest I've ever read."[34]

As many people became confused over whether Tutt existed, popular periodicals tried to explain what drove so many readers to insist that the autobiography proved that Tutt was a real person. In fact, the *Saturday Evening Post* and the *American Bar Association Journal* both compared Tutt to another mythical being whose existence is sometimes doubted—Santa Claus. While at first blush the comparison may seem odd, these periodicals maintained that just as adults grappled with the true identity of Ephraim Tutt, children faced a similar predicament as they weighed their doubts that perhaps Santa Claus did not exist against their genuine desire that he might. With Tutt there were many readers who remembered Train's fictitious stories about Tutt, but upon reading *Yankee Lawyer,* they wanted to believe that a man like Tutt could exist. Despite their awareness that Tutt had only appeared as a fiction for years, these readers allowed their desire to trump reason. They chose to overlook the facts that weighed in favor of Tutt's nonexistence and instead to believe that Tutt was a living lawyer to fulfill their hope that all he represented could be real.

Just as Virginia O'Hanlon wrote to the *New York Sun* in September 1897, stating: "Dear Editor. . . . Some of my little friends say there is no Santa Claus. Papa says 'If you see it in The Sun it's so.' Please tell me the truth, is there a Santa Claus?"—almost fifty years later, adults mailed letters to Charles Scribner's Sons asking the same sort of question about the existence of Ephraim Tutt. In commenting on this phenomenon, the *Saturday Evening Post* published an article titled, "Sure, Virginia, There's a Mr. Tutt," and playfully referenced the *New York Sun*'s response to Virginia's letter:

> Yes, Virginia, there is a Santa Claus. He exists as certainly as love and generosity and devotion exist, and you know that they abound and give to your life its highest beauty and joy. Alas, how dreary would be the world if there were no Santa Claus! It would be as dreary

as if there were no Virginias. There would be no childlike faith, no poetry, no romance, to make tolerable this existence.[35]

Just as Santa Claus gave children faith and hope and made the world seem less bleak, so did Tutt for his readers. The letters sent to Scribner's show that those who wrote desperately wanted to believe in Tutt, but had enough of a doubt that they needed to write for clarification. While the *Saturday Evening Post* made it clear that Arthur Train had written *Yankee Lawyer*, the article doubted that devoted Tutt fans would succumb to this reality.

Beyond the *Saturday Evening Post*, the *American Bar Association Journal* also noted the similarity between Tutt and Santa Claus. In a review of *Yankee Lawyer*, the journal commented that in trying to answer the question of whether Tutt existed, it was reminded of "the refrain of the New York *Sun's* ageless editorial response to the little girl," and noted:

> [As with Santa Claus,] so of "Eph." Certainly he lives in the brain and breast of every lawyer worth his salt—the wistful, perhaps whimsical, fancy of himself as a some-time-to-be modern combination of Henry Esmond, Chevalier Bayard, and Frank Hogan—gracious and gallant, but ready and able by artful expedients to aid the poor, rescue the defenseless, and confound the arrogant, all in the cause of a "more perfect justice."
>
> "Eph" is of the same stuff as the dreams and hopes which warm the heart, start the song, and give importance to even the commonplace in the lawyer's life and work. Isn't this *reality*?[36]

Clearly, Train had created quite a mess for himself, but that did not stop him from taking a few liberties in perpetuating the idea that perhaps Tutt did exist. Although in a September 1943 letter to Perkins Train admitted to feeling "distressed" by the confusion, he was also having the time of his life watching as *Yankee Lawyer* wreaked its havoc. For in the same letter in which he described the anguish he felt at having tricked a fragile elderly woman, he also commented that "the reviews seem to be uncommonly good, enough to justify the expectation that Tutt may get to the bestselling list. Do you think so? The one in the Wall Street Journal was a peach!" He also made a rather cryptic inquiry as to whether "the window display [was] a success," which likely refers to a Charles Scribner's Sons store display, which may have housed a cane and top hat belonging to Tutt. The letter proceeds with Train asking whether "they still have Mr. Tutt's long-headed cane downstairs," and, if "they" did, "why not send it along with his hat to be auctioned off in Providence on the 23rd?" In a postscript, Train even added: "Should think the cane would bring a good price in War Bonds with Kip Fedderman as auctioneer." Unfortunately for Train, the cane was never auctioned off. "The ivory headed cane belongs to Mr. Wilcox and he is unwilling to part with it permanently," Perkins informed Train.[37] These letters indicate that although Train claimed he did not wish to deceive anyone, he committed a few good-natured misdeeds in order to perpetuate the idea that Tutt was alive and practicing.

Confusion swept the United States and quickly spread across the world. When Tutt's autobiography was published in 1943, the United States was in the throes of World War II. American soldiers were stationed across the world, and there was one book, in particular, that caused quite a sensation when it reached the front lines.

Arthur Cheney Train, circa 1930. Photo by Kaiden-Keystone. Photo courtesy of Princeton University Library.

Judge Harold R. Medina, author of the foreword to *Mr. Tutt at His Best*. Photo courtesy of Princeton University Library.

Ephraim Tutt. Photo courtesy of
Princeton University Library.

Stories about Ephraim Tutt were popular among the servicemen in World
War II. Many people were inspired by Tutt's example. Photo circa 1945.
Photo courtesy of Princeton University Library.

According to *Yankee Lawyer,* this is an image of Pottsville, New York, in 1895. Photo courtesy of Princeton University Library.

Various photographs of Ephraim Tutt were included in *Yankee Lawyer.* This one was said to be of Tutt at the age of five. Photo courtesy of Princeton University Library.

Yankee Lawyer included photographs of Ephraim Tutt's mother and father, Margaret and Enoch Tutt. Photos courtesy of Princeton University Library.

Ephraim Tutt's fishing stories were legendary. Demonstrating his fondness for the sport at a young age, this photograph of Tutt on a fishing trip during his college years was included in *Yankee Lawyer*. Photo courtesy of Princeton University Library.

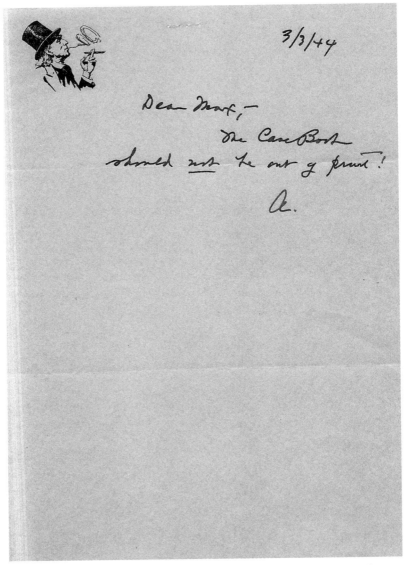

3/3/44

Dear Mart,—

The Case Book
should not be out of print!

A.

Arthur Train had stationery printed, with Tutt's likeness in the upper left-hand corner, which he used to write letters to unsuspecting book reviewers and, in this case, to his longtime editor, Maxwell Perkins. Photo courtesy of Princeton University Library.

"Tutt" stated in *Yankee Lawyer* that this portrait by Arthur William Brown was the one "by which I am best known to the public." Photo courtesy of Princeton University Library.

Lewis R. Linet, a public-spirited attorney, filed a lawsuit against Arthur Train, Maxwell Perkins, and Charles Scribner's Sons alleging that *Yankee Lawyer* was a fraud on the public. Photo courtesy of Lewis R. Linet Jr.

Will Wright, a popular radio and film actor, played the role of Ephraim Tutt in the CBS production *The Amazing Mr. Tutt,* which aired in the late 1940s. Photo courtesy of CBS Radio and Landov.

This photograph, said to be of Esther Farr, was included in *Yankee Lawyer.* Photo courtesy of John Train.

5
"As Popular as Pin-Up Girls"

Mountains of books—good books, including classics, current best sellers, history, biography, science and poetry—are being distributed among our fighting men overseas by a novel publishing arrangement between American book publishers and the Army and Navy.
—*New York Times,* April 30, 1944

The confusion over Tutt's existence proved a welcome distraction during the early 1940s as World War II was raging overseas, and Americans were prompted to actively join the hostilities after the attack on Pearl Harbor. It was a dire time, with a generation of Americans being sent across the globe to join the fight, meeting ruthless war tactics and conditions for which perhaps no training could prepare them. As millions of American men joined the military, those who remained on the home front sacrificed in other ways—by volunteering, rationing their household's use of certain goods and materials, and securing employment outside the home, often in factories manufacturing the supplies needed for the front lines.[1] In the midst of all of this, the image of Tutt—a friendly faced, respectable, clever old gentleman of the highest morals and constitution—provided comfort at home and proved to be a source of repose overseas as well. During World War II Tutt served as a symbol of America and provided inspiration to those fighting the war. Just how Tutt made it to the front lines requires a bit of background before delving into his reception there.

Soon after America declared war on Japan and Germany, concern arose over keeping American morale strong—especially among those who joined the armed services. As early as January 1942—one month after the attack on Pearl Harbor—the army focused on the importance of supplying its servicemen with books. The press announced that "the role of books in maintenance of morale and for recreation has been considered of such importance that the morale branch of the Army and the service clubs have established libraries of varying size at all camps." In reality, while the "government provide[d] libraries in the larger [training] camps, smaller units ha[d] no libraries at all and even in most camps where libraries exist[ed], the demand for recreational reading [wa]s said to be far greater than the supply." In response to this shortage of books, the Victory Book Campaign was created, with the goal of collecting ten million books to send to soldiers, sailors, and marines. In New York City, a quota of two million books was set, and over seven hundred donation sites were established, including inside "libraries, stores, theatres and schools and other depots in all reaches of the city." Although "a landslide" of books was donated when the campaign first began, some collection sites reported that the majority was "junk, fit only for sale as waste paper." Dedicated volunteers pleaded with their communities to donate books:

> This is true for any time, but the book as a symbol of freedom means more now than it has for many years. In country after country books have been destroyed because they stood for liberty of thought and expression. They have been burned and banned. Men's minds as well as their bodies have been rigidly controlled. Our public libraries are the pledge of our belief in intellectual freedom.
>
> But there is another and deeper reason for sending books to the men in camp for their brief hours of relaxation. These men have given up temporarily their freedom of action to work as they please, to live as they choose with their wives and children, in order to defend with their lives our precious liberty. They have done it willingly. We cannot at the moment ease the restrictions placed upon them; we cannot give them back their careers, their homes, their friends, their families. But we can give them the freedom of the book. It is our ack-

nowledgement of their service for us; it is our gratitude for their sacrifice; it is our pledge of a future liberty for them and for all of us.[2]

Articles in newspapers also coaxed the public to donate quality books. "A donator can't go far wrong if he gives books he has read, enjoyed and would like to keep." The Red Cross asked that when donating, "Be sure they are of the kind your own son would want to read if he were in the service." The Victory Book Campaign advertised that "appropriate books in good condition" were needed, and noted "just as foodstuffs are being rationed at home to provide the best in vitamin values for fighting men, there must be no shortage of mental nourishment for the fighting forces." The press published a light chiding every so often to address the donation of books that were unsuitable for the servicemen because they were "ragged or shaky of binding." "All the services are hungry for good books. They know many hours of tediousness. Books are their surest recreation. Like most of the rest of us, they want fiction and detective stories first. Like most of the rest of us, they hunt best sellers and like to be reasonably up-to-date. They will eat up entertaining biography and memoirs. . . . Give them any book that has interested you. But ascertain first that there are no missing or defective pages and that the cover will stay put." "The soldiers' preferences are for fiction, biography, history and technical works in that order," according to a 1942 announcement on the book campaign.[3]

Although the book drive was supposed to last only two months, it ended up being extended for over one year. As the number of Americans in the armed services—and the popularity of books among them—continued to increase, it became clear that the demand for books exceeded ten million volumes. Some cities turned to creative partnerships to try to boost donations. In New York City, the book drive collaborated with the city's milkmen so books could be collected as milk was delivered to people's homes— "since a mountain of books won't come to the Victory Book Campaign from the homes of New Yorkers, the book drive will go to the mountain," the *New York Times* announced. President Roosevelt made a plea for the "cooperation of all citizens, newspapers and radio stations" to help with the book drive, and he and Eleanor Roosevelt personally donated books. In the end the Victory Book Campaign resulted in the collection of seventeen million books; however, in December 1943 the drive was discontinued. Although the Victory Book drive surpassed its original goal, far more books were needed than what could possibly be collected. In addition, "too many people looked upon the voluntary campaign as an opportunity to get rid of books that nobody would want."[4] A new program was devised in 1943 that would result in distribution of quality books to servicemen on a massive and unprecedented scale.

In 1942 it was announced that the Council on Books in Wartime was going to take over the responsibility of sending books to the servicemen. Before 1942 the council concentrated on the role of books in the lives of those who remained on the home front, but its most important contribution to the war effort was what it accomplished for America's sailors, soldiers, and marines. Its slogan was "Books are Weapons," for "books are great builders of morale," and the council found that they served as "companionable 'weapons' against fatigue, boredom and fear." The council's goal was to organize publishers, authors, and others in the book industry and create a united alliance dedicated to sending Americans in the armed services a selection of wholesome and interesting books for their leisure hours. This organization was managed by Philip Van Doren Stern and had a directorate of more than "twenty prominent figures in the book world." An unpaid advisory committee—composed of publishers, authors, librarians, book critics, booksellers, "and other members of the [book] industry"—met twice each week to screen titles to recommend for the armed services and drafted monthly proposed lists of books fit for the front lines.[5]

According to an early report, to "meet the demand of the troops for worthwhile books," the council had arranged for the "purchase [of] large numbers of titles available from regular publishers." However, this plan was not very practical considering the cost of books and their unwieldy size and weight. Thus the council altered its goal to republishing "the best of current fiction, biography, history, philosophy, science, poetry and the drama . . . in pocket-size form." The army and navy had the final word on what books were published, and the books chosen for publication were selected for their perceived likelihood of providing "recreation and entertainment." The council worked closely with the US Army and Navy since after the books were selected and printed the Special Services Division of the Army Service Forces and the Bureau of Naval Personnel had to orchestrate the shipment and disbursement of the books to the servicemen stationed all over the world. In the spring of 1943, the Council on Books in Wartime announced that it planned to send thirty-five million copies of "American books" to the armed forces.[6]

One of the first considerations was the need to provide servicemen with books of a size and shape that could be stowed in a backpack or pocket without burdening its carrier by its weight. It became clear to those who were involved in this endeavor that the configuration of most books— hardcover, too bulky to fit in a pocket, and heavy—just would not do. Besides, with books costing a few dollars each, the council's goal of providing thirty-five million books to the armed services was going to be a prohibitively expensive one, unless modifications were made. It seemed that the only way to provide books to the armed services, without encumbering troops by their size and the army and navy with their cost, was to rebuild the chosen books from the binding to the pages themselves.

To this end a new, troop-friendly book design was created, called the "Armed Services Editions." These books were "pocket size, with a paper cover, bound along the short edge," and had "two columns to the page and type designed for easy reading." This format was revolutionary. Beginning with size, each Armed Services Edition, regardless of its word count, could be tucked away easily by its reader, since even the longest one—which was 512 pages—was "just big enough to slip into a hip pocket," while shorter books were produced so as to "fit snugly into a breast pocket." The Armed Services Editions were bound by several staples, which proved significant, since many servicemen were stationed in locales where insects would feast on a glue binding or the dampness of jungles and other wet climes would cause books with sewn bindings to mildew. The cover of each book was

re-created, with most Armed Services Editions exhibiting a large thumb-
nail image of the original cover, with the title and author written in large
letters. Whenever possible, the covers would exhibit "colored pictures taken
from the jackets of the original editions." The Armed Services Editions
were designed and produced so each volume weighed one-fifth or less
of the amount of a "normal book." In a nutshell, the books were small
enough to be carried by the troops, and a range of titles was offered to appeal to a diverse audience of tastes.[7]

However, how were these books to be printed? No printing presses were
designed to manufacture books of this size, shape, and weight. In addition, paper was being rationed, and the cost of producing the books had
to be kept as low as possible, since no money was going to be made from
selling the books (servicemen were not charged for them) and the government was already overtaxed in costs for traditional supplies for warfare—
ships, munitions, and such. In this case, necessity proved to be the mother
of invention. When it became clear that the "book press capacity available was insufficient for such an enormous project," the revolutionary solution proposed was to print lightweight, portable books "on high-speed
magazine presses, on paper of about the same grade as newsprint." Since
the rotary presses used to print the Armed Services Editions "were designed for magazines, not for pocket-sized publications," the books were
printed "two up, or in pairs, one book above the other, and then [were]
separate[d] . . . by a horizontal cut." The same presses that printed the
Reader's Digest were used to print some of the shorter books chosen, with
the resulting books measuring 5 ½ by 3 ⅞ inches. Larger presses for "pulp
magazines" were used for some of the longer titles, resulting in books that
were 6 ½ by 4 ½ inches.[8]

This new process of printing was incredibly efficient and "achieved [a
level of] mass production, believed to be unprecedented in the history
of American publishing." Such efficiency also resulted in lower production costs—with the initial average cost of each book at only slightly more
than seven cents per copy. These lower costs were passed on to the army
and navy, as the books were purchased at cost. What's more, as time wore

on and production increased, the price decreased to six cents per copy, and in 1946 to five and one-half cents per copy—a price that factored in a one-cent royalty, per copy, to be divided between publisher and author. The printing of the Armed Services Editions marked the beginning of an era in which books were being printed "at the lowest cost in the history of the industry."[9]

While the production of the books was taking place at home, the members of the armed forces were alerted to the new titles they could expect to find in their next delivery of books through a monthly list sent to them. Each month's shipment ranged from twenty-five to fifty new titles. The Council on Books in Wartime strove to ensure that roughly half of the books distributed in a given month were fiction, and the rest nonfiction, resulting in a variety of genres, "including a few classics, mysteries, and Westerns." The army and navy ordered each book in minimum editions of fifty thousand copies, with 80 percent of the Armed Services Editions being distributed to the army and the remainder of the books being divided among "the other services."[10]

Although censorship of books on the home front was deemed absurd, interestingly, restrictions were placed on the types of books and viewpoints that could be sent to the servicemen. Of all things, federal legislation proved to be an unexpected obstacle to providing servicemen with a variety of books. "The controversy arose over Title V of the new Federal Voting Law, an amendment to the Hatch Act, which was intended to prevent the Government from financing, distributing or sponsoring any political information for influencing the votes of Americans in the armed forces." The effect of the amendment, which Senator Robert Taft wrote, was to prohibit "any agency of the Government to issue any 'literature or material' containing 'political argument or political propaganda of any kind designed or calculated to affect the result of any election.'" While Taft's main concern was not censorship—he was worried about the spread of "party propaganda in an election year" that would be favorable to President Roosevelt's quest for a fourth term—Title V had a far greater reach. As a result of this legislation, the War Department "refused to circulate in its libraries books such as 'The Republic,' by Charles A. Beard, and 'Yankee from Olympus,' Catherine Drinker Bowen's biography of the late Supreme Court Justice Oliver Wendell Holmes." Further, education courses for those in the armed services were impacted, as the War Department ceased using "six books on American history and economics because they contained statements of opinion about the acts of the Roosevelt Administration."[11]

Since any kind of censorship was antagonistic to America's position in the "war of ideas," some viewed Title V as an anomaly to the general spirit of the country. One commentator noted that there were probably "worse things in the Bible or Shakespeare," than in the books being banned. Another commentator noted, "we had better address ourselves to the real disability of a disfranchised Army and Navy than to the imaginary menace of infection from the wisdom of Justice Holmes or the idealism of Woodrow Wilson, or the impact of the day's news objectively presented." In the end, "Congress amended and drastically liberalized the new law."[12]

Aside from Title V, the provision of books to the servicemen generally proceeded smoothly. The first shipment of books was printed in June 1943 and consisted of fifty thousand copies of twenty-five different titles, including *The Song of Bernadette,* by Franz Wefel; *The Forest and the Fort,* by Hervey Allen; *The Human Comedy,* by William Saroyan; *Tom Sawyer,* by Mark Twain; and *Green Mansions,* by W. L. Hudson.[13] This shipment of books was not actually delivered to the army and navy for transport to the front lines until September 1943. Subsequent shipments of books included titles by Marjorie Kinnan Rawlings, Jack London, Ernest Hemingway, Carl Sandburg, C. S. Forester, Booth Tarkington, James Thurber, F. Scott Fitzgerald, Harry Emerson Fosdick, Willa Cather, John Steinbeck, Edith Wharton, Ogden Nash, and Stephen Vincent Benet. "In short order, 'bundles of these books [were] flown into the Anzio beachhead by plane. Others were passed out to the marines on Tarawa within a few days after the last remnant of Japanese opposition had been extinguished on that atoll. They have been dropped by parachute to outpost forces on lonely Pacific islands; issued in huge lots to the hospitals behind the combat areas in all points of the world; passed out to soldiers as they embarked on transports for overseas duty.'"

And were they popular? "As Popular as Pin-Up Girls," a headline in the *New York Times,* reported.[14] The *Chicago Daily Tribune* stated that the Armed Services Editions, "dog-eared, and moldy, and limp from the humidity . . . go up the line. Because . . . they can be packed in a hip pocket or snuck into a shoulder pack, men are reading where men have never read before. . . . I've seen G.I.'s . . . hungry on . . . iron rations after being up to their waists in that terrible Hollandia marsh mud, but there they were, guarding a captured Jap plane against souvenir hunters, or in their shack in the beach camp, or mooning out after chow, reading a book." Charles Rawlings, a war correspondent, witnessed the excitement a delivery of books caused:

> I was attracted by a crowd in front of a PX in a bomber camp, and jammed the brakes of the jeep and got out to see why. Even the ice cream handout counter was deserted. There had been a rumor that some cigarette lighters were due and I figured nothing less could have caused the furor, and I needed one of the things myself. But it was the books. They had come in those taut-corded paper bundles and the PX was cutting the bundles open and dumping the things into a big bin.
>
> The line went past. No time to shop and look for titles. Grab a book, Joe, and keep going. You can swap around afterwards. 'That Brooklyn Tree'! The guy who got that one howled with joy. He'd have to sleep on it to keep it long enough to finish it.[15]

Soldiers who received the Armed Services Editions "read them avidly whenever they had time." Soldiers, sailors, and marines eagerly awaited the publication of the next month's list of titles and made their appreciation of the Armed Services Editions known. For example, one armed service member wrote from New Guinea: "I want to say thanks a million for one of the best deals in the Army—your Armed Services Editions. When ever we get them they are as welcome as a letter from home. They are . . . popular . . . especially over here, where we just couldn't get books so easily if it weren't for your editions." Another soldier expressed his appreciation for the quality of the titles chosen for Armed Services Edition publication, noting that when he first heard of the program, he was skeptical, as he thought there would be "plenty of comic books which weren't funny, unwild Wild West stories, and pretty awful mystery novels." However, he found that "when I saw the first batch contained Conrad, Melville, Steinbeck and good humor via 'H. Kaplan,' my incredulousness was being shattered." This soldier found the program to be a "victory" and noted his delight in reading the "gripping fantastic murder mystery in W. Sloan's 'To Walk the Night,' which kept me up after 'lights out' last night to learn more of Selena. My grateful appreciation for your selections and ask you to 'keep 'em coming.'" Another soldier remarked that the provision of a "good book" likely kept many servicemen "out of trouble."[16]

By early 1945 the popularity of the Armed Services Editions had grown. American soldiers were requesting more books—"any kind of book"— and, according to Lieutenant Colonel Ray L. Trautman, chief of the Library Section of the Special Services Division, Army Service Forces, "the fighting man's interest in reading books . . . has reached the pitch where he is willing to pay another soldier just for the privilege of being next in line to read his book." For the year of 1945 Philip Van Doren Stern, who continued to manage the production of the Armed Services Editions, assured that books would be produced "at a rate of 7,000,000 copies a month, 8,000,000 a month by July," which brought the total number of books printed by the end of 1945 to eighty-five million.[17]

Beyond the benefits of providing servicemen free books for their entertainment and comfort, the council also saw its provision of books as being aligned with the purpose of the Allies and for that which they were fighting. The work of the council revealed "the difference between the two ways of life and thought now locked in battle throughout the earth. People of the Axis lands are prevented by force from knowing the facts of the time and are told what to think. People of this free nation are supplied with the truth as free men see it and are confidently left to think for themselves." It is not surprising that the Council on Books in Wartime received the *Saturday Review of Literature*'s award "for distinguished service to American literature" in the summer of 1945. The provision of these books to servicemen continued through October 1947, when the "final shipment of 18,000 copies of Armed Services Editions to Army and Navy distributing depots" was scheduled to be completed. It was reported that, "consisting principally of contemporary fiction, westerns and mysteries in twelve titles, this shipment will bring to 122,059,388 the number of the paper-bound books distributed here and overseas."[18]

The unprecedented use of mass-printing techniques to produce low-cost books seemed to hold the potential to transform the publishing industry. However, during the war, and insofar as the Armed Services Editions were concerned, the use of these printing techniques, and the concomitant magnanimity in pricing, started and ended with benefiting those who belonged to the armed forces. The books were purposely made so that they were not particularly durable, not only to keep the cost of their production low but also to stymie concern that the books could flood the postwar market. "The goal is to have them passed on from hand to hand until they finally disintegrate," one newspaper reported. "No copies will be available for sale for civilians now or ever," the *New York Times* explained. The *Chicago Daily Tribune* noted, "you won't see the books. They are intended solely for the soldiers and sailors and will not be distributed in the United States."[19]

Through the Armed Services Edition program many members of the armed forces either met Tutt for the first time or were warmed to find a book with the tales of an old friend. *Yankee Lawyer* was Train's first book to be made into an Armed Services Edition, and from what evidence survives to this day, the servicemen loved it. A second book of Train's, *Mr. Tutt Finds a Way*, was also made into an Armed Services Edition, shortly after *Yankee Lawyer*.

❖

On the home front, patriotism was running high, and the Trains' feelings were no exception. In addition to cooperating with the Council on Books in Wartime, in facilitating the publication of *Yankee Lawyer* and *Mr. Tutt Finds a Way* as Armed Services Editions, the Trains were also involved in other activities to raise money for the American Red Cross, contribute to the United Service Organization (USO) drive, and bolster troop morale. For example, on July 12, 1942, while spending time in their summer home on Mount Desert Island, the Trains hosted a luncheon for officers stationed at the nearby Naval Section Base and the Army Signal Corps Station. However, this luncheon was not an exceptional act of kindness by the Trains, for they had a habit of hosting naval officers at their summer home, since the officers were stationed in their neighborhood. Even an act as simple as sending a very fine radio to the naval base, so the officers might pass their time more enjoyably, was the type of behavior you could expect from the Trains. The Trains' patriotism did not just exist during World War II—even when World War I was raging, Train, at the age of forty-five, enlisted for service, and before enlisting he "occup[ied] [him]self with propaganda for Liberty Loan, etc., and the writing of patriotic fiction."[20]

During World War II, Helen Train devoted herself to a number of activities to support the American officers. For instance, she arranged for the periodic publication of a small blurb in the *New York Times,* just below the bridge column—from 1942 to 1945—that stated: "Playing cards, new or used, and parlor games of every description are needed for members of our armed forces. Readers are invited to send them to Mrs. Arthur Train . . . who will distribute them on behalf of the Citizens Committee for the Army and Navy, Inc." In order to raise money for the American Red Cross, the Trains volunteered to be one of nineteen estates in Bar Harbor that were "opened to the public" on July 30, 1939, and donated all proceeds from this "open house" event to the Red Cross. Mrs. Train was also active in the USO drive and went so far as to join the "committee in charge" to ensure that Bar Harbor met its quota of the national fund.

In addition to volunteering her time, Mrs. Train also contributed to the women's special gifts committee for the Red Cross War Fund. These are just a few examples of the volunteerism, patriotism, and humanitarian activities to which the Trains devoted themselves during World War II.[21]

While Train was, no doubt, a Good Samaritan and patriot, he was not immune to the old saying "no good deed goes unpunished." There is no indication that Train had any intention of deluding servicemen into believing that Tutt existed by allowing *Yankee Lawyer* to be published in the Armed Services Edition format. The truth of the matter was that "the tastes of the men overseas show[ed] a remarkable similarity to those of the reading public at home, as reflected in the best seller lists. As soon as a book becomes popular [in the United States] the demand for it arises abroad . . . apparently as the result of its mention in letters from home." One member of the book selection committee noted that "the book that reaches best seller popularity next week will be on the next month's list for the armed services." *Yankee Lawyer* appeared on best-seller lists and received favorable reviews and high praise by major newspapers. Thus it seems that the Armed Services Edition of *Yankee Lawyer* was the result of, at least in part, the book's popularity at home, in addition to Train's cooperation in having it published for those in the military.[22]

In any event, it seems that the servicemen abroad gained more amusement than grief from the advent of the possibility of Tutt's existence. Some of the most memorable and heartwarming letters sent to Scribner's, Train, Tutt, and Perkins were those from the servicemen. As dour as their circumstances were, the writers of these letters seemed to find humor in their predicament over Tutt. The letters are littered with colorful prose and humor-filled sentences, alongside words of heartfelt gratitude for the Armed Services Editions. The servicemen joked good-naturedly about their confusion, or for having been fooled into believing that Tutt existed. However, it is interesting that even those who were duped often remarked that even if they learned that Mr. Tutt were not real, such knowledge did not lessen their admiration for what he represented.

Some letters from Americans in the armed forces stated their inquiry plainly and succinctly. One such letter, written in February 1944, from a sergeant in the Air Corps who was stationed in Tucson, Arizona, at the time, stated: "I have recently read the book 'Yankee Lawyer' which . . . purports to have been written by Ephraim Tutt. I have previously read numerous articles by Arthur Train regarding Mr. Tutt who was apparently a fictitious individual." Despite his inclination to believe that Tutt was a mere character and not a living person, this Air Corps sergeant wanted his suspicion to be confirmed: "I should appreciate it very much if you could advise whether the author of Yankee Lawyer was really Ephraim Tutt and whether he is a real or fictitious person." Another letter to Scribner's, written by Alfred Segal, a captain in the Coast Artillery Corps (CAC), noted: "Practically all of the officers of this battalion have read the book 'Yankee Lawyer,'" and "now an argument has arisen which we would like you to settle for us."[23] He asked whether the beloved old gentleman, whom the entire battalion adored, was a real person?

Men stationed in places far from the United States also wrote to Scribner's. One letter, from the Philippine Islands, dated February 1945, was sent by a sergeant who had just finished "and enjoyed" *Yankee Lawyer,* but he noted that the book was the source of "a disagreement between myself and one of the boys here with me." The sergeant explained, "I claim it is an autobiography and was written by Ephraim Tutt and therefore is a true story of a real person. My friend claims that the story and character is purely fictional and that the book was written by one, 'Arthur Train.'" Either way, he was glad to have read the book, but the sergeant was hopeful that he might receive word from Scribner's to settle the matter.[24]

A serviceman stationed in Luxembourg wrote, in a letter dated February 1945, that he had "read a number of Tutt stories published in the Saturday Evening Post" and was "delighted last week to find 'Yankee Lawyer' . . . in the overseas distribution for the Armed Forces." The serviceman explained that after he finished reading *Yankee Lawyer,* he recommended it to another member of his battalion, who was a former attorney. Apparently, his attorney friend read the book and then informed the serviceman that Train had authored *Yankee Lawyer*. However, the serviceman was "persuaded, since reading this book, that Ephraim Tutt is a real person," and was so certain of Tutt's existence he "made a wager of 1000 francs" with his attorney friend. He even sent a self-addressed stamped envelope for Scribner's to use in sending its response. That this man's belief was so strong that he was willing to place a bet on it speaks volumes to what Tutt meant to him, and the act of writing to Scribner's for clarification exhibited the value he placed on being assured that someone like Tutt existed. Another serviceman, this one stationed in India, wrote to Scribner's requesting a response as to who wrote *Yankee Lawyer* and whether Tutt ever existed. He explained that he had bet his "'jungle ration' for three months" that "such a person as Ephraim Tutt existed, that he wrote 'Yankee Lawyer,' and that he was a noted attorney in New York City."[25] One can only imagine how Train and Perkins felt when faced with letters such as these.

Considering the danger and daily challenges the members of the armed forces faced, it is remarkable that they became so preoccupied with whether Tutt existed that they bothered to write letters to a publishing company to learn the truth. Yet they did in large numbers. In June 1945, Charles Scribner's Sons received a letter from James Shaw, who began by noting, "at present, I am a paratrooper stationed in Austria." He explained that a "buddie and myself have a bet on one of your books, Yankee Lawyer. . . . He says Tutt is an imaginary character created by Arthur Train, while I think he is a real person." Shaw requested that Scribner's settle the bet.[26]

Another impressive attribute of many of the letters that were written regarding Tutt's existence is the humility with which the servicemen wrote. In June 1945 a captain in the Air Corps, John Farese, did not even bother to trouble Train or Scribner's; instead, he wrote to William Embree, an attorney who practiced law in New York City. Farese must have known that Embree had served as an assistant district attorney on the staff of William Travers Jerome at the same time that Train worked in that office, and thought Embree would be able to answer his question. In his letter, sent from Casablanca, French Morocco, Farese meekly began: "At the risk of encroaching on your valuable time in what may seem to be a piddling inquiry to you, and yet what is important to us, I am taking the liberty of asking you a question which has been the source of much discussion at this foreign base." After such delicacy, Farese went on to explain that one of the officers at his base had a copy of *Yankee Lawyer*, and apparently the book had made its way around to many of the men stationed there. At the time of his letter, two sides had formed in a great debate: "one side contends that there is no such person as Ephraim Tutt and that Mr. Tutt is a fictitious character of Arthur Train. The other side contends that there is an eminent lawyer in New York City by the name of Ephraim Tutt who has been used by Arthur Train for the writing of various stories." Farese merely wanted to know the truth.

The response to Mr. Farese's letter is quite telling of the scope and grip that Tutt had on the readers of his autobiography. Plus, it's one of the few letters not written by an interested party—Train, Perkins, or Scribner's—that illuminates just how pervasive the belief that Tutt existed was. Embree noted that he was "very glad" to be able to answer Farese's letter and that he happened to be "in [a] position to give you an accurate answer." Embree explained:

> I saw several of [Train's] stories in the making. Many of them were based on our experiences in the District Attorney's Office. Ephraim Tutt is purely fictitious, and Mr. Train and his publishers have so informed the public time and again and yet to this very day I think there are more people who believe that Tutt is a real person with a distinguished career in New York as a lawyer than know of his fictitious character. Only the other day my dentist asserted the fact that he is a real character.
>
> On receiving your letter I telephoned Mr. Maxwell E. Perkins of Charles Scribner's Sons, the publishers of 'Yankee Lawyer' and other books by Arthur Train. Mr. Perkins thereupon sent me the most recent Train book 'Mr. Tutt Finds a Way.' The first sketch and the last sketch in the book tell the story of the unexpected impression of

the reading public and the efforts made by Mr. Train and Mr. Perkins to correct this.

I am mailing the book to you and I hope it reaches you.

Upon receiving the copy of *Mr. Tutt Finds a Way*, Captain Farese sent a letter of thanks to Embree, for both the clarification and for sending Train's latest Tutt book. Farese noted that *Mr. Tutt Finds a Way* would "be circulated among the members of the military personnel at this base and it will afford many enjoyable hours to these men who are far from their homes."[27]

Other letters were infected with humor and gusto. One such letter, which appears to have been sent to Scribner's from Japan, states:

Gentlemen:

Your book "Yankee Lawyer" by Ephraim Tutt has become a source of controversy in this outfit. One chap claims that Ephraim Tutt is not a real person. Another says that "Charles Scribner's Sons" would not perpetrate a fraud on the public.

Be that as it may the book "Yankee Lawyer" has been the source of so much enjoyment to its readers that it could in no way be called a fraud.

However, the fat is on the fire and we are waiting for your answer to settle sundry bets.

Did or did not Arthur Train write the complete book "Yankee Lawyer" "The Autobiography of Ephraim Tutt" in addition to the introduction. In other words are Arthur Train and Ephraim Tutt one and the same?[28]

Another letter, from three men in the US military—a sergeant, a captain, and a "T5," or technician fifth class—was sent from Okinawa Island, Japan, on May 24, 1945. The letter writers explained that among the group of men with whom they were stationed, there was an ongoing, "never ending discussion." The "question raging back and forth is whether Ephraim

Tutt is a real or a[n] imaginary character." The letter noted that while many of the men stationed overseas had read Train's stories in the *Saturday Evening Post,* which "we have readily taken for fiction," Tutt's autobiography was quite another matter, and it had "divided us into two camps as to the authenticity of the character." The three men explained, "at the moment we are fighting two battles, one with the Jap[anese] on Okinawa and the other among ourselves about your particular book. We have no doubt as to the outcome of the argument with the Jap[anese] but are certainly up in the air about Ephraim Tutt. Real or imaginary, Ephraim is a hell of a lot better ideal and inspiration to fight for than blue berry pie and a chance to boo the Brooklyn Dodgers." These men also expressed their thanks to Charles Scribner's Sons for publishing Armed Services Editions of their books and providing them to the men fighting in the war. They noted that "most of us over here have read more books in the last two years overseas than we have had the previous ten years. Keep up your good work and let us have more of Ephraim Tutt, or at least stories that portray his philosophy and outlook on life." This final sentence suggests that even if Tutt were not real, the ideals he represented made the readers of *Yankee Lawyer* respond so strongly to this character.[29]

Many servicemen expressed their gratitude for the Armed Services Editions in the midst of expressing their confusion over Tutt. A member of the navy wrote to Scribner's in 1945, noting, "we have in our ships' library a copy of Yankee Lawyer, the Autobiography of Ephraim Tutt, which has been widely read by the crew. There has been quite a bit of controversy concerning the author. . . . Would you please clarify this question?" While the first part of this letter was typical of many others, the next part might have tugged at the consciences of the parties responsible for sending *Yankee Lawyer* to the front lines: "I would like also to take this opportunity to thank you for the fine thing you are doing for the servicemen overseas by making available to the 'Editions for the Armed Services, Inc.,' such fine manuscripts as this. It is such gestures as this that constantly remind us that the people at home are also doing their part in many ways. I feel that medals also should be given to organizations such as yours for the part they have played in the building of the high morale that has made our fighting men the best in the world."[30]

A lieutenant (MC) in the US Navy wrote to Scribner's in 1945, first noting that *Yankee Lawyer* had "furnished [him] with several hours of good entertainment, which is rather scarce at present." However, beyond providing entertainment, the book placed him in a state of bewilderment. "The identity of Mr. Tutt has been the subject of discussion among the officers of the Squadron for several days with more basis for argument than the 'Baker Street Irregulars' have for the actual existence of Sherlock Holmes. I hope that you, as Mr. Tutt's publishers, will give me a final authoritative answer." Before closing his letter, however, the lieutenant felt it necessary to "repeat, Mr. Tutt's autobiography afforded me a great deal of enjoyment."[31]

Another serviceman came to the defense of Train in a letter to Tutt, dated June 15, 1944. What is impressive about this letter is that it is a handwritten note, scrawled in what appears to be a rushed cursive, with a brief disclaimer opening the letter: "at the moment in the jungle, on an island in the South Pacific." However, this serviceman felt compelled to address some of the things written in Tutt's autobiography that were critical of Train. He noted that although Tutt was "probably muttering to himself 'with all of the damned things by Train [written about me],'" the serviceman was writing "in defense of Mr. Train, and doubting that he needs it, he has created a character akin to the late Will Rogers." The serviceman stated to Tutt, "You perhaps may not see the similarity, or deem the statement as a compliment, but it exists as one nevertheless," and noted that many of the servicemen considered Tutt a "pretty swell guy." What made Tutt so likeable was that Tutt's "profession was, and is viewed by the laity with suspicion," and "law, as practiced, is looked upon not so much as right and wrong, but what one can get away with." The letter continued:

So, when Mr. Train creates a character of the people, they cannot much be blamed for rallying around his banner.

Although there are undoubtedly many times when you must squirm from embarrassment from ephemeral appreciation, there has to be more than a few gleams of truth in [Train's] stories, with your own collaboration.

Frankly, I confess my approbation both for his stories and your "defense."

I've gotten many grins, while sitting on a rotting log in the jungle, from evidence, both by the account and the defense.

The letter concluded: "In any event, we like you—Mr. Tutt."[32]

James D. Cargill, who was stationed on a ship in Hagushi Wan, a bay near Okinawa, Japan, in September 1945, sent a letter to Scribner's in which he noted that *Yankee Lawyer* "is at present enjoying great popularity aboard our ship and at the same time it is the cause of quite a few heated discussions." Cargill explained, "Some of us aboard remember Mr. Tutt and the many stories of him written by Arthur Train [and] contend that Ephraim Tutt is a fictitious character created by Mr. Train. Others of us aboard are equally positive that Ephraim Tutt is not a brain child of Mr. Train but one of the outstanding lawyers of our country." Cargill politely requested that Scribner's "be so good as to let us have the facts," as it "would be greatly appreciated."[33]

It seems that far fewer letters were sent to Scribner's when the writer knew *Yankee Lawyer* was written by Train; however, one serviceman, who was "At Sea" on July 20, 1945, wrote a short note to Scribner's remarking that he had read the Armed Services Edition of *Yankee Lawyer*, and it was "excellent." He went on to explain that he "especially liked, however, the so-called 'autobiography.'" This serviceman revealed that he came into the knowledge that Train had written *Yankee Lawyer* when a "fellow member" "on board" revealed the truth to him.[34]

While many of the servicemen took Train's ruse in stride, not all did. One letter written in 1946 plainly showed how peeved the writer felt at having been fooled. This naval officer, belonging to the Chinese Amphibious Training Group stationed in San Francisco wrote:

Dear Mr. Train,

At last the ludicrous truth about Ephraim Tutt comes out. During the war I came across your book "Yankee Lawyer," and read with great delight of the legal knowledge that one man contained. Being in close contact with lawyers from practically every state of the union, I spoke much of Eph's exploits, and was disappointed at that time that none had ever heard of him.

Just recently another of your books "Mr. Tutt Finds a Way" came into my possession and the truth was out about Eph.

I do not agree particularly in your article "The Best Tutt Story of [A]ll" where you say "Yankee Lawyer was not intended as a 'hoax.'" Rather on the contrary I should like to refer you to the Armed Services Edition of "Yankee Lawyer" on the jacket blurb wherein it states in part "Ephraim Tutt . . . is undoubtedly the best known lawyer *now alive!*" and further . . . it goes on to state "the reputation probably nearest akin to his perhaps was that of his friend the late Clarence Darrow, with whose ideas he had much in common."

Maybe the book was not intended to "hoax" the reading public, but you certainly have to admit, the public believes most of what it reads, and there being nothing contrary to doubt this fact they go ahead and believe. Had I not been able to put the two books together and see for myself I would still be believing Eph was alive and practicing law in New York.

I have read "The Saturday Evening Post" for years, but lost contact with it during the war, and this may be why I never recall seeing any of the articles you have written on Eph. If I had, I might well have recalled them and wouldn't have been "hoaxed" like the people you write about.

There is no particular point in my mind for writing you, but since in your books you have always taken the side of right, I thought you would like to see how "out of character" the jacket blurb is with the real facts that have now come to light and how it has left wide the door of public misconception for believing what they read.[35]

Although this naval officer was clearly upset at having learned Tutt was not a real person, on the whole it seems that the provision of copies of *Yankee Lawyer* and *Mr. Tutt Finds a Way* to the servicemen did more good than harm. While it seems that many servicemen were fooled into believing that there was a Mr. Tutt, alive and practicing law in New York, it also seems that the servicemen had a genuine appreciation for the entertaining story *Yankee Lawyer* provided. Also, a few of the letters suggested that though the writer wished to be informed that Tutt did exist, even if he did not, the image of Tutt and all that he represented gave meaning to the sacrifice they were enduring. To fight for justice and for a version of America where people help their neighbors and do the right thing—these were ideals worth fighting for, more so than pie and baseball, as some servicemen termed it. Hoax or not, the value of *Yankee Lawyer* to those in the armed services was that its descriptions captured a version of American life that epitomized a society worth protecting and coming home to. The example of Tutt rising from a humble farm background to becoming a successful lawyer in Manhattan was inspiring. Watching as Tutt dedicated his life to ensuring that justice and a moral outcome would trump a nefarious result, even if it meant some degree of personal sacrifice—wasn't that also what the troops were fighting for?

Ironically, Train wrote such a convincing and detailed fictitious "life" for Ephraim Tutt that people became certain that Tutt actually existed. The book was such a unique volume—as a fictitious autobiography—it tricked many unsuspecting readers, who simply accepted the book at face value. Train's provision of photographs, a detailed index in the back of the book, the copyright by Tutt, the dedication to Esther, the name-dropping of well-known real people, and the explanation that Tutt had merely given Train permission to write stories about his law practice made the entire book seem so real.

However, after all was said and done, it really did not much matter whether Tutt was real. His autobiography *felt* as real as any other, and people wanted him to be a living lawyer. The public liked Tutt, they responded to his stories and rooted for him to win his courtroom battles. He was an extremely popular figure, and, as with many popular figures, his ability to attract people's confidence and trust did not go unnoticed by those with commercial interests. In fact, Tutt is probably one of the few fictitious characters who became so popular and desirable that he practically needed a publicity agent to deal with his endorsement, radio, television, film, and play requests.

6
Mr. Tutt, the Celebrity

Many an author has written affectionately about his favorite cigars—
Thackeray, Tennyson, Kipling, Huxley, Mark Twain, Winston Churchill
to name but a few of the many. . . . Now, we whose pleasant duty it is
to increase the popularity of cigar smoking, hope to "move the spirit"
of some of our present day writing brethren so that they, too, might set
down on paper their appreciation of the fragrant leaf. . . . Would Arthur
Train write such a piece for us?
                            —Letter from the Cigar Institute of America, Inc.

By the 1940s Mr. Tutt, the fictional character, had become so famous that
he was considered as popular, if not more so, than the celebrities of the
day. Tutt was a household name, and his image was easily recognized because of the lifelike, practically photographic, sketches that accompanied
Tutt stories. In 1945 Train surmised that "in all probability, Ephraim Tutt
is more widely known than any justice upon the United States Supreme
Bench." When his autobiography was published, one review noted that
Mr. Tutt "has not only achieved an international reputation during his
fifty years of legal practice but has also acquired during their crowded span
a following of 'Tutt fans' which would turn a movie star's hair straight with
envy." By the 1940s it was estimated that Tutt had appeared in more than
200 million copies of the *Saturday Evening Post,* and since many of these
copies were passed from one person to another, the number of people who
actually read the stories was likely even higher.[1]

There were two main ingredients for the recipe yielding Tutt's fame.
First, Train's writing captured the world of Mr. Tutt so vividly and descrip-
tively that the stories seemed to be cloaked in truth. As a result, readers
felt connected to Mr. Tutt, as if they had known him intimately for years.
However, another important component to the development of Tutt's fame

was the artwork that accompanied Train's stories. In nearly every *Saturday Evening Post* Tutt story there were sketches and portraits of Tutt, engaged in a courtroom battle or pensively thinking over a fine legal point. These renditions made Tutt feel more real.

Train had the good fortune of working with premier artists who were guided by Train's stories in crafting lifelike representations of Tutt's appearance and fictional world. These drawings were finely detailed and captured a feeling of movement, emotion, and spirit; they provided physicality to Tutt's world and brought an air of authenticity to Tutt's life. In addition, the drawings brought some continuity to Tutt; as a single artist, Arthur William Brown sketched nearly every portrait and courtroom scene, from Tutt's early appearances in print through his last. Because of Brown's familiar style, the public came to know Tutt as a dignified and respectful gentleman, whose appearance conveyed a sense of benevolence, compassion, and approachability.

Arthur William Brown was born in Ontario, Canada, in the late 1880s, received formal schooling until he reached the age of fourteen, and then came to New York in 1901, with little more than $400 in his pocket and the "cutdown" suit he wore, which belonged to his uncle. In order to raise the money he needed to come to New York, Brown worked for a brief time as a newsdealer on a steamboat, during which he spent countless hours filling notebooks with sketches of the passengers and personalities he encountered on board. During this employment Brown compiled an ample portfolio. One day he selected one of his sketches for submission to the editor of a local newspaper in Hamilton, Ontario, *The Spectator.* Much to his delight his illustration was accepted for publication, which gave him confidence in pursuing his dream of earning a living as an illustrator and caricaturist. Brown thus began his career as a freelance artist; he continued to submit drawings to various newspapers and other publications and was pleased to find that his artwork was worthy of fetching a price. Perhaps the biggest "break" in his early career was when the editor of *The Spectator* asked Brown to sketch "a six-column picture of the sinking of the battleship Maine in Havana harbor in 1898." The *Spectator*'s editor approved

Brown's rendition of this tragic scene, published it, and Brown's career as an artist was sealed.

Once in New York, Brown entered the Art Students League, where he studied for approximately two years under the tutelage of Walter Appleton Clark—it was Clark's use of his first, middle, and last name that gave Brown the idea to do the same. Brown quickly made a name for himself in New York, and in 1910 he was elected to the Society of Illustrators—a group of which he later became president. In 1964 this society honored Brown as its eighth member to join its Hall of Fame.

Brown became a great success over the years—he is attributed with "bobb-[ing] the hair of F. Scott Fitzgerald's flappers and . . . dr[awing] the first airmen's fashions for Montague Glass's early aviation stories." Yet the work for which he was most famous was drawing dozens of poses and scenes featuring Ephraim Tutt. The partnership between Train and Brown began almost contemporaneously with the first published appearance of Tutt. In a 1944 article about Brown, the *Toronto Globe* reported that "Brown did the first illustrations for a story about Tutt written by Arthur Train. Since then the two have teamed to keep the character alive until Tutt is now the oldest continuing character in current fiction." In order to capture the likeness of Tutt, Brown "thought about all the kindly, shrewd, just, genial and fiery old-timers he ever knew, then he put these characteristics into his drawing. And Tutt has stayed the same ever since." Brown claimed that he "drew [Tutt] out of my head," but he also used two models (the first died, forcing him to find another). While some drawings might capture a scene or a person in a dull and lifeless way, Brown's sketches of Tutt were so skillfully done that they seemed to bestow vitality and spirit on Tutt's image. Some sketches captured Tutt in the midst of a courtroom battle, tugging at the lapels of his worn suit coat, looking rather grave, but not defeated. Another picture, drawn by Brown, shows Tutt, donning his stately top hat, graying locks peeking out from underneath its brim, with brows furrowed and mouth pursed, on the cusp of making some great legal argument.[2]

Even in his autobiography, Tutt pays credence to Brown's work. Tutt noted that in over one hundred stories, published in eleven volumes, Brown had provided the illustrations for them all. Tutt remarked that "his drawings of myself are said to be excellent and I can personally vouch for the accuracy of those of my office force." Tutt noted that "Brown's pictures are an important factor in the popularity of the stories, and I have heard Train say that if he is my literary father, Brown is my pictorial mother."[3] (Surely Brown is one of the few artists to gain the approval of even the fictitious character he portrayed.)

Due to Brown's portraits and sketches, Tutt was one of the most well-recognized creatures of fiction during the first half of the twentieth century. Brown once explained that he believed that his task, as a modern artist, was to be a "darned good photographer."[4] Since Tutt certainly could not be photographed, Brown's consistent drawings were critical to establishing Tutt's appearance and the public's sense of familiarity with him. During the decades he spent sketching Tutt, he essentially provided Tutt's audience with a photographic history of Tutt's courtroom performances, fishing expeditions, office wranglings with his staff, and city scenes of Tutt in his daily life. Drawing after drawing captured the same essence of Mr. Tutt; each was cast within a backdrop suited for the particular story it was accompanying, whether for a *Saturday Evening Post* article or to enrich the reader's experience with the latest Tutt book.

As adroit a writer Train was, without Brown's faithful representations of Tutt actually experiencing the scenes and escapades Train wrote of, Tutt likely would not have gained the sense of life that he did. And a life unto his own did Tutt acquire. This character of fiction garnered such great interest among the public that some companies wished to use Tutt in their advertising. Tutt's fishing acumen, as Train described and Brown depicted, seemed worthy of mention in actual books on fishing. Publications devoted to documenting the most noteworthy living persons wished to include Tutt within their pages. Plus, as with other celebrities of the day, Tutt was beckoned to join other media—from radio and television programs to having some of his court exploits portrayed on the Broadway stage. At the height of his popularity, it was even rumored that a movie was going to be made about Tutt's life.

Endorsements

Two of Tutt's favorite pastimes, smoking stogies and fishing, had become so closely associated with his name and likeness that Tutt seemed a natural choice to serve as a spokesman for companies, organizations, or enthusiasts seeking to profit by Tutt's celebrity and example. For instance, just before Tutt's autobiography was published, the Cigar Institute of America, Inc., sent a letter of inquiry to see whether Arthur Train would be willing to write an advertising piece that might discuss cigar smoking in a favorable light. The letter notes that "many an author has written affectionately about his favorite cigars—Thackeray, Tennyson, Kipling, Huxley, Mark Twain, Winston Churchill to name but a few of the many. We believe that cigars have a proper niche in the literature of the day—that many authors would write about their own favorite form of smoking if they realized the magnitude and intensity of interest in cigars." With its "pleasant duty . . . to increase the popularity of cigar smoking," the Cigar Institute of America wished to "help 'move the spirit' of some of our present day writing brethren so that they, too, might set down on paper their appreciation of the fragrant leaf." "We want a few stories of about five hundred words from popular authors. They would be published in leaflet form and distributed to smokers by dealers when their customers stop in for their chosen tobacco ration thus to flatter the cigar smoker and to persuade him who has not yet tasted of tobacco in its purest form."[5]

There probably could not be an easier task for Train to accomplish than to write a short Tutt story that might include some mention of Tutt smoking a stogie. Many of Train's stories featured a scene in which Tutt reaches for his cigar for a moment's enjoyment or to more intimately consider some fine legal point—accompanied with lifelike drawings of him, with pipe or cigar in hand, sending a small plume of smoke upward. In fact, Train even printed stationery, which he used to jot notes to Perkins, or sometimes to unsuspecting book reviewers, that had an image of Tutt in the upper left-hand corner, looking rather jovial as he held a cigar in his hand and exhaled rings of smoke. Based on his growing celebrity, as well as his reputation for having an affinity for tobacco products, Tutt was an obvious figure for the Cigar Institute's campaign to promote the popularity of cigars.

Train's publishing house believed Tutt would be a natural choice for the type of story the Cigar Institute wished to purchase. In a letter to Train, it was noted that he could easily write a piece featuring Tutt and his stogy, especially considering Train's "original conception of Mr. Tutt in which you could never separate him from a cigar." It did not seem that there was "any harm in doing it, and if Tutt could be brought in, he would gain some advantage." While Train was perfectly willing to write a piece, he was not willing to do so for a small fee. The Cigar Institute was informed that Train, "would not write anything for advertising for less than a thousand dollars," and thus it was assumed the Cigar Institute of America would not be interested in acquiring a story by Train. While Train was well aware that Tutt's popularity was on the rise, he perhaps overshot the Cigar Institute's interest, or the depth of its pockets, in obtaining a Tutt-smokes-a-cigar story. A dearth of records following Train's ultimatum suggests that Train's wish to fetch such a high fee cost him the opportunity to write any piece for the Cigar Institute.[6]

Anyone familiar with Train's stories is likely aware of Tutt's love of fishing. The stories about his angling escapades exude a genuine esteem for the sport. This enthusiasm was an extension of Train's own, for Train loved the outdoors—from being perched in his writing house in the deep woods of Maine to taking hiking trips both around his Maine home and in places much more exotic. His love of nature included a passion for fishing. Thus when he wrote about Tutt's enjoyment in taking a brief sojourn to his favorite lake in upstate New York—requiring nothing more than a fishing rod and bait to spend an afternoon most pleasantly—Train was really writing autobiographically. In fact, Train even incorporated one of his favorite places to fish, New Brunswick, Canada, into some of his Tutt stories. Train included the people and experiences he encountered on his trips there. For example, when Train sent Tutt on a fishing expedition, Tutt was left in the able hands of his guide, "Mac." In reality, Mac was modeled after Donald McKay, who was a famous angler and guide for those who fished for salmon in the waters of the Miramichi River in New Brunswick, Canada. Train's skill, likeable personality, and easygoing manner caused him to become a favorite with some of the New Brunswick locals. He was even recognized in June 1931, when "the government of New Brunswick paid tribute to Arthur Train . . . at a dinner in his honor . . . at the camp of Jack Russell at Porter Cove on the Southwest Miramichi. Premier C. D. Richards attended the dinner, at which Mr. Train received a silver-mounted moose hoof bearing the inscription 'Presented by the Province of New Brunswick.'" Train had obviously made quite an impression in the place where he most loved to fish. Considering Train's own love of the sport, it is not surprising that when he wove a tale of fishing into his Tutt books, he was able to provide a realistic description of the locale and the way one might go about catching a fish (as well as the necessary hyperbole on the size of his catch).[7]

Tutt knew so much about fishing, and developed an expertise for fishing in certain waters, that he won the respect of avid outdoorsmen. In fact, according to Train, "the old man [Tutt] has a large and loyal following among salmon fishermen," and their admiration for Tutt even materialized with gifts of "handmade flies and invitations to try his luck on their private waters." Unfortunately, "to his great regret he has never been able to accept any of the opportunities so kindly offered."[8]

Among the admirers of Tutt's fishing escapades was the Derrydale Press, which specialized in publishing "sporting books and prints." In 1938 Eugene Connett, the founder of this press, wrote to Maxwell Perkins to see whether Train might be willing to contribute a series of Tutt stories of his fishing adventures and philosophies. "The Arthur Train stories of Mr. Tutt as a fisherman are grand and I personally am keen about them," Connett remarked. In the end, Connett did not finalize a deal with Scribner's, since the entire idea for the book was scrapped because Derrydale Press had to reduce its "program materially, as we look for a bad year"—the enduring effects of the Great Depression plagued the project. However, Train liked Connett's idea. Around the same time as Connett's letter, Train received a suggestion that perhaps "there were enough anglers who are also friends of Mr. Tutt, to warrant a special deluxe edition of a collection of the old man's fishing stories."[9]

Ultimately, one of Train's Tutt stories did make its way into a fishing book. Posthumously (in relation to Train), a fishing anthology, *The Fireside Book of Fishing: A Selection from the Great Literature of Angling,* was published by Simon and Schuster, in which a series of articles and stories were collected to amuse and advise even the staunchest fishing fans. The volume was composed of instructive pieces—such as "Some Field Problems and Their Solutions," which provided a "narrative of trout experiences," and "Spinning for Fresh and Salt Water Fish," which, evidently, involved advice for someone encountering the "limestone streams of Pennsylvania"—as well as fictionalized accounts that were "not always closely hooked up to fishing or even fish," one reviewer warned. Some of the stories bent less on instruction and more on amusement and entertainment included Stephen Vincent Benet's "Daniel Webster and the Sea Serpent," Ernest Hemingway's "Big Two-Hearted River," and Arthur Train's "Black Salmon."[10]

Aside from the Cigar Institute's wish for an endorsement piece and Tutt's fishing wisdom making its way into a fishing treatise, requests to include Tutt in other types of publications and mediums were sent to Scribner's. For example, Faith Life Library, located in Nellisville, Wisconsin, sent an amusing inquiry to Charles Scribner's Sons in 1944 asking "whether, if I retained Ephraim Tutt, he wouldn't find a way of getting around your copyright, since it is in the name of a fictionalized person?" In the end, Faith Life just wanted permission to reprint "a stickful of matter from *The Yankee Lawyer,*" namely, a scene involving a clergyman. Scribner's replied that they had no objection to the use of the material, so long as credit was given to the book and publishers in a suitable way; however, as to the copyrighting matter, it was noted, "one can copyright safely under a pseudonym if it is sufficiently distinctive. Ephraim Tutt must be so."[11]

Tutt on Broadway?

In the late 1930s through the early 1940s, one of the more juicy pieces of gossip floating around the New York stage was that a play was being written about Ephraim Tutt. A Tutt theatrical was such a desirable event that even a mere glimmer of progress was enough to fuel a report about it in the *New York Times*'s theater column. However, progress on a play was continually hampered, often because of the difficulty in writing an appropriate script or in securing suitable stage and production talent. The result was a protracted media-driven roller-coaster ride, as every "rumor" buzzing around Broadway about the imminence of a Tutt play was reported with some regularity. In the end, it seems a dramatic production could be written on the painstaking efforts to get this ill-fated project off the ground.

It appears that the first mention of Tutt coming to Broadway was in February 1937, when the *New York Times* merely noted, in passing, that Owen Davis, the famous playwright, was undertaking a new comedic script for a project titled *Mr. Tutt Comes Home,* to be written by Davis and Train together. "Mr. Davis was always one to keep a finger on the popular pulse, and this perhaps confirms what the showmen have been saying: that the public is in a mood to laugh and will pay for anything that lets it do so." A few months later, a more definite pronouncement of the project was made: "It might appear that one of the Fall's major events will be the arrival on Broadway of Ephraim Tutt, attorney at law." It was reported that "Owen Davis, Arthur Train and Max Gordon are signing the necessary papers for a production of 'Mr. Tutt Comes Home'"—readers were told to "set it down tentatively for mid-October."[12]

Many theatergoers were thrilled that Tutt's play was on its way to the stage. Plus, Davis's participation was significant, since he was such a capable playwright that he reputedly "could and did write a play and have it cast and before an audience in twenty-four hours." In June 1937, news spread that Train and Davis had completed the script for *Mr. Tutt Comes Home.* One week later there was even a rumor that the "Max Gordon Plays and Pictures Corporation will enter the motion picture field during the 1938–39 season with a program of three pictures," and it was "understood that the second might be based on the 'Tutt and Mr. Tutt' Saturday Evening Post stories by Arthur Train." The prospect of a Tutt movie must have delighted Train and Perkins to no end.[13]

In August 1937 more progress seemed to have been made with the Tutt play, since it was reported that Walter Huston, a popular actor, had dropped out of another play, making himself available to play the part of Tutt in *Mr. Tutt Comes Home.* It was reported that Tutt could be expected to grace the stage as a "Christmas week number." However, it appears that there had been a falling out with Max Gordon since it was reported that "no director has been signed for it." In November 1937, the play still seemed likely to manifest and was described as "all in shape now," but there was a delay because Huston was "finish[ing] a picture."[14]

Aside from the gossip and newspaper reports, Train and Perkins, who were in constant communication, were also discussing the prospect of Tutt on Broadway. In a June 1937 letter, Perkins wrote to Train: "I am delighted that Tutt is to go on the stage, and I hope it will be a great success. It might lead to ever so much. Mr. Tutt ought to get into the movies, for one thing." In June 1938, Perkins again commented that he was "delighted about the Tutt play" and that "now the old man should get his full due, and it ought to react favorably all around." Perkins was so certain that the play would be a success, he even offered that Scribner's "ought to put the play into the final Fall list, even though you would not be able to give us [a] copy until the early Fall, I suppose." Even more promising was a letter Perkins wrote in September 1938 reminding Train that the "play ought to be published as close to production as is possible. I suppose you won't be able to give us a final version until after rehearsals have begun but the sooner we can get it the better." In an undated letter, Train wrote to Perkins, noting in a postscript that "Huston is going to act Tutt. We are re-writing the last two acts. It will be ready about July 1."[15]

Yet, as of January 1938, it seemed that the play was not imminent. "Well, Mr. Tutt is not coming home, after all. Not this season, anyhow," the *New York Times* reported. "It seemed that he was about to, because Owen Davis and Arthur Train had finished their play; and Walter Huston, who was to have starred in it, offered only minor objections. Nor has Mr. Huston any known stage or screen commitments." It seemed that the play was ready to move forward, yet inexplicably it did not. "It is all a bit mysterious," a miffed *New York Times* writer reported. The remainder of 1938 brought no new rumors about Tutt's play.[16]

In early 1939 the *Times* playfully noted that, "At about this time of year, every year, this corner begins to worry slightly about Ephraim Tutt, that Arthur Train legal character who for some time has been bound toward the stage in a play entitled 'Mr. Tutt Comes Home.' Well, you now have it on the word of Max Gordon that Mr. Tutt will be along, perhaps next season, in the person of Walter Huston." However, by the fall, the *Times* divulged the unfavorable news that "the long-waited dramatization of Arthur Train's 'Mr. Tutt Comes Home' . . . was still being worked on." Yet, 1939, 1940, 1941, and 1942 passed, with no stage production.[17]

In late 1943, after a few years of silence on the topic, rumors of the Tutt play again began to circulate. With a new director at the helm—Guthrie McClintic—and a new actor to play Tutt—Raymond Massey—it appeared that the play might actually ripen into an actual production. In September 1943, Raymond Massey sent a telegraph to Train stating, "We are overjoyed to report that Guthrie McClintic who is clearly the top producer and director in the business thinks even more highly of Mister Tutt for the stage than we or even you. He wants exactly the play you and we want and considers it can and must be done, but we need a playwright." Massey added that McClintic "sees the play as a great force to remind America of what America has been and must remain." The newspapers confirmed that once again, "it begins to look as if Ephraim Tutt, Arthur Train's illustrious legal character of fiction, is really serious about coming to Broadway after

all. Sure . . . something like this has been disclosed to a breathless popu-
lace before—let's be conservative—about a half dozen times. And yet Mr.
Tutt has steadfastly remained in the wings." The article continued, "Well,
the word is that this time Mr. Train is chained to his desk and is tackling
the job of dramatization himself. Two acts have been completed. Further,
the plans for the production have remained constant. . . . What's the date?
Be patient. They say next season."[18]

In January 1944 the *Times* happily announced, "Arthur Train has completed the dramatization of his legal character of fiction, Ephraim Tutt,"
and was expected to read his finished work to Massey. However, those who
followed the theater news closely might have noticed a serious obstacle—
Massey had already committed himself to acting in another performance,
in the lead male role for *Lovers and Friends* at the Plymouth Theatre, "presumably for one of those lengthy engagements here and a subsequent one
on the road."[19]

Clearly, there was a market for a Tutt play—his popularity only seemed
to grow, and with the publicity that his autobiography received, he would
have easily been able to fill the theater with eager fans. Yet what was in-
hibiting this play from a successful adaptation from the page to the theater? Train wrote a script, then rewrote it, and a new director and lead actor committed themselves to the project, yet the play just could not get
off the ground. It seems that Train had created a character in his stories
that was larger than life—it was impossible to portray Tutt in only a matter of hours, through a single story. No script could do him justice, thus
no script was ever good enough. In fact, when in 1944 it was once again
reported that the Tutt play was going to make it to the stage, Raymond
Massey, in an interview, was asked to verify this rumor. After all, "since
Mr. Tutt's Broadway debut had been promised many times before and the
elusive Mr. Tutt still had insisted on remaining offstage, it was necessary
for Mr. Massey to explain why really this time was 'it.'" "The trouble in the
past," Massey expounded, "has been that almost every time a Tutt script
was completed it turned out to be a whodunit. If it wasn't that then Mr.
Tutt emerged as nothing more than a cracker-barrel philosopher, a cliché

character of no significance. Now that's all wrong. Mr. Tutt is one helluva fellow and he's gotten bigger with the war. He has come to stand for justice opposed to evil. He's too great a character to be subordinated to the story. He's bigger than any story." It was said that "Mr. Tutt's biographer had completed a dramatization that was fine, [and] if everything worked out, next season would behold a 'great American play.'" This rumor even went so far as to include a report that in August 1944, rehearsals for the Mr. Tutt play had commenced, and "the venerable barrister should be seen on Broadway the week of Oct. 30 after four weeks out of town." There were to be thirty cast members and five sets. Yet the project completely stalled, and no play made it to Broadway.[20]

The last word on the project was in 1947—Max Gordon and Henry Kurnitz were working on a settlement with Train's estate for production rights to adapt a series of Tutt stories into a stage performance. However, a few months later, it was reported, "another of the literary clan [is] having script trouble," as Harry Kurnitz, who was undertaking the script writing, had already taken "two tries," but still believed "he'll pin the old boy yet." It would not be the first time that Mr. Tutt posed this difficulty— "Mr. Tutt, you may recall, has jammed more than one playwright's typewriter over the years," the *New York Times* commented.[21]

Although Broadway had brooded over a Tutt play for nearly a decade, "nothing ever came of the project."[22] Tutt had become too complex a character, and he had come to mean too much to his fans and those involved in any production that each script fell far short from capturing the full essence of America's beloved barrister.

Television and Radio

Although the Tutt play never came to fruition, Tutt did appear on television. In 1951 Tutt made his debut on New York's channel 4. Parker Fennelly played the role of Mr. Tutt. Thereafter, there was enough interest in more Tutt programs, and additional television shows based on Train's stories about him were made. For example, in 1956 Parker Fennelly played

Tutt in a rendition of Train's story "Mr. Tutt Goes West," which was shown during the *Robert Montgomery Presents* show.[23] Also, requests to put Tutt on the radio were received from New York, Chicago, and California. Large radio corporations, such as the General Artists Corporation and National Broadcasting Company, Inc., wrote to Scribner's seeking information on securing the radio rights to the Tutt stories. In the late 1940s, CBS Radio produced the program *The Amazing Mr. Tutt,* which featured the popular film and radio actor Will Wright as Ephraim Tutt. Requests were also made by individuals who worked with regional radio stations. For instance, one Virginia man wrote to Scribner's asking whether there was a fee "for using the stories of Arthur Train, namely 'Tutt & Mr. Tutt,'" which he wished to make into a radio script "for local audiences." Another man, writing from Chicago, explained to Scribner's that "while serving overseas with the Army Air Forces, I had in my possession Mr. Tutt's Case Book," and, "being a radio writer by profession and searching for a vehicle to reestablish my career, I was struck by the great possibilities for turning the Tutt stories into a radio show."[24] In the end, Tutt was featured in many radio plays, which only added to his popularity and celebrity.

Who's That?

In 1943 the A. N. Marquis Company Publishers contacted Charles Scribner's Sons to request background information on Ephraim Tutt. The inquiry consisted of a short questionnaire for Ephraim Tutt to complete, in order to ensure that his name would be included in the pages of A. N. Marquis's well-known publication, *Who's Who*. Train, happy to oblige, realized that the information needed to complete the *Who's Who* application could easily be derived from the contents of Tutt's autobiography. Thus Train prepared the following blurb:

EPHRAIM TUTT, Lawyer; b. July 4, 1869, Leeds, Vt; S. Enoch & Margaret (O'Conner) Tutt; A.B., Harvard, 1891, L.L.B., 1894; LL.D. (Hon.) Columbia, 1942; admitted to N.Y. state bar, 1894; in general practice Pottsville, N.Y., 1894–1898; ass't dist. atty., N.Y. Co., 1898–1902; mem. firm Hotchkiss, Levy & Hogan, 1902–1907; mem. firm Wiegand & Tutt, 1907–1922; mem. firm Tutt & Tutt, 1922–1942; retired from active practice 1943. Clubs: University, Harvard, Colophon, Players, Lambs, Bibliophile, Salmagundi (New York), Cosmos (Washington), Bohemian (San Francisco), Canadian Anglers (Montreal). Hon. bencher Gray's Inn (London). Author: *Yankee Lawyer: The Autobiography of Ephraim Tutt*. Address: 597 Fifth Avenue, New York, N.Y.

Believing the information to be fair and accurate based upon Tutt's personal history in *Yankee Lawyer,* Train submitted the completed application to the A. N. Marquis Company.[25]

When Charles Scribner's Sons learned of Train's action, the publishing house felt that Train might have overstepped whatever boundaries might exist with respect to his hoax. Maxwell Perkins was given the fool's errand of telling Train that something would have to be done to ensure that Tutt's biographical information was not published in *Who's Who* under the auspices that Tutt was a real person. In response, Train sent a short, handwritten letter to Perkins, stating: "*Re:* Tutt: I understand that you (*not* I) are to call the attention of Who's Who to the fact that Ephraim is not a real person, so that unless you tell me to the contrary, I shall do nothing."[26]

Charles Scribner's Sons prepared a letter to the A. N. Marquis Company, with the purpose of cautioning that if they chose to publish Tutt's information in *Who's Who,* they must first understand that Tutt did not exist and did not complete his own application. The letter read:

Dear Sirs:

Some days ago we received from you an invitation addressed to Ephraim Tutt to contribute his biography to "Who's Who in America." You no doubt considered Ephraim Tutt to be the actual author of "Yankee Lawyer: The Autobiography of Ephraim Tutt."

As a matter of fact, no such person as Ephraim Tutt exists. He is a fictional character who has figured in scores of stories published in the last twenty-five years, by Arthur Train. The biographical sketch that was sent you should therefore be withdrawn from "Who's Who in America."

After nearly two weeks elapsed, and having received no answer from A. N. Marquis Company Publishers, Charles Scribner's Sons dispatched another letter, with a copy of their previous letter. This second letter reiterated, "The biographical data you requested from Ephraim Tutt, a purely fictional character, was in the form of proof, and we wish to make sure that you are apprised of the fact as to the non-existence of Ephraim Tutt and that you withdraw this material from the forthcoming WHO'S WHO IN AMERICA." Shortly after this second letter was mailed, the general manager of *Who's Who* sent his response. The letter noted that "Over the years Mr. Tutt has almost become a real character so I can not much blame our editorial assistant who selected his name and I certainly thank you for calling the matter to our attention now so that WHO'S WHO IN AMERICA may still be a book of fact rather than fiction."[27]

While Scribner's and Sons and the A. N. Marquis Company Publishers were satisfied with the outcome of this latest episode in the Tutt drama, Train was not. According to Train, his publishing house "yielded to the admonitions of their consciences, or perhaps of their lawyers, and intervened just in time to prevent [Tutt's] inclusion in *Who's Who* for 1945." As far as Train was concerned, Tutt *was* someone "who had 'accomplished some conspicuous achievement—something out of the ordinary, so to speak—something which distinguished him from the vast majority of his contemporaries.'" Train thought Tutt deserved to be in *Who's Who,* and he did not hide his anger when Tutt's application was removed from consideration. "What the cowards saw fit to do is no affair of mine. As far as I am concerned, I remained true to Eph—faithful, as it were, unto his literary death," Train exclaimed.[28]

The Big Screen

Perhaps all the talk of a Tutt play prompted the film industry to tip their ears toward Tutt. As early as 1940, Charles Scribner's began to receive a few letters from people in the film industry seeking information on whether a Tutt movie might be of any interest to Train, Tutt, or Scribner's. One film promoter living in California, L. W. Babcock, wrote to Scribner's, stating that while he was reading *Mr. Tutt's Case Book,* it occurred to him that "this book would, with its lovable characters, make beautifully into a motion picture." He explained that "with the basic theme of love thy neighbor, [such a film] would catch the public at a time when it is spending itself in hate." Babcock offered his services in "arousing interest among the studios," and was "confident I can sell your motion picture rights at a handsome price." However, Babcock was too late. Scribner's informed him that the motion picture rights had already been purchased.[29]

In 1946, Maxwell Perkins received a letter from Morey and Sutherland Productions, of Los Angeles, California, asking whether "any motion picture contract or agreement has been made by or for the various works of Arthur Train"; they wished to discuss "the possibility of adapting Mr. Train's books for motion pictures." Another offer, made in 1961 by the Landers Agency, of Beverly Hills, California, was sent to a Scribner's editor asking whether there was an "agent involved" with Arthur Train's *Mr. Tutt at His Best* volume, since it "sounds interesting as a motion picture possibility."[30] Unfortunately, like the play, none of these inquiries materialized into a Tutt movie.

Dead, alive, or nonexistent, it was no matter. Tutt was beloved by his fans, and even the commercial sector of society recognized the value and importance of Mr. Tutt. He had Hollywood, the airwaves, and the New York stage knocking on his door, and meanwhile, he enjoyed the support of a loyal fan base that consisted of both "everyday people" and members of the bar and judiciary. In fact, Tutt was even the subject of a January 1946 letter to Charles Scribner's Sons from the Astor family, who asked for "a list of all of the books published by you of which . . . Arthur Train was the author. I am particularly interested in the Ephraim Tutt series and am wondering whether by any chance you anticipate publishing a volume containing all of those stories."[31] Tutt's appeal had no boundaries.

To be associated with Tutt was, no doubt, a positive thing. People bonded with Tutt while reading the stories about him, and they were always eager to learn more of him. In fact, some people developed such an attachment to Tutt—whether they were longtime readers of the *Saturday Evening Post* stories or were newly acquainted with Tutt through reading his autobiography—that they began to feel as if they knew him. Readers related to Tutt's rise from a humble background, admired him for living the American Dream, and applauded his self-made success in life.

When Tutt's autobiography was published in 1943, Train thought he was providing the public with an amusing situation: a fictional character writing the story of his own life. However, Train did not fully appreciate how badly the public wanted to believe that Tutt existed. When their desire was met with Tutt's autobiography, it seemed that their wildest dreams had come true: even though Tutt had appeared as a creature of fiction for decades, it now appeared that he was, in fact, a real person who kindly allowed Train to write romanticized tales of his legal and personal adventures. People found solace in losing themselves in the world Train created for Tutt—being transported to another era, when the world's progress seemed slower and the times seemed easier—and found their troubles and worries temporarily soothed. Between the ideals that he embodied and the optimism he instilled in his readers, it certainly seemed that Mr. Tutt should exist. And with the advent of his autobiography, what "should be" seemed to become a pleasant reality.

7
Pygmalion and Frankenstein

Max Perkins says that fifty years hence, as between Tutt and myself,
Tutt will be remembered as the real person and I as the fictional character. And that, if anyone asks who Arthur Train was, the answer will
be: "Train? Why, he was the character that Ephraim Tutt invented as a
stooge in his autobiography. There wasn't any such person. Tutt just put
him in to explain how he came to write the book and to give himself a
chance to tell in the introduction what a great chap he was."
                            —Arthur Train, "Should I Apologize?"
                            Saturday Evening Post, February 1944

Six months after *Yankee Lawyer* was published, Arthur Train decided to issue a public statement addressing the bewilderment that plagued some of
his readers. However, what response would be appropriate? To apologize
would suggest that he intended to trick readers, but to take no responsibility for their confusion might cause even more agitation. Issuing any
statement would be a delicate task. From Train's perspective, any critical
reader should have recognized that Tutt could not have written his own
autobiography. In fact, Train stated that he "would as soon have expected
the general public to believe [Tutt] to be an actual person as Little Orphan
Annie." On the other hand, Train had engaged in several mischievous deeds
that perpetuated the hoax—from printing "Tutt" stationery and sending
notes to unwitting souls, to writing a book review for his own book and
auctioning off a top hat that purportedly belonged to Tutt. Although these
extra flourishes may have caused more confusion, Train did not undertake these shenanigans with the purpose of deceiving people—he was enjoying the opportunity he had to take a character from his own pages and
briefly give it the appearance of reality.

In the history of literary hoaxes, when an author admits that a book is not what it appeared to be a public backlash typically results—against the author and the book. However, Train's literary prank was different. The press did not attack him, and the public did not revolt against Train or *Yankee Lawyer*. It seems that the main distinction between Train's and other literary hoaxes is that the latter tend to feature an intentional deception, whereas Tutt's autobiography seemed unlikely to fool anyone. Train's motive in publishing it was innocent—he recognized that the public wanted to know more about Ephraim Tutt and that an "autobiography" was the most ideal format to provide a personal and detailed account of Tutt's history. Thus while many hoaxes have resulted in public apologies, Train did not feel that he needed to apologize because his reason for writing *Yankee Lawyer* was pure and the truth about Tutt was in plain sight all along. Therefore, when he wrote an article telling his side of the story, he titled it "Should I Apologize," and it contained Train's defense of his actions and explanation for why an apology was not warranted. In order to appreciate how unique Train's position was in the history of literary hoaxes, an examination of society's perspective on, and reaction to, other literary hoaxes is necessary.[1]

Americans have always been fascinated by tales of redemption—of unlikely victors who overtake their rivals, of underdogs who persist against all odds and ultimately prevail. However, when such stories are published as autobiographies or memoirs, they take on a special aura—the book becomes more personal to the reader and there is some amount of trust placed in the fact that it identifies itself as a true story. Works of nonfiction define the bounds of human perseverance and strength. When reading a "true story," readers become emotionally invested in whether the author's tale ends in failure or victory. The ultimate triumph is not just the author's—for having lived through the incidents described in their book—it is also the reading public's because the story feels like a triumph for the human experience. While the power of a true story is immeasurable, the effect of a literary hoax can be devastating.

When James Frey confessed that his "memoir," *A Million Little Pieces*, did not tell his entire story accurately, a public uproar followed. Millions had read the book, all believing that Frey had really undergone the misery he described and had successfully left his self-destructive lifestyle behind. The book had become spectacularly popular because it told a human interest story that catered to the cultural interests of the time, from the obsession of learning the most personal details of others' lives (for example, consider the fascination with "reality" television shows and the demand for details of every aspect of a celebrity's life), to the "popularity of recovery-movement-reminiscences" (as illustrated by the public's infatuation with talk shows such as Oprah Winfrey's or Dr. Phil's). Part of the appeal of Frey's book was that it demonstrated that a person could turn his life around, and it provided optimism and encouragement to those who wanted to make a change in their own lives. People relied upon the representations in Frey's book and found meaning in Frey's story. However, when Frey explained that the book was *mostly* true, and that he embellished parts of it only to tell a better story, questions arose as to whether "concepts like 'credibility' and 'perception' [were] replac[ing] the old ideas of objective truth." Did America still value "the efforts of nonfiction writers to be as truthful and accurate as possible," or was it acceptable to just shrug off minor discrepancies and turn a blind eye to accountability? Cultural values were suddenly at stake, all because a book claimed to be something it was not.[2]

The reason literary hoaxes cause so much turmoil is because books are used to define American culture, and what that culture values. There are many reasons why people read books—some people look for inspiration in the stories they read, others look to books for entertainment and are happy to be lost in a tale about another time and place, and sometimes people seek factual information and turn to books for authority or reference. While a "hoax" can still inspire and entertain, it can wreak havoc when a reader relies on a book's claim that it tells the truth only to later find that it does not. Yet for as many readers who feel outrage, disappointment, or discomfort at having been fooled, there are others who are amused at the prospect of having believed in a great tale that wound up being a fiction. In hindsight, many readers can even laugh that they had believed such wonderful stories with so many convenient moments of serendipity and drama that lent the book's finale an added sense of importance and triumph. Therefore, two sides tend to emerge when society is ensnared in a literary hoax—there are those who feel that such books have little worth and are simply a "mass of lies," while others enjoy experiencing this time-honored literary tradition and value such books for the unconventional entertainment they provide. With high-profile hoaxes, these two sides often come to a head publicly, as society examines whether something should be done to prevent future literary hoaxes and the related issue of whether society continues to place value on "truth."

For example, shortly after the public learned that James Frey's *A Million Little Pieces* was not (entirely) a true story, the media began to explore the consequences of Frey's embellishments. The dilemma posed was not as simple as being "a case about truth-in-labeling or the misrepresentations of one author: after all, there have been plenty of charges about phony or inflated memoirs in the past," one newspaper writer commented. The real trouble was that it called into question "how much value contemporary culture places on the very idea of truth." The unpleasant issue that Americans faced was whether America's desire for entertainment had somehow allowed "truth" to become a relative term. James Frey contended that "having 5 percent or so of his book in dispute was 'comfortably within the realm of what's appropriate for a memoir.'" Some people wondered whether there would be any future for nonfiction if Frey's belief was indicative of society's. Those who found Frey's book reprehensible were unwilling to adopt his loose definition of "truth." After all, what would it say about society if all works of nonfiction were allowed to have a 5 percent margin of error and still enjoy the distinction of being described as "true"?[3]

As some lamented over the future of nonfiction, others defended Frey's book because it still delivered a valuable message—whether the book was true or not, it still inspired and entertained its readers. In fact, some people straddled this line between admiring the message of Frey's book and despising it for not being entirely truthful. For example, when murmurings began to circulate that Frey's "memoir" was not entirely true, Oprah Winfrey famously defended the book, clinging to the "'underlying message of redemption' that resonated with her." However, days later, Oprah Winfrey spoke again on the matter, apologizing for her earlier comment, as it had the effect of giving "the impression that the truth does not matter." What did people in America value most? If book sales have any bearing on the answer to this question, within weeks of the revelation that *A Million Little Pieces* was not a true memoir, sales dropped to half of what they were when it was believed to be true.[4]

The quality of the story had not changed—the text remained the same—but the perceived value of Frey's experiences was greatly diminished because the experiences related were no longer based on actual facts. One critic noted that *A Million Little Pieces* had not become a best-selling book because of its "literary merits" (noting that the "narrative feels willfully melodramatic and contrived"); the book was popular because it fed the public's appetite for a story about one man's courage in facing his destructive lifestyle and transforming his life into a positive one. For James Frey, by exaggerating aspects of his experiences in order to seem more notorious than he really was, his account of how he escaped his addictions and triumphed over his pernicious habits was made that much more gripping and dramatic. However, it came at a price.[5]

The question of what Americans value has been tested by many literary hoaxes, most of which have resulted in a clear message: truthfulness does matter. Some authors of literary hoaxes have paid dearly for their mischief—Clifford Irving was imprisoned over his publication of a bogus autobiography of Howard R. Hughes in 1972, David Rorvik's *The Cloning of a Man* resulted in a lawsuit and congressional hearings, and James Frey and his publisher were sued for defrauding readers and were forced to issue a massive refund to anyone who purchased the book before its true nature was revealed. The intervention of the courts and government suggest that society has found that literary hoaxes are something from which the public needs protection. By requiring payment of large legal settlements, courts have sent a message to publishers and authors that their publication of a false memoir will not be condoned. By threatening legislation and regulation of the publishing industry, more care might be given to fact-checking books that are purportedly true. However, in the midst of the public scoldings and backlash against literary hoaxes, one is almost forced to wonder, is modern America taking literary hoaxes too seriously? Are Americans losing their sense of humor with respect to this centuries-old tradition?

While many literary hoaxes from the past have prompted cries for regula-tion and sparked fears over lowered literary standards, Train's hoax did not. This is because Tutt's autobiography was not a hoax in the tradi-tional sense since, if viewed objectively, the public knew or could have known that Tutt was not a real person and could not have written the book. To state it bluntly, a fictitious character cannot write his own auto-biography. Since the truth was evident to those who read magazines and Train's books, Train's "hoax" was not viewed in the same light as Joan Lo-well's, James Frey's, or others. For, before *Cradle of the Deep* and *A Mil-lion Little Pieces* were published, the public had no knowledge of who Joan Lowell or James Frey were. However, for decades before *Yankee Lawyer* was published, readers knew that Ephraim Tutt was the marvelous public-spirited lawyer that Arthur Train invented and wrote about in his stories. Plus, *Yankee Lawyer* did not humiliate and embarrass its publisher and re-viewers by tricking them into unknowingly presenting the book as non-fiction. The media knew that Tutt had not written his autobiography, but were comfortable in publishing reviews that playfully patronized the idea that he had. Charles Scribner's Sons was not fooled into publishing the book—it was common knowledge at that publishing house that Ephraim Tutt was a figment of Arthur Train's imagination. The hoax was considered transparent enough that when an irate reader sued Train and his editor and publisher, the media took Train's side and defended his publication of Tutt's fictitious autobiography. Newspapers even belittled, insulted, and ridiculed the man who felt he had been defrauded. There was no clamor for Train's arrest or that he be fined for his literary prank; at worst, he had to endure the endless stream of inquiries as to whether Tutt was real and the related guilt of disappointing thousands of people who had come to believe that Tutt was—and all of the ideals he represented were—real.

Train was not censured for his hoax because it was never meant to deceive anyone and was only meant to amuse and entertain. Adding to Train's state of innocence was the fact that Tutt had publicly appeared as a creature of fiction for decades—there really should not have been any doubt that he was anything but an imagined persona. However, hoaxes such as Clifford Irving's, David Rorvik's, and James Frey's clearly fall into another class altogether—all three authors wrote books that were presented as nonfiction, the authors did not disclose to their publishing companies, books reviewers, or readers that their books were actually embellished or untrue, and the public and courts found all three to have engaged in behavior warranting a punishment and an apology.

After reviewing other literary hoaxes, it becomes clear that when Train published his article "Should I Apologize" in the *Saturday Evening Post* in February 1944, he was justified in feeling that an apology was not entirely necessary. However, since his book had fooled thousands of readers, many of whom were upset with Train, he took great care to explain his reaction to the public's response to the book and his reasons for publishing *Yankee Lawyer.* In describing his relationship to Tutt and his great hoax, Train noted that he felt empathy for Pygmalion and Frankenstein—the one creating a sculpture that he loved so dearly it came to life; the other creating a homicidal monster he was unable to control. Train admitted that he felt a "similar experience of seeing a character of my own become infused with unexpected vitality," and he noted that he was "astound[ed]" by the public reaction to Tutt. After all, Train noted that for over twenty-five years, Tutt had "wandered in and out of the pages of The Saturday Evening Post, defending the rights of the underdog and inventing legal stratagems for rescuing the legally guilty but morally innocent from the toils of justice." He estimated that Tutt had appeared "in 200,000,000 copies of The Saturday Evening Post and 100,000 printed books all under my name," and that "Tutt is more widely known than any justice upon the

United States Supreme Bench." Despite this widespread exposure, Train found that the "seemingly incredible, preposterous but certainly appalling fact has become apparent that a multitude of people are firmly convinced that [Tutt] is a living human being, and refuse to be persuaded to the contrary."

Train maintained that "Mr. Tutt's previous audience either must have been far smaller than I had supposed or less discerning as readers, for both the publishers and myself have been deluged with letters and telephone calls showing that what was undertaken as an amusing literary stunt, without the slightest intention to deceive, has been widely accepted in all seriousness." The aftermath of his literary caper was described as "ludicrous," "regrettable," and "revealing." Train explained that he wanted to provide his account of the whole ordeal, with "these tears and this *apologia pro vita sua.*" (In using the phrase *apologia pro vita sua,* Train may have been making a reference to a book of the same name, whose title translates to a "defense of one's life." The book that was so entitled was written by Cardinal John Henry Newman as both an autobiographical work and a response to what he perceived as an unwarranted attack on his religious opinions.)

"Now, of course, Ephraim Tutt is a fictional character pure and simple, like Sherlock Holmes or Tugboat Annie, and there has never, throughout his long literary life, been a suggestion that he was anything else." Yet Train was drawn to the idea of creating an "autobiography" of Tutt to allow for the development of this character, one "well worth ampler treatment than it had yet received and to explain the genuinely serious purpose behind this series of nearly a hundred stories about an old lawyer." Train explained that he wanted to undertake a meticulous examination of the background and motivations that he had envisioned for Tutt, which could not be conveyed adequately in his usual short stories. An "autobiography" would allow him to delve into "the passion for justice which is rooted deep in American character and ideals," and, "like a large proportion of works of fiction," he wrote the book in the first person—but "it was never for an instant intended as a hoax."

Train found the process of "construct[ing] . . . this life story of a man who never existed . . . not only interesting but highly educational." Train explained that he based the information on Tutt's childhood "on that of his supposed friend Calvin Coolidge," Tutt's college experiences and stories of being an assistant district attorney were based on Train's experiences, Tutt's "career as a youthful practitioner in the town of Pottsville was wholly imaginary," and the remainder of Tutt's experiences were those that "any active trial lawyer" might have had. The photographs appearing in the book were actually from Train's family photo albums and scrapbooks, and, on the whole, Train maintained that the majority of Tutt's life was based on his own—Tutt's "social ideas and philosophy" were Train's, as was Tutt's "world, politically, socially, legally." In a nutshell, "Yankee Lawyer was half Tutt and half Train—partly fancy, mostly true."

If the book were to have any semblance of reality, Train determined that he could not publish it as: "*The Autobiography of Ephraim Tutt,* by Arthur Train"—it would be treated as "just another Tutt story." As a result, Train explained that it was necessary to publish the book as if Tutt wrote it (even copyrighting it in Tutt's name) "to enhance the effect of actuality, but without the slightest expectation that anyone would accept the name of Ephraim Tutt as that of a real person." Yet despite what Train perceived to be a known truth, he found himself confronted with the reality that "a substantial minority of the reading public had been unintentionally deceived, and, come hell or high water, firmly intended to remain so." As he became inundated with mail and inquiries, Train's attitude changed from believing the writers of such letters to be nothing more than "members of the lunatic fringe" to discovering that many sensible "men and women . . . had conceived an admiration and even an affection for [Tutt]."[6]

One letter, in particular, caused Train to realize "Mr. Tutt had started something." This letter, "written in a rather shaky hand and signed by an elderly woman of evident refinement," stated:

Dear Ephraim Tutt—If I may so address you—Many times since reading your autobiography I have started to write you a letter and then laid down my pen appalled at my temerity. Never in my life before have I been so bold, so egotistical, so—shall I say?—unabashed as to write to a stranger. My excuse is that you are not so to me, but an old friend, and I, a lonely old woman, your contemporary, have spent so many happy hours before my fire in your company that I am sure you will forgive me when I say that the privilege of knowing you would be a great joy and consolation to me. Will you not do me the great honor and give me the equally great pleasure of coming to see me some afternoon?

This letter was sufficient to pierce Train's belief that only the "lunatic fringe" could believe that Tutt existed. Train grew anxious over how to respond to such a letter since it was clear that this woman "had fallen, and fallen rather hard, for Mr. Tutt . . . [and] the discovery that he did not exist might prove a grievous shock, apart from her probable embarrassment at having been duped." After debating it with Perkins for a week, Train "wrote her a frank letter, couched in the kindest phraseology . . . confessing the truth, in which I said that though I was distressed at having unintentionally deceived her, I could not but feel a selfish gratification that I had succeeded in portraying so convincing a character." Train offered to take Tutt's place, "however unworthy," and was surprised to receive a telephone call in response, inviting Train to afternoon tea, which Train attended. The two chatted like old friends, and Train left on the best of terms.[7]

"But other cases did not have so fortunate an outcome." Other Tutt admirers presented much more difficult conundrums—to tell some of Tutt's admirers that Tutt did not exist posed the risk of "weaken[ing] [their] faith in human nature." In fact, Train reported that one woman who "was accidentally switched onto Max Perkins' private wire refused for a long time to accept his assurance that there was, in fact, no Ephraim Tutt. 'But there must be a Mr. Tutt!' she almost sobbed, and, when finally convinced, burst into tears." Tutt's account of his "life" had become intertwined with how some people viewed society—and this was perhaps the most unpleasant aspect of Train's creation of a Tutt autobiography. By giving the book the appearance of being a true and authentic account, readers who did not recognize that the book was fictitious were disappointed to learn that the values the book espoused were nothing more than a fairy tale. In addition, just as Frey's *A Million Little Pieces* had inspired and encouraged many, some of Tutt's readers were so inspired by Tutt's example that they attended law school or planned to do so—obviously placing reliance on Tutt's account of his legal practice and philosophies. In this respect, even though Train's literary hoax may have been executed with innocent intentions, it still produced some of the same difficulties as those hoaxes that were intentionally deceptive.

Whether Tutt's autobiography told a true story was a sensitive topic for many people, and Train acknowledged that the book was so meaningful to some readers that the very suggestion that it was fake could cause quite a disturbance. For example, from the letters he received, Train learned that there was a small town "in the northern tier where Mr. Tutt has occasioned little less than civil war." Another town reported that in its local library, "a vehement discussion arose as to [*Yankee Lawyer*'s] authorship," resulting in the creation of a "Tutt party and an anti-Tutt—or Train—party and they became so bitter about it as to occasion several breaches of the peace." Train explained that "[t]hese rows usually occurred in the lending library, which was connected with the local drugstore, during which all business had to be suspended." As he was informed that there was only a single copy of *Yankee Lawyer* in the town, Train suspected that "the altercation will doubtless continue with increasing violence until the last voter has read it."

Train confessed that he was at a loss as to what he should do. He surmised that the reason for the public's bewilderment, and his difficulty in trying to clarify the matter, was that "while the readers of Ephraim's legal adventures know that they are pure fantasy, this in itself does not preclude the possibility of there being an actual person of that name upon whose experiences they are based." Further, Train believed that many people who had read his Tutt stories over the years might have forgotten just how they knew about Tutt. Therefore, when Tutt's autobiography was published, some readers may have recalled "only that they have vaguely heard of such a person; thus swelling the ranks of those who are not only bewildered but actually deceived." With these thoughts, Train exhibited an understanding that there was some potential for confusion.

"Should I Apologize" concluded with a fine piece of gamesmanship. Clearly indicating that Train was not apologizing, he reverted to a playful denouement that catered to the great spirit in which Tutt's autobiography was published. He noted, "it is, of course, possible that there is an Ephraim Tutt. Who can tell? My personal denial is not conclusive. He may still exist, even if I honestly believe and assert the contrary."[8]

Weeks after Train's "Should I Apologize" article, the *Saturday Evening Post* decided to include a follow-up piece since it had been so inundated with mail from readers who were irate that Train should suggest that Tutt did not exist. In this article, the *Post* expressed surprise at how seriously some readers treated the issue of Tutt's existence. The article began with a disclaimer: "Just so that no one will misunderstand us, to the best of our knowledge, eyesight and belief, Mr. Arthur Train exists in the flesh and Mr. Ephraim Tutt exists only in Mr. Train's and his readers' imaginations. Let us hold to that thought." The article went on to note that although Train's article did clarify for some readers that Tutt was not real, "in other cases he only stirred up more hornets' nests, and not a few faithful readers started buzzing at him again. Many, it appears, are still unable or unwilling to believe that the lovable old lawyer, Mr. Tutt, is a fictional character."[9]

Perhaps the most earnest letter submitted to the *Post* was a missive by a professor of chemistry at the University of Nebraska, noting that Train's "Should I Apologize" article left him "not only unconvinced but puzzled about [Train's] motives in denying the existence of Mr. Tutt." In fact, this gentleman claimed that his "grandfather was born in Pottsville, New York—once Mr. Tutt's home—as attested by the family Bible. That I have never been able to find this town on any map does not incline me to doubt my grandfather's existence or my own. The place has doubtless since been given a more dignified name." This professor noted that while he did not doubt Tutt's existence, he was dubious of Train's. In fact, the professor surmised that perhaps "Tutt now seeks to retire into nonexistence. . . . [s]o he invented Arthur Train." Since he could not be sure if one or both men were real, he concluded his letter by warning: "do not be surprised if it turns out that [Train], if you exist, or your co-conspirator [Tutt], if he does, or both of you, should receive a summons to appear in court in what used to be Pottsville, New York, to make clear whether you are not conspiring together to obstruct the course of justice." The advice that the *Saturday Evening Post* had for Train was "to forget the whole thing and take a good, long rest—better still, go on a fishing trip with Mr. Tutt."[10]

❖

Although the truth about Tutt could have been evident to most anyone, the hoax still caused harm. The very possibility that Tutt was a real person caused many people to grapple with whether Tutt's representation of American culture was authentic, even if Tutt was not. Just as Frey's book gave his readers hope and inspiration that they could change their lives, Tutt's autobiography gave his readers hope of what American society could be like. "You have restored my faith in mankind and especially Americans," one reader wrote to Tutt. For servicemen, Tutt proved to be an ideal and inspiration. Many women were taken by Tutt's charm and character. "I really was not aware men of such honesty and caliber were circulating today, especially in the legal profession," one admirer commented. Tutt's example so moved some readers that they were inspired to study law, and one man wrote that he hoped to "apply the character, tenets, and principles of . . . Mr. Tutt to my cases and in these parts." For these readers it was important for Tutt to be a real person because they were relying on his view of the world to shape their own. However, when the truth was revealed, these readers were disappointed that such an admirable character suddenly appeared to be a fraud. As one woman explained in a letter to Scribner's: "You will perhaps forgive a feeling of profound sadness that a character so fine should be a travesty of all that it proclaimed to champion!"[11]

One of the most fascinating characteristics of Ephraim Tutt is that this virtuous figure became mired in controversy, and suddenly the character that was known for saving victims in desperate circumstances needed to be saved. While many people expressed shock and disappointment when they learned that Tutt did not exist, one individual became so upset that he felt compelled to do something to protect those who had been fooled and demoralized by the Tutt hoax and those who had yet to read the book and suffer these consequences.

8
Mr. Tutt's Day in Court

I am seriously disturbed about the price of $3.50. . . . I can't imagine the
average book buyer not saying "Why on earth should I be asked to pay
$3.50 for that, when I can buy [other books] for $3.00." . . . I think even
the critics will comment on $3.50 for the novel . . . and it will certainly
stand in the way of the book's success.
                            —Arthur Train to Maxwell Perkins, July 18, 1943

I don't believe anyone would make the slightest adverse comment on the
price, which is fully justified by the cost of manufacture per copy, and
also by the fact that the book is an autobiography, not a novel.
                            —Maxwell Perkins to Arthur Train, July 20, 1943

On March 2, 1943, before *Yankee Lawyer* was published, Train received
a letter from the Albany Institute of History and Art, located in Albany,
New York. At first blush, it appears the letter, from J. D. Hatch, the director of the institute, sought only to "complete our uncompleted business officially," with respect to the sale of two drawings that Helen Train
had purchased and other artwork Train selected. However, after resolving their matters of art, Hatch added a paragraph to his letter, providing
a word of caution to Train. Apparently, Hatch and Train had discussed an
idea of Train's for a character to be included in an upcoming book or story.
After the two parted, Hatch realized that he had heard of a person quite
the same as the character Train had pitched. Once aware of this similarity,
Hatch worried that Train might "get into trouble by describing his having
habits . . . so uncomplimentary that he would not appreciate it." However, Hatch jocularly noted, "it might be good publicity for Tutt though,
if this gentleman was living and could sue you." In the margin, a bracket
was drawn alongside the paragraph containing this interesting sentence,

and in what appears to be Train's handwriting, the word "Max" was written next to the bracket.[1] Five months later, *Yankee Lawyer* was published.

Within one year after Hatch's letter to Train, Lewis R. Linet read *Yankee Lawyer* and was content in believing that Ephraim Tutt was a living attorney practicing law in New York. However, when he read the February 26, 1944, *Saturday Evening Post* and found an article by Arthur Train titled "Should I Apologize," his feelings about the book sharply changed. Much to his shock and chagrin, Linet learned that Tutt's "autobiography" was not an autobiography at all. Being a public-spirited lawyer who spent his time guarding the interests of his community, Linet felt that he needed to take action to prevent others from being tricked and fooled as he had been. He turned to the place he felt most comfortable resolving disputes: court. Although the press treated Linet harshly in reporting the news that he filed a lawsuit against Train, Perkins, and Scribner's based on his belief that *Yankee Lawyer* was a fraud, a brief look at Linet's background and character reveals that he did not bring the lawsuit as a publicity stunt or for selfish reasons. It would seem that Linet's philosophy mirrored Tutt's, for when Linet perceived what he believed to be an injustice against the reading public, he felt the victims of Train's hoax deserved a day in court.

From the time he graduated from Temple Law School in 1924 until his retirement in 1994, Lewis Linet practiced law out of a small law office in Philadelphia. Over the course of these years, not only did he serve as an effective advocate for his clients, but he also became a voice in—and for—his community. During his youth Linet began building a name for himself as a masterful orator, as local newspapers reported the many awards he won for his local debate team. Throughout his life Linet was an active participant in politics, community service, and in his synagogue. In fact, after practicing law for only six years, a local newspaper described Linet as a "well known" attorney in his community. Linet participated in various community activities—he worked with several charities and organizations and volunteered in programs that would improve the lives of others.

In 1950 Linet led an "orphan home drive," and was committed to raising $50,000 for Philadelphia's Downtown Jewish Orphan Home.[2]

When it came to his legal practice, Linet was quick to take cases whose resolution would ultimately benefit the public and stop an injustice. For example, when servicemen reported that they were being overcharged for the purchase of gifts in Philadelphia, George F. Richardson, an inspector in Philadelphia's Detective Bureau, contacted Linet, who was then serving as counsel for the legal aid and small claims division of the municipal court. Richardson told the press, "Fortunately, there are only a few places stooping to this mean practice . . . and I have asked Mr. Linet's cooperation in breaking it up. We are going to get rid of these wolves." Linet vowed that "civil action will be taken in any case of overcharge . . . and, where possible, criminal action, too." Linet felt duty bound to ensure that servicemen, who were willing to risk their lives for their country, would not be wrongly overcharged by his community.[3]

In the 1930s, as the Great Depression permeated the nation, Linet became involved in the banking difficulties plaguing Philadelphia. When the US State Department closed the Northwestern Trust Company due to the significant amount of loans it issued to home builders before the housing market became depressed, Linet was retained as counsel for the "depositors' committee." Linet worked to assemble the entire group of depositors so the bank and its customers could reach an agreement and avoid a local financial disaster. A meeting was held, with more than one thousand depositors assembled, and an employee who worked at the bank for twenty-three years, Charles Finley, addressed the audience as Linet stood by. Finley noted that "the bank was closed because a great number of home owners, business people and depositors could not pay the money due" on their loans. He further explained, "They call it frozen assets. If the money you folks owe was available[,] assets would not be frozen and the bank would be open. The bank stood by you in your trouble. Now you stand by the bank." The speech was met with an "outburst of applause." Staying with their bank is exactly what the depositors did. Subsequently, Linet announced that the majority of the Northwestern Trust Company's depositors—three thousand in number—approved plans for the bank to reorganize and reopen. In fact, the depositors agreed to purchase stock in Northwestern Trust Company, amounting to almost $2.5 million.[4]

As he helped his community by utilizing his skills as a lawyer, mediator, orator, and leader, Linet's reputation grew. He was known for being "friendly and witty," and the Philadelphia press dubbed him a "hard and earnest worker and an excellent co-operator," whether he was engaged "in business or other activities." One newspaper described him as "the type of lawyer who is a distinguished member of his profession."[5]

Beyond his duty to his community, Linet wished to also serve his nation. During World War II, Linet enrolled in a special thirty-day training camp at Fort Meade, paying his own expenses, living in barracks, and taking courses in military equipment and training. Linet also served as a goodwill delegate, and as the official representative of the city of Philadelphia, to Mexico. While serving in the latter capacity, Linet had a private audience with Mexican president Manuel Ávila Camacho, was invited to a reception by the American ambassador to Mexico, was a guest of the Mexican national government, and was invited to speak in the Mexican legislature.[6]

Linet's impact on the city of Philadelphia and its neighboring towns was significant. In the field of real estate, his work was so highly esteemed that Philadelphia's Oxford Circle Realty Board, along with a host of individuals who worked in the realty profession in Philadelphia, created the Lewis R. Linet Award in 1978, to be awarded annually "to a person who by service and accomplishment has distinguished himself or herself in the real estate field." Upon announcing the creation of this award, the chairman of the Philadelphia Board of Realtors sent a letter of personal congratulation to Linet and noted, "I sincerely know of no finer gentleman than yourself on which they could have bestowed this honor." Linet's skill as a lawyer was recognized when he was considered for an opening on the bench of the Philadelphia Orphans' Court.[7]

Looking back at his career at the time of his retirement at the age of ninety, Linet identified his retention on a case that other attorneys had rejected as one of the "proudest memories of his career." In the early 1950s a group of Philadelphia firemen and police officers visited Linet's law office, inquiring whether Linet had any interest in representing them. They explained that in 1949 George Branden—a nonveteran—took a civil service examination for promotion to the position of captain of the Fire Bureau of the city of Philadelphia. In December 1949 a list of those eligible for the promotion was published, and both Branden and a group of veterans appeared on this list. Although Branden's raw score was the highest, the veterans were entitled to "a ten point bonus [to their scores] under the provisions of the Veterans Preference Act." As a result of this bonus, the veterans' scores were higher than Branden's raw score, and the veterans were promoted and Branden was not.

The firefighters and police officers explained to Linet that they wished to challenge the validity of the statute that gave this ten-point "preference" to veterans for promotions because it jettisoned the chances of qualified nonveteran firefighters and police officers to attain higher positions. Linet's potential clients had already requested the assistance of the two largest firms in Philadelphia, both of which declined the case because they believed the law was discriminatory but constitutional. According to Linet, he "said to the men, I know nothing at all about the law in this case, about what you have to pass to become a policeman and to become qualified for promotion." Linet told his future clients that he would research the law and "[will] either take the case or I won't. If I feel I can't win it, it won't cost you a nickel." Linet and an assistant spent the next two days reading cases and briefs that challenged similar laws in other states, and Linet found a unanimous verdict: such laws were constitutional. Despite this wall of authority that seemed to tower over Linet, there was one case in which a court remarked that although the law was constitutional, the judge felt "that the public gets hurt." These words struck Linet, and he realized: "why do I have to argue constitution? This is public policy . . . if you don't have a good fireman, it's the public who suffers." With this epiphany as his guide, Linet agreed to take the case.

With decades of precedent against him, Linet initially met defeat; the

Pennsylvania trial court rejected Linet's argument and dismissed the case. However, Linet appealed this decision to the Supreme Court of Pennsylvania, which, seemingly against all odds, ruled in his favor. The court found that to provide veterans with a ten-point bonus to their scores for promotions (in addition to a ten-point bonus when they were first hired) led to "a totally unjustified appraisal of the value of their military training and [was] highly prejudicial to the public service." When Linet won on appeal, the nation took notice, and Linet received a shower of requests from judges and lawyers across the country for a copy of his brief. While Linet enjoyed his legal victory, it was not simply because he won his case despite the precedent that was stacked against him. Linet felt he was helping the public by ensuring that the firemen and police officers employed in his community were those who would be the best at performing such jobs.

After nearly seventy years of practice, Linet's law school interviewed him for its quarterly newsletter. When he was asked what he liked best about his profession, Linet responded: "helping people."[8]

In reviewing Lewis Linet's background, principles, and philosophy, it becomes clear that Linet was a lot like Tutt. Both "men" were honest, hardworking servants for the public good. Linet ran his own private practice, and he acted like the type of lawyer most anyone would want to hire: a lawyer bound by a conscience and who was willing to put his name on the line and take cases even when they might not clearly have law on their side. He chased what he thought was right, even when it was not popular. Linet represented people who needed his help and worked to achieve an outcome that was deserved. He was the type of person who commanded the respect of his colleagues at the bar, and also his fellow townspeople. He may not have resorted to tricky strategies to win cases as Tutt did, but the two had similar ideals and philosophies on the role that lawyers should play in their communities.

When Linet read *Yankee Lawyer,* he undoubtedly connected with Tutt; he understood what Tutt's small-town practice was like and the challenges of being a solo practitioner. Linet saw his own belief system in Tutt's, for he was willing to take worthy cases, even when losing them seemed likely. He was honored to represent people who were wronged and to try to set things right. For Tutt and Linet, it was the principle at stake that would often drive them to make the legal decisions they made, or to take the cases they agreed to take. Only, for Linet, it was all real. For Tutt, it was not. And thus we have our adversaries—Linet and Train—both of whom admired Ephraim Tutt to such a degree they became embroiled in litigation over him.

Shortly after he brought the lawsuit, Linet was asked why he decided to take Train to court. "It's not the publicity . . . [or] to get back the $3.50 he paid for the fictional and fictitious 'Yankee Lawyer,'" but to "stop Arthur Train, Publishers Charles Scribner's Sons, and others who may care to emulate them, from fooling the public," Linet told his local newspaper. Linet further explained, "the book is a hoax. Lots of its 100,000 readers were fooled. They believed in Tutt and his smart tricks. They came to their lawyers and wanted to know why they couldn't do likewise. That's embarrassing to a lawyer." Armed with Train's published article of "apology," Linet noted, "Train thought it was poetic license. I say it was a fraud. The book was carried by booksellers as nonfiction. I am taking this up as a public matter."[9]

In March 1944 Linet's lawsuit came to fruition when he caused a summons and complaint to be served on Arthur Train, Charles Scribner's and Sons, and Maxwell Perkins. The complaint stated that these defendants had engaged in fraudulent conduct by writing, publishing, distributing, and selling a book that proclaimed to be written by and about "an eminent, successful, and famous New York lawyer." Beginning with the foolhardy dust jacket, Linet demonstrated how the book goaded the public into being scammed by its appearance and representations. The complaint provided an excerpt from the dust jacket and noted that it suggested that Tutt was "alive" and friends with a famous lawyer: "Ephraim Tutt is undoubtedly the best known lawyer now alive. Others may have achieved greater eminence in their profession, but their fame has been local or special to the bar, while his is popular and international. There are probably a thousand persons throughout the land that know Mr. Tutt, for every one who can name the present Chief Justice of our United States Supreme Court. The reputation probably nearest akin to his perhaps was that of his friend the late Clarence Darrow, with whose ideas he had much in common." As for Train's introduction to his own book, Linet reproduced the entire thing in his complaint, since it included so many bold assertions by Train—including that Tutt had asked Train to write the introduction.

Train's "fun," taken at the expense of unsuspecting readers, was something Linet took very seriously. He argued in his complaint that between the dust jacket and Train's delusive, inaccurate, and disingenuous introduction, there could be no countering the fact that the defendants intentionally manufactured the book to create the illusion that Tutt was a real, living lawyer. Linet also charged that the defendants, by publishing Train's introduction, acted so as "to convince anyone who had any prior acquaintance with the fictional short stories written by defendant Arthur Train concerning Mr. Tutt that his prior fictional stories were based on actual experiences of a famous living lawyer." In addition, Linet highlighted the fact that the defendants even caused to be published text within *Yankee Lawyer* in which "Tutt" referred to Train "in such a way as to indicate that the stories of Arthur Train were based on facts supplied by the writer, Ephraim Tutt, a living lawyer." Passages of *Yankee Lawyer* were quoted in the complaint, illustrating incidents of "Tutt" chastising Train and taking umbrage with the way Train portrayed certain facts about him in Train's stories. One example included in the complaint was when "Tutt" stated, in *Yankee Lawyer:* "The Tapley suit happens to be an instance where Arthur Train in writing his story was for once obliged to stick closely to the truth for the reason that being complicated, it left him no space for romancing. Usually, however, he lets himself go to such an extent that before he has finished, I can hardly recognize my own case."

The complaint also outlined a list of other characteristics about *Yankee Lawyer* that had no other purpose but to deceive its readers into thinking that Tutt existed. These included the publication of "certain photographs purporting to be those of Mr. Ephraim Tutt at various ages and others purporting to be those of his father and mother," and the inclusion of various "statements and anecdotes" that involved "many prominent men and public officials who were the contemporaries of Mr. Ephraim Tutt and with whom he purportedly associated." The complaint argued that the defendants had taken all of these actions in order to convince the reading public that the book was a "genuine autobiography," when in fact such a representation was "false and untrue" since the "book is wholly imaginary and fictional and not the autobiography of Mr. Ephraim Tutt, a well-known lawyer." As a result, the publication of *Yankee Lawyer* was nothing more than "a deceit and fraud and is a hoax upon the plaintiff and the reading public." What's more, Linet described Train's "introduction" as nothing more than "an additional mass of lies and deceits."[10]

Making his way to the relief he desired, Linet explained that he was induced to buy the book based on the representation that it was the autobiography of a real person. Because of this, he was willing to part with $3.50 to purchase the book, "whereas [if it were] a pure fictional story . . . [it] would not [have been] sold for more than $2.50 to $3.00." Thus contrary to Perkins's assurances to Train—that no one "would make the slightest adverse comment on the price"—Linet, and others, took great offense to the amount of money the book cost. As one newspaper noted, "we are with the plaintiff in our touchiness about the $3.50. When a book costs that much money a buyer should get some meat, butter and gasoline with it."[11] Linet complained that he was not only induced to spend his money, but also his time reading a book that was supposed to be a "true autobiography of a famous attorney." For these injuries, Linet demanded a refund—in whole or in part—for the purchase price of the book to prevent the defendants from collecting a windfall for a work of fiction. Linet also wanted to stop the defendants from profiting from their "false and fraudulent representations" by requesting a court order enjoining the defendants from "producing, printing, advertising, distributing, offering for sale, or selling the said book," so long as it was described as an "autobiography" by "Tutt."[12]

Meanwhile, Charles Scribner's Sons' advertising department was busy securing advertising space in newspapers across the country. Even shortly after the lawsuit was filed in May 1944, Scribner's published advertisements featuring *Yankee Lawyer* in its "Check List for Good Reading," which noted that "EPHRAIM TUTT in this bestselling autobiographical volume tells the full, uncensored story of a rich and eventful life." The following month, Scribner's published an advertisement for *Yankee Lawyer* noting that "at 75, Ephraim Tutt the lawyer has given us a full-length portrait of Ephraim the man."[13]

Beyond any advertising space Scribner's purchased, the book received a bonanza of free "advertising" with all of the media coverage of Linet's lawsuit. As can easily be imagined, once word of the lawsuit spread, newspapers and magazines had a field day with the story. The *New York Herald Tribune* announced that "Mr. Tutt Faces His First Battle in a Real Court," and the headline in the *New York Times* read: "Real Lawyer Goes to Court Here Charging Ephraim Tutt Is 'Fraud.'" The *Washington Post* named the case the "Suit of the Month," and noted jokingly that copycat lawsuits were going to abound, and that Betty Smith could face legal troubles if a customer "claimed he thought 'A Tree Grows in Brooklyn' was a publication on landscape gardening." The *Washington Post* continued: "Elmer Twitchell is suing Somerset Maugham on the ground he bought 'Razor's Edge' as a treatise on shaving, and Ima Dodo is seeing her lawyer about proceedings against Mr. Marquand for his book 'So Little Time.' The saleslady sold it to her as a technical book about grandfather-clocks." Finally, the *Washington Post* surmised on what a court transcript would look like if any of these lawsuits made it to trial:

We avail the transcript of a court proceeding:
 Q: You are the author of the book in question?
 A: Guilty as charged.
 Q: Are you familiar with the allegations in this suit against you?
 A: No, but I'm familiar with the sales jumps since the action
  was filed and I wish to thank everybody concerned.

Q: Did you have any help on this book?

A: Not until the plaintiff sued me.

Q: Do you know the plaintiff?

A: No, but I have developed a great regard for him.

Q: Are you willing to give him his money back?

A: Not only that, but I will put him on the payroll.

Verdict

Judge: The decision of the court is that this suit should never have been brought.

Author: So, you're unfair to authors, eh![14]

One Connecticut newspaper reported that "an 'out-of-town lawyer'" by the name of Lewis R. Linet "wants his money back and something to boot for the 'deception' he suffered when he bought a copy of 'Yankee Lawyer: The Autobiography of Ephraim Tutt,' by Arthur Train." The article surmised that "Mr. Linet would have to live a long way back in the sticks not to know that the Train hero, immortalized in at least nine novels published in this century, is a brilliant figment of the author's creative imagination. True, there are said to be some Tennessee mountain backwoodsmen who have never heard there's a war on. Maybe Mr. Linet never heard of the *Saturday Evening Post* or of Arthur Train. Maybe!" Even *Time Magazine* covered the story, noting that Tutt "had some real lawyer trouble to worry about." *Time* stated that *Yankee Lawyer* "had caused considerable pain to the person of Lewis R. Linet," who was "suing for $3.50 worth of fraudulence." Ironically, although the media did not provide a definitive account of who wrote *Yankee Lawyer* when it was first published and reviewed, when it came to reporting Linet's lawsuit, the media had no sympathy for his initial confusion.[15]

While the press was having its fun with the lawsuit, the records Charles Scribner's Sons kept confirm that the defendants were taking the suit very seriously. Although the press was initially suspicious of whether the lawsuit was Train's creation—believing that perhaps Train wished to gain publicity by manufacturing fictitious details about an irate attorney suing him for fraud—records show the suit was very real. In fact, in May 1944 Perkins wrote to Train noting that he had received a variety of requests for information from newspapers and magazines that wished to run exposé-type articles on "the whole story [on] Tutt." Perkins exclaimed, "the daily papers just can't believe that it is not a publicity stunt, or, as the PM man said to me when I persuaded him it was genuine, they are afraid that their readers will think it is a publicity stunt." However, they didn't. Newspapers seemed to exhibit no small amount of concern over the Tutt lawsuit, and people generally wanted to see that Tutt triumphed and did not become a victim of the legal system from which he always protected others. For example, the *Hartford Courant* noted that although Train "does very well for himself and has been diligent in searching out authorities to support his defense," "one can only wish that the author would call upon Ephraim Tutt to handle the brief."[16]

Ephraim Tutt did not file an appearance to be an attorney on behalf of Train, Perkins, and Charles Scribner's Sons, but these defendants were well aware that they would need to hire an attorney—and a very good one at that. Shortly after being served with the summons and complaint, the defendants contacted John W. Davis to see if Davis would be willing to represent them. At the time Davis was a household name, as he had a distinguished career in public service and was a prominent attorney in Manhattan. Davis served in the US House of Representatives from 1911 to 1913, was solicitor general of the United States from 1913 to 1918, was the United States' ambassador to the United Kingdom from 1918 to 1921, and was the Democratic Party's presidential candidate for the 1924 election. He argued countless cases before the Supreme Court of the United States, and was well respected within the profession of law and without. In the 1940s he was a partner in the firm Davis Polk & Wardwell.

In April 1944 Charles Scribner, concerned with the cost of the looming litigation, wrote to Davis and explained the limitations he wished to place on the perpetuation of such a suit. Scribner noted that he believed that there was a "good chance" the case would be dismissed upon the filing of a motion for such relief. However, to file such a motion would "rob" the case "of any significance or publicity value." On this note, Scribner stated, "personally I would like to see it come to trial, but as president of Charles Scribner's Sons it is naturally my duty not to involve the company in expenses that far outweigh the benefits." Next, Scribner, apologizing for being so frank but making no qualms about his feelings on the lawsuit and its cost, explained:

> Mr. Train has always insisted in his authors' contracts with us that we cancel the usual clause whereby the author agrees to reimburse the publisher for any legal costs or damages that may be incurred in the publication of a book. Also he has not intimated that he would agree to assume any [s]hare of the costs incurred by this firm in defending the suit, although any publicity that might come from it would be far more to his advantage than to ours, inasmuch as the play, and perhaps also a motion picture are still to be produced. Charles Scribner's Sons are willing to assume a moderate expense of perhaps two or three thousand dollars in fighting it out in Court this interesting but on the whole academic question, but if our [s]hare is apt to far exceed this sum we would naturally prefer to see the case settled with the least possible cost.[17]

In response, Davis wrote to Scribner assuring him that Davis did not "anticipate that the expense of this suit will be great and I think you may safely assume that my charge will be within the bracket which you suggest." As for the next step, Davis filed a motion to dismiss Linet's request that the court order Train, Scribner's, and Perkins to cease selling *Yankee Lawyer* as Tutt's "autobiography." This type of legal relief—equitable and injunctive—generally cannot be awarded when whatever injury the plaintiff suffered can be remedied through the payment of a money judgment. With this in mind, Davis argued that whatever harm Linet faced, the harm occurred in the past and could be ameliorated, if necessary, with money. In addition, Davis also argued that Linet could not bring his lawsuit on behalf of others, since he did not have "standing" to do so. The theory behind the concept of "standing" is that when a lawsuit is commenced, a person actually being harmed by the conduct alleged in the lawsuit is usually the best person to complain of the injury being inflicted. Davis noted, "It is significant that the plaintiff's nomination remains unseconded by a single member of the great multitude whose protection he professes to seek and who, strangely enough, seem to remain blissfully unconscious of the grave and irreparable peril that awaits them within the covers of an innocent looking 'autobiography' now resting upon the shelves of the bookstores of the Country!"[18]

Linet filed opposition to Davis's motion to dismiss his lawsuit, in which he recounted all of the details in *Yankee Lawyer* that made the work so convincing as a piece of nonfiction and maintained that "the defendants have utilized every deceptive device and every false representation possible to make the book appear to be a genuine autobiography and to have persons purchasing same buy it under the representation that it is the autobiography of a famous New York lawyer." With regard to Davis's "sarcastic prowess" in stating that Linet had not been joined by any other members of the public who "remain[ed] blissfully unconscious" of the harm lying in wait for them, Linet noted that the defendants "have admitted that many persons have been deceived by the book and after reading it have, as they were supposed to do, believed that it was the autobiography of a living genuine attorney." In addition, Linet noted that since the amount of damage to each individual may not be great, many injured readers might hesitate to bring litigation; however, he argued this "should not prevent equity from restraining these defendants from continuing to perpetuate a fraud upon the public."

Linet also described his lawsuit as involving one party trying to protect "truth," while the other was peddling a falsity. Just as with many other literary hoaxes, Train's publication of Tutt's autobiography caused many people to question whether a book identified as an "autobiography" should be anything short of nonfiction. Linet was not just asking the court to resolve his case; he was seeking an answer to whether American culture would tolerate a fictitious work of nonfiction. Linet explained: "We have in this case a question of truth as against falsity. The defendants would make a joke of truth and would honor fraudulent representations by pointing out how well deceived the public were in that they remained blissfully unaware of the deception. A fraud undiscovered is a fraud just as much as one that is discovered. It happens that the plaintiff here has discovered the fraud whereas many thousands of purchasers of the book may not have discovered it and may remain unaware of the fraud that has been perpetrated upon them." Linet stated that the damage suffered was not speculative, but "definite and actual." Linet did not care about his $3.50, he wanted a court of law to tell the defendants—and any other publishing company or author who might try to do the same as Train, Perkins, and Scribner's— that publishing fiction under the auspices of nonfiction would not be tolerated by the public.[19]

Ultimately, the motion to dismiss Linet's request for injunctive relief was granted—"on the ground that no man could of his own volition constitute himself the champion of the public and demand relief on their behalf." All that remained of Linet's lawsuit was his request for a refund for himself and all others who purchased *Yankee Lawyer* believing it to be nonfiction. In the end, however, Linet's lawsuit ended inconspicuously and undetected by the press, with the filing of a "stipulation of discontinuance" on May 2, 1947.[20] By this time Train had passed away, and perhaps Linet no longer wished to litigate the case. In any event, the reason the case was "discontinued," or under what terms the discontinuance was secured, remains a mystery. The fire that burned when Tutt's courtroom battle commenced seemed to slowly smolder until it went out, without even the smallest whimper.

Before Train died, he published an account of his feelings about Linet's lawsuit in the chapter titled "Mr. Tutt Pleads Not Guilty," in *Mr. Tutt Finds a Way.* Train, who never met Linet, described the latter as "partial to biography [and] . . . antipathetic if not allergic to fiction," and he stated that Linet "would never have purchased the miserable book if he had known its true character." Train explained that Linet suffered various injuries to his "body and soul," including "the waste of his time involved in reading nearly four hundred pages which he supposed to be true but which were in fact nothing but tosh and piffle—and—inferentially—there was his chagrin and mortification on learning that he had been hoaxed." Train commented that Linet wanted to be reimbursed "a dollar, or at least fifty cents, plus adequate damages for his loss of time, mental anguish and general discombobulation" and wanted to stop "further publication or sale of said book."

Train maintained that at first the defendants believed that Linet was indulging in a publicity stunt, and they searched for information on the mysterious plaintiff who had sued them. However, their search revealed neither "hide [n]or hair of him." Wondering whether Linet was bringing his lawsuit in good faith, the defendants questioned Linet's attorney, and they received an "emphatic" answer that Linet was "a serious-minded, public-spirited citizen, who not only was exceedingly angry over his own deception, but felt . . . duty bound to act as champion of all such as had already been deceived, as well as of all others born and as yet unborn who might be similarly swindled hereafter." According to Train, "Mr. Linet meant business and was eager to get into court."

Train took Linet's suit very seriously—both legally and personally. In fact, while thinking about the case, Train invented a defense that sounded very much like one that Tutt would invent. According to Train, he "recalled that towards the end of the last century someone had drawn a crude caricature consisting of eyeglasses, teeth and sombrero on an otherwise unaddressed letter, which, having been mailed, had been promptly delivered to Col. Theodore Roosevelt." Believing the same would happen if he mailed a picture of Tutt, he pasted upon a blank envelope the image he had created for his stationery (see page 114).

Train happily reported that "within twenty-four hours it was deposited by the postman at my front door, bearing the endorsement: 'This is for Arthur Train, 113 E. 73rd St., New York City—Postmaster.'" With the power vested in the US Postal Service to deliver mail to its rightful owner, how could a court of law find Train guilty of fraud for publishing Tutt's autobiography when the Post Office deemed him to be the alter ego of his famous fictitious character, Ephraim Tutt?[21]

Although Train kept a sense of humor about the suit, it is apparent that he was upset—or at least feigned to be—for having been sued and accused of perpetrating a fraud against the public. Perhaps it was Train's faithfulness to Ephraim Tutt that might explain Train's outrage at being sued by Linet. Or perhaps Train was merely exaggerating his displeasure in order to support his defense that he had no idea people would be fooled into believing Tutt existed. On the one hand, Train reaped obvious benefits from the lawsuit, since it attracted the attention of newspapers and magazines, and it secured the public's continued curiosity about the book. On the other hand, Tutt was a character that Train had meticulously developed over the course of decades—Tutt was undoubtedly dear to Train. In fact, Train described Tutt as a penumbra of himself; Tutt was Train, Train was Tutt. Thus being sued for fraud over the "autobiography" of Tutt likely struck a very personal chord with Train. In this way, boosted book sales or not, the lawsuit felt like an attack on Train. Linet did not seem a victim, but a villain who was discrediting a character who stood for good and right and was as innocent as one could be. Tutt was no fraud, at least not to Train.

The irony about the lawsuit is that Lewis Linet shared so many of Tutt's characteristics, but Train did not know this because he had never met Linet. Train was unaware of the countless articles written in Linet's local newspapers, describing the various cases Linet took and the type of legal practice he conducted. Not knowing that Linet really *was* just a public-spirited citizen who was trying to protect others from what he believed was a wrong being perpetuated against them, Train was left to conclude that Linet was either suing with bad motive or lacked a sense of humor and was out of touch with reality. Unfortunately, Train's death prevented the two from ever meeting, though I would like to think that if they had ever met, they would have been able to resolve their differences and would probably have parted with a mutual respect for each other—Train would have admired Linet for conducting a legal practice much like Tutt's, and Linet would have credited Train for having created a character who, though shady at times, strove to do good and protect the public.

In the hoaxes that have followed *Yankee Lawyer,* authors and publishers have not escaped from their shenanigans unscathed. In fact, just as Linet raised allegations of fraud, lawsuits were filed across the United States alleging that James Frey and Random House had "defrauded them by selling the book [*A Million Little Pieces*] as a memoir rather than as a work of fiction." The case ultimately reached a settlement, which provided that Frey and Random House did not admit any wrongdoing, but consumers who bought Frey's book before January 2006—when the true nature of the book was publicly revealed—could obtain "a full refund." The total amount for which Frey and Random House were responsible was "no more than a total of $2.35 million."

After the Frey settlement was reached, an attorney for one of the plaintiffs commented that his client was only seeking "a refund of the [cost of the] book and clarification about whether it was fiction or nonfiction.'"22 Fifty years earlier, when Linet brought a lawsuit seeking practically the same relief, the media laughed at him, and his suit was considered frivolous litigation. Despite Linet's request for a refund on behalf of everyone who had been hoaxed, Train and Scribner's were not forced to pay a cent in reparations, and public support was generally on their side. The divergent paths these cases took can be explained by either a growing intolerance for literary hoaxes with the passage of time or the fact that Tutt was a creature of fiction and Frey was not—it was far more egregious for a real person to write a fictitious autobiography than for a fictitious autobiography to be written about a known fictitious character.

One of the most severely punished literary hoaxes was Clifford Irving's. Irving got so carried away with his hoax that he was fined and imprisoned for the actions he took to keep his ruse afloat. His trouble began in December 1971, when the McGraw-Hill Book Company announced that it planned to publish an autobiography of the reclusive Howard Hughes, which was based on over one hundred tape-recorded conversations between Hughes and the author of the autobiography, Irving.[23] From the beginning, Hughes insisted he had not spoken to Irving, and had not provided any details about his life for an autobiography. However, "McGraw-Hill claim[ed] to have a substantial amount of signed and handwritten communications from Mr. Hughes, including agreements . . . an edited manuscript with his handwriting on it," and endorsed checks; Hughes maintained that "there was no such material written by him." Handwriting analysis was conducted, and early reports revealed that there were matches between Hughes's handwriting and the documents in McGraw-Hill's possession. Matters were further complicated when a longtime aide to Hughes, Noah Dietrich, reported that as far as he could tell, the autobiography was authentic. Dietrich surmised that Hughes was denouncing the autobiography because Hughes had a change of heart about the publication of the details he revealed to Irving.

In short order, Hughes filed a lawsuit to block publication of his purported autobiography. As soon as all parties were shepherded into court, Hughes's attorneys declared that they could produce witnesses to prove that the autobiography was a hoax, and Irving filed a sworn affidavit detailing his contact with Hughes in preparing the manuscript of the autobiography. Just as the two parties seemed to be coming to a head, Irving's story began to crumble. It was rumored that two days after the court hearing, Irving and his attorney were preparing a defense based on a "theory that the novelist had been a victim of a hoax by a 'gang of six to eight people.'" Meanwhile, news spread of three checks from McGraw-Hill, totaling $650,000, which had been deposited in a Swiss bank account that was opened in the name of Howard Hughes. Soon Zurich police and the FBI were investigating this mysterious bank account, and Irving confessed to the New York District Attorney's Office that his wife had opened this bank account, posing as "Helga Hughes," and that she had withdrawn the money from that account. However, Irving maintained that Howard Hughes "had requested that the bank account be opened by the novelist's wife and that Mr. Hughes had supplied the false Swiss passport that [Irving's wife] had used for identification." Soon a joint investigation by the US Attorney's Office and the New York County District Attorney's Office commenced, with over one hundred subpoenas issued to secure witnesses at a federal grand jury proceeding to determine whether state or federal law had been violated with respect to the incidents surrounding the purported Hughes autobiography.[24]

As Irving's web of lies slowly unraveled, *Life* magazine, which had gained the right to publish excerpts of Irving's Hughes autobiography, canceled its plans to publish any portion of it and declared the manuscript a "'hoax' perpetrated by Clifford Irving." It was soon reported that Irving's autobiography appeared to be "almost exactly like the manuscript based on the recollections of Noah Dietrich." In March 1972, after approximately three months of drama over the Hughes autobiography, Clifford Irving, his wife Edith, and Richard Suskind—Irving's "researcher" for his Hughes autobiography—were indicted on charges of grand larceny, conspiracy, perjury, mail fraud, and possession of forged instruments.[25] Days later, the Irvings appeared in federal district court in Manhattan, where they pleaded guilty to charges of conspiracy and then proceeded to plead guilty in state court to charges of grand larceny and conspiracy (Suskind pleaded guilty only to the state charges). A solemn Irving admitted, "I conspired to convince the McGraw-Hill Book Company that I was in communication with Mr. Howard Hughes and, in fact, I was not." Edith Irving was ultimately sentenced to a two-month term of imprisonment for her role in the conspiracy, Suskind received a six-month sentence, and Clifford Irving was sentenced to two and one-half years of imprisonment.[26]

Although Clifford Irving expanded the literary hoax to criminal proportions, Arthur Train, Maxwell Perkins, and Charles Scribner's Sons engaged in some behavior that was similar. For instance, Train printed special stationery that had a drawing of Tutt in the left-hand corner, which he sometimes used for correspondence that was customarily signed (or perhaps "forged") "Tutt" or "Eph." Train playfully communicated with those who were writing book reviews on *Yankee Lawyer* by sending notes on this stationery. While reviewers generally knew that Train was the author of Tutt's autobiography, many of Tutt's fans did not, yet Train also used this letterhead to respond to Tutt's admirers in the same fashion. Although Train's "Tutt" letters certainly did not rise to the level of forged endorsements on checks, it cannot be said that Train's behavior was entirely innocent—especially when he communicated with unsuspecting Tutt admirers. But should Train's conduct be criminalized? Could the signature of a fictitious character be "forged?" Could Train even be prosecuted for writing a counterfeit letter purporting to be written by his own character of fiction? It certainly seems unlikely, though these issues appear to be unprecedented.

While Train may not have been guilty of criminal forgery, what about the actions by Train, Perkins, and Scribner's in conspiring to publish the book? Just as Irving, his researcher, and his wife were convicted of conspiracy, would it have been possible to press such charges against Train, his editor, and his publishing company? It cannot be denied that the three parties worked together to publish an autobiography of the "best known lawyer now alive" (or, at least, that's what the dust jacket they printed stated). Yet when letters were sent to Train, Perkins, and Scribner's for clarification, they promptly dispatched truthful letters, explaining that the book was a work of fiction written by Arthur Train. Whether any criminal charges could have been pressed against Train, Perkins, and Scribner's might be fodder for a lively legal debate, but on the whole it seems their actions were far less egregious than Irving's or Frey's. Since Tutt was clearly a creature of fiction for decades leading to the publication of his autobiography, the actions Train, Perkins, and Scribner's took were innocent compared with the motives for and actions taken in other literary hoaxes. For instance, with Irving's hoax, harm to the reputation of a real person—Howard Hughes—was at stake, whereas the publication of Tutt's autobiography presented the unlikely scenario of a fictitious character being harmed. While McGraw-Hill had no idea that Irving's book was not written with Howard Hughes's help, Train's publishing company knew *Yankee Lawyer* was a "false autobiography." In these ways, it is clear that Irving's conduct was reprehensible, while Train's was not.

Train, Irving, and Frey were all guilty of publishing books that gave the appearance of being true—by being labeled as autobiographies or memoirs—when they contained, in whole or in part, imaginary details. However, Irving and Frey were punished because their stories were supposed to be about real people and their actual experiences. When Frey admitted that his memoir was embellished and Irving finally confessed that Hughes's autobiography was not written with the cooperation of Hughes, the public faced the dilemma of what value should be placed on "truth." The intervention of courts in settling disputes over whether a literary hoax should go unpunished has shown that society has increasingly viewed this literary tradition with disdain and is not willing to allow "truth" to become a relative term. It seems that Train escaped this public wrath because, at its core, *Yankee Lawyer* could never have actually been a work of nonfiction, and people generally recognized that Train had not published it with a nefarious motive. Most people embraced Tutt's autobiography with a grain of salt and a sense of humor. And although there were many who were fooled by it, most readers came to terms with the fact that it would have been impossible for Tutt to publish the book. However, the hoaxes by Frey and Irving could not enjoy this same lighthearted forgiveness because Howard Hughes and James Frey were real people, and the term *nonfiction* was a definite one for them. If Tutt had lived, his story may well have been the one that Train told, but the public did not fault Train for having provided a full account of their favorite character's fictitious life. Since Hughes and Frey did live, the public and the courts did not tolerate the idea that their books could be published under the term *nonfiction* when the very premise of Irving's book was a lie, and Frey's account of his own life was riddled with falsities.

In the end, Irving's autobiography of Hughes was never sold to the public, and therefore the public was never fooled into believing that the book contained real facts about Hughes. However, an amusing article published on the whole Irving/Hughes affair suggested the public did suffer some disappointment; the reporter lamented, "No more fantasizing on the subway, no more speculating at cocktails—damn you, Clifford Irving, you've taken our fun away. All those lovely Machiavellian schemes we'd been devising to explain how you really did write Howard Hughes's 'autobiography,' all gone."[27]

9
Life after Death

Equally capable as a lawyer and writer, Train received his greatest tribute as an author last year when Ephraim Tutt, fictional lawyer with the stove-pipe hat, became the subject of a legal wrangle.

—"Arthur Train, Ephraim Tutt Creator, Passes,"
Los Angeles Times, December 23, 1945

While Train gamely dealt with all of the publicity and inquiries flowing from Tutt's autobiography, his health was quietly declining during the 1940s. At the time, Train was in his mid-sixties, and although he appeared to be robust and healthy, he suffered from intermittent illnesses. Perhaps these growing health concerns fueled his desire to complete a meticulous account of Tutt's "life," so as to ensure that his finest character, unlike its brainchild, would enjoy immortality.

During Train's hospitalizations, his friendship with his longtime editor, Maxwell Perkins, proved a constant comfort. After more than twenty years of working together, Perkins lifted Train's spirits, sending him letters and books, and promising future visits. Train's optimism that his condition would improve was apparent from his letters. "I am glad to be able to inform you that all goes well and that I am looking forward to going back to Maine in a couple of weeks," Train wrote Perkins from the Massachusetts Hospital. "I hope to stay there and get the benefit of the clear autumn weather so that by the time I get back to New York, towards the end of the month, I shall be my own vigorous self," he noted. During his recovery, Train critiqued the books Perkins sent to him, and the two discussed the possibility of meeting after Train was released from the hospital. Train told Perkins that "it would be wonderful if you could come down [to Maine] for a few days, so that we could go over some of the points of Mr. Tutt's Autobiography and more or less take some walks." Train's health improved after this 1942 hospitalization, he went on to publish two more books, and he and Perkins had a wonderful time watching as their literary mischief took the world by storm, with the publication of *Yankee Lawyer*.[1]

As 1945 came to a close, the lawsuit Linet had filed remained pending in court, but it simply was not a priority for Train at that time. Arthur was suffering from an illness he could not shake, and in mid-December he was hospitalized at Memorial Hospital in New York City. After an unsuccessful operation, on December 22, 1945, at the age of seventy, Arthur Train died. Although he had struggled with his health over the preceding years, he never gave the appearance of ill health. In fact, to his colleagues, Train gave no hint of how grave his health problems were; one week before he died, he was even reelected to his post as president of the National Institute of Arts and Letters.[2]

Maxwell Perkins learned of Train's passing through a Western Union telegram that was delivered to his New York City office. In its rigid, formal font, it read: "want you to know father died this morning following an operation. Feel it is best to have only immediate family at funeral," signed by Train's daughter, Lucy. It was by means of this terrible slip of yellow paper that Perkins learned he had lost a confidant, pen pal, collaborator, legal advisor, conspirator, book reviewer, client, and friend. In describing Train's last year of life, Perkins once noted, "he went through a full year of operations and all the time grew . . . in wisdom and tolerance, and in a kind of spiritual serenity. It was something much better and far high[er] than what we call heroism." Perkins remained in contact with various members of Train's family after Arthur's death; however, he had forever lost a close friend.[3]

Train left this world when he was approaching the height of his popularity. And the tributes and obituaries written about him reveal how much Train meant to the public and how sorely missed his stories and contributions to society would be. One newspaper lamented that "the death of

Arthur Train has ended a life devoted equally to law and to letters." It was noted that the world would be forever grateful for how he "humanized Ephraim Tutt and the kindly Mr. Tutt in turn humanized our concept of the law." Known as a "keen-witted, legal-minded humanist," it was believed Train would be remembered not only for his legal achievements—"acting without pay for the Legal Aid Society, gang-busting, exposing fraudulent department store operators or helping clean up Tammany"—he would also "be remembered for his services to literature." And as for his literary creations themselves, "the incorruptible Ephraim Tutt is certainly one of the finest flowers cultivated in this garden of his imagination. Both creator and protagonist now belong to the great tradition of American literature."[4]

Similar tributes were written in other papers. The *Chicago Daily Tribune* remarked how Train's sense of fairness, a quality with which Tutt was well endowed, was evident even when Train first began to practice law. In fact, it was noted that when Train was an assistant district attorney, "he maintained amiable relations with the men he prosecuted instead of browbeating them before juries, and even the defendants seemed pleased when he obtained convictions, as he usually did." Newspapers were grateful for the hundreds of stories that Train provided about Tutt, "the Yankee lawyer with the stovepipe hat who was forever interrupting fishing trips to appear in court on behalf of some deserving person caught in the technicalities of the law." In remembering Train, his literary prank could not be overlooked—many newspapers commented on not only Train's hoax, but also on the delight he took in having Tutt confused with reality. One reporter remarked, "equally capable as a lawyer and writer, Train received his greatest tribute as an author last year when Ephraim Tutt, fictional lawyer with the stove-pipe hat, became the subject of a legal wrangle."[5]

Naturally, when Train died there was some concern about what would happen to Tutt. In the city Train called home, a small piece was written days after his death, which examined the role that Train and Tutt had fulfilled over the course of the last several decades. The *New York Times* stated that it was "the fate of Arthur Train to see his own personality submerged in a character of his imagination. Many persons who felt that they knew Ephraim Tutt intimately could not have told you for the life of them the name of his creator. In fact, many persons believed that there actually was a tall, stovepipe-hatted barrister-above-reproach by the name of Mr. Tutt." Train had expressed many of these sentiments over the course of his life. The truth was by 1945 in many ways Tutt had become such a part of Train's life that the two were practically indistinguishable. In fact, Train had even commented that he was "habitually introduced as 'Mr. Tutt,' and [his] wife as 'Mrs. Tutt,'" when they went to parties or were seen around town. Train also liked to joke that between him and Tutt, Tutt would be remembered and Train would be forgotten. In fact, in 1931 Train commented that "nobody remembers what cases I prosecuted as an assistant district attorney . . . but a great many people know 'the Tutt family' and, if I am remembered at all after I am dead, it will be as 'the fellow who used to write those Tutt stories.'" Train felt so strongly in his creation that he took comfort in the thought that Tutt would outlive him.[6]

Turning to Tutt, the *New York Times*'s tribute remarked that he did "great good for the bar," and that "one could not read of his achievements without a warm, kindly feeling toward the profession that produced him." Although some of Tutt's tactics could be criticized for being a little too sly, cagey, or nearly illegal, his devotion to his professional duty to take any case that came his way was commendable. Plus, Tutt had a way of humanizing the law—when his clients did not deserve to be punished but seemed to be caught between unyielding legal precedents, Tutt could find a way to explain why the law would allow an exception in his client's case. Because of Tutt's example, many people became interested in becoming lawyers and joining the profession that Tutt fashioned as a means to do good. The *Times* remarked that "no one can know how many less noted lawyers were influenced to worthy, if poorly paid, deeds by his example. Doubtless many were inspired, after pondering one of Mr. Tutt's famous stratagems, to make another search for the legal precedent that would enable them to extricate some client from a situation where he might be legally guilty but morally innocent. That was Mr. Tutt's forte."

Apart from Train, Tutt left an unmistakable impact on the public and the profession of law. And so, although Train had passed on, his influence (and, by extension, Tutt's influence) was far from dead. What's particularly convenient for a character of fiction is that death does not come as suddenly as it does to those actually living. In concluding its tribute, the *New York Times* declared: "Mr. Train is dead, but Mr. Tutt is not. The kindly character the former created still remains, and will for many years, on the shelves of many a library, a gentle and well-loved friend of leisure hours."[7]

Tributes to Train and Tutt sprouted across the country. In Connecticut, a short piece was published noting that despite Train's death, "there lives after him the most famous of his creations, Ephraim Tutt, the country lawyer who has become as fabulous and indigenous an American folk hero as Paul Bunyan." Further, there were innumerable people who were moved by Tutt's example, and those who were influenced by the Tutt stories would continue their work in the world. "There are today countless legal lights in the country, venerable members of the bar in high professional standing or young and up-and-coming lawyers, who have confessedly profited from the example of Mr. Tutt, that salty, Down-East Yankee ever on the alert to find in hoary precedent the way out for those legally guilty but morally innocent."[8]

Memorializing Train, *American National Biography* remarked, "Ephraim Tutt made Train famous. A defender of those victimized by the law, Tutt owes his success . . . to 'the general impression that the laws of man, like those of nature, often work deep hardship.'" This tribute went on to note that "Train used the Tutt stories to demonstrate what he saw as the frequent conflict between law and justice," and through the combination of "Train's straightforward narrative style and Tutt's sympathy for the underdog made these stories spectacularly successful."[9]

The "success" of the Tutt stories, and their general appeal, was not tied to Train's mortality. And in writing *Yankee Lawyer,* it seems that Train was well aware of this idea. In fact, Train once joked with Perkins that fifty years after *Yankee Lawyer* was published, people would have forgotten all about who "Arthur Train" was. In fact, of the two (Train and Mr. Tutt), Perkins believed that Mr. Tutt would be remembered as a real person. "If anyone asks who Arthur Train was," Perkins stated, "the answer will be: 'Train? Why, he was the character that Ephraim Tutt invented as a stooge in his autobiography. There wasn't really any such person.'" As the two men chuckled at the prospect of Tutt outliving Train, Train presciently responded, "There is no longer any doubt about it."[10]

So, did Tutt "die" with Train? He most certainly did not. Tutt served too important a role in American culture for him to suddenly disappear from the world of literature. Tutt had helped a generation of Americans as they weathered the Great Depression and World War II. Over the years, he attained a status that placed him in the company of American legends such as Uncle Sam and Paul Bunyan—he came to represent what it was to be an American. At Train's death, Tutt had appeared in print for more than twenty-five years. His cultural contributions and the role he served in providing Americans hope and faith were not erased or forgotten upon the death of his literary creator. In short, Tutt was an American icon, and he would retain that status for decades to come.

In addition to having become a symbol of American life, he also served an important role by representing the type of lawyer Americans wished they had in law offices across the nation. For as long as there have been courts, the American public has been fascinated by the legal system and has despised the lawyers who practice within it. But Tutt was different from other lawyers—he really cared about his clients, he would even work for free when he felt compelled to intervene on behalf of someone who had experienced an injustice but had no means to pay for an attorney to right it. When his court cases seemed to be all but lost, Tutt's conscience would not tolerate an innocent person's conviction—Tutt felt compelled to find a way to help his client, even if it meant that he, himself, would be punished or fined. Tutt's principled practice of law, and his common-sense approach to his legal cases endeared him to the public. Tutt's stories remained relevant and important to American literature and society because Tutt had set an ideal for the legal profession with which most anyone sympathized.

Trials have always had the potential to captivate the nation; they have the power to mesmerize the public as the full panoply of the human experience unfolds before a jury and judge, exposing the ugliest crimes and the noblest intentions. The public cannot get enough of ghastly crime scenes and those who created them and the anguish and emotional devastation of the victims of a perceived injustice. Modern Americans track trials on television, devour every word of testimony, examine the evidence admitted, and ponder the proper verdict in the search for "truth." Time and again the public places its trust in the sacred forum of the courtroom, where the naked facts are supposed to be revealed and revered. Yet despite the assurances of lady liberty's blindfolded eyes and her perfectly calibrated scales, morally repulsive verdicts are sometimes returned. When this happens the public could not care less that evidentiary rules had been followed, the precious constitutional rights of the defendant were safeguarded and respected, or that bias and prejudice had not played a part in the verdict. Rather than feeling that the search for truth had led to a proper verdict, a different truth rears its ugly head—that real life does not always fit well within the compartmentalized confines of rules and laws. While humans can understand the emotional complexities of a case, and can get a feeling about what was right or wrong, the law operates by imposing rigid rules to a colorful array of facts, and the two combined are supposed to yield justice. However, while the law seeks to remain objective and fair, humanity is inherently subjective—the inevitable clash between the two can result in verdicts the public is wroth to accept.

When this imperfect system generates a verdict that "makes sense legally and can be explained and justified by judges, lawyers and law professors simply by conforming, in some formalistic sense, to precedent and procedure, but ultimately feels emotionally and morally wrong to everyone else," the American legal system appears to produce "justice that doesn't feel just, but instead feels like a colossal misnomer."[11] It is in these types of situations that Mr. Tutt would somehow even the scales, and then tip them in favor of the verdict that was satisfying because it felt right and just. Mr. Tutt's forte was infusing a subjectivity and morality into the law that did not otherwise exist. He was guided by an infallible moral compass and a clever mind—the two combined ensured that an injustice would not slip through a judge's fingers. As people felt swindled out of their life savings with the stock market crash and felt cheated out of their jobs and livelihoods during the Great Depression, the symbolism of Ephraim Tutt was extraordinarily powerful. When America entered World War II and the world felt dark and people's hope in the future was shaken, Tutt provided comfort because his stories showed that even when it was doubtful, justice would triumph in the end. For a generation, Americans found comfort in Tutt's stories, and they consistently turned to him to recharge their faith in society. Tutt represented the idea that though the public might be harmed by forces largely out of their control, there were people in America who would ultimately ensure that a just outcome would prevail.

Many people are motivated to become lawyers because they believe in the "three virtue myths" of the American lawyer: "(1) lawyers have a dedication to a transcendent concept of justice—they do not just want to fight to win; they want to serve the cause of justice; (2) lawyers have a special relationship with their clients and care about their clients in a special way; the client is not just an entity you bill, but one whom you honorably serve; and (3) the practice of law is more than 'just another business'; money is not everything." Tutt possessed all of these characteristics—he was a slave to justice, he sympathized with his clients and cared about their cases, and he did not practice law to make money, but to do good. It was precisely these characteristics that caused so many people to value Tutt and his law practice. However, so far as the actual practice of law is concerned, some deem these "virtue myths" "impossible to honor in a world of human fallibility."[12] But through all of the confusion over whether Tutt actually existed, Tutt had the effect of making it seem possible that there could be lawyers who possessed these virtues. After all, many people sincerely believed Tutt was a real lawyer—and some would never believe otherwise.

Thus, even when Train passed away, society was not willing to let Tutt, and all that he represented, pass also. His books continued to be popular, and the example Tutt set continued to touch the hearts and minds of the public. Perhaps the clearest indication of his continued vitality is that even after Train's death, Scribner's and Sons' mailbox continued to fill with letters seeking affirmation that Mr. Tutt was a living, breathing attorney, wandering the streets of New York, rendering justice to all causes worthy of it. A sampling of such letters shows that Tutt maintained a healthy existence (and that many people still did not know—even after Train's public confession and the media frenzy over Linet's lawsuit—that Tutt was a mere fiction).

One noteworthy letter that was mailed to Scribner's after Train's death was from a woman—Mrs. Boley—who had written months earlier and, in rather scathing language, let it be known that she was extremely disappointed and depressed at having learned that Tutt was not a real person. Upon hearing of Train's death, she was prompted to send another letter. "A sense of guilt pursues me, since the demise of Arthur Train," she wrote. Apparently, her last letter created enough of a stir that Scribner's sent this woman a complimentary copy of Train's *Mr. Tutt Finds a Way*, perhaps because that book contained the nearest thing to an "apology" by Train for fooling so many people. In any event, Mrs. Boley referred to her past letter, noting, "I was extremely angry and disillusioned, this fall, concerning the Ephraim Tutt fiction," and she apologized for failing to "acknowledge receipt of your kind gift of Mr. Train's last book." Interestingly, Mrs. Boley's previous ire seemed to have cooled. She noted, "I think perhaps Arthur Train was more Ephraim Tutt than Arthur Train, anyways, and it is fitting that he should be remembered [as] thus." Maxwell Perkins personally responded to Mrs. Boley's letter; he thanked her for remembering him, as "such remembrances happen very seldom nowadays," and noted, "you are right in thinking that Arthur had much of Ephraim Tutt in him."[13]

After Train's death, there were the usual inquiries as to whether Tutt was a real person. One such letter was sent in January 1946 from a woman a literary group had chosen to review *Yankee Lawyer*—she admitted to feeling "confused" and asked that Scribner's clarify whether Mr. Tutt was "a real person or . . . a fiction[al] character." Other readers wondered whether Tutt had interacted with their relations or friends. For instance, one woman wrote in January 1946 about whether Tutt's grade school principal might have been her grandfather. She addressed her letter to Tutt and explained that "a friend of ours—an attorney—loaned me 'Yankee Lawyer.' I had always read your stories—in Saturday Evening Post—and admired greatly your interest in the 'underdog.'" Although she had "truly supposed [Tutt] to be a fictitious character," she was rather delighted at the "surprise [she] had" when Tutt referred to his time as "a student at Black River Academy—and refer[red] to a Mr. Pickard." This reader explained that Mr. Pickard may have been her grandfather or one of her grandfather's siblings and hoped that Tutt would respond to her letter.[14]

In replying to such letters, Scribner's continued to break the truth as delicately as possible, while providing some explanation of the hoax. For instance, in response to the letter regarding whether Tutt might have known the reader's grandfather, Scribner's stated, "you were right in your first supposition: Ephraim Tutt is a fictitious character—although a great many of the things recorded in his autobiography did actually happen to Arthur Train himself. It is quite possible too that your grandfather was known by reputation to Mr. Train, and that he had him in mind, but there is now no way of ascertaining this since Mr. Train died several days short of last Christmas." In the event that a reader might want additional information on Train and his publication of *Yankee Lawyer,* Scribner's often noted in its letters to confused readers that Train provided a full explanation of the hoax in *Mr. Tutt Finds a Way.*[15]

Another letter, to which it was likely more difficult for Scribner's to send a meaningful and sufficiently compassionate response, was sent from Pennsylvania in April 1949 to Tutt. This Tutt fan was blind, and she had come to learn the details of Tutt's life by listening to a "Talking Book Record" of *Yankee Lawyer.* As the name suggests, the "Talking Book Record" was a popular method of providing books to those with visual impairments. After listening to the entire story, this reader wrote:

Dear Mr. Tutt:

Although you wrote your delightful autobiography in 1943, I have just read it by means of Talking [B]ook [R]ecords. . . .

Your story brought hosts of distinguished names and childhood memories back to me. . . .

But the most beautiful memory which your story called to mind was that of Esther Farr. My mother too, was an ardent feminist. She knew Esther Farr and, I know, their paths met from time to time. It was not until you mentioned that she became President of Ramona College that I was sure she was the same admired and beloved Ester Farr. I never read anything more lovely anywhere than the account of your reunion with Miss Farr on the day you both received honorary degrees from Columbia University. I put that record on and listened to it over and over again. How marvelous it was that you kept your relationship on such a high, spiritual plane and yet how warm and real your devotion was. I understand now that it is not necessary to have the bodily presence of a loved one in order to love him, as my devoted husband died three years ago this month. For nearly thirty years he was eye for me as well as many other things. We met as students in the U of C at a time when a little understood eye disease was threatening my eye sight.

I don't know where to send this letter, but I feel that I want to send it in the hope that you will get it.

A prompt response was sent by Scribner's, which stated: "Your letter . . . would have brought great pleasure to Arthur Train. Ephraim Tutt was his creation, but he was in a true sense his alter ego, and the autobiography of Ephraim Tutt which you read was in a very real way the autobiography . . . of Arthur Train." Scribner's noted that although Train had died years earlier, "he would have found your letter most rewarding."[16]

While it was a rare occurrence for readers to respond to Scribner's after learning the truth, this reader did. She graciously conceded that it must have been difficult for Scribner's to respond to a letter "written to a strictly 'legendary character,'" but noted that Scribner's "did it most admirably." She stated that before contacting Charles Scribner's Sons, she had called Curtis Publishing Company, the publisher of the *Saturday Evening Post,* and spoke with someone who "assured [her] that Mr. Tra[in] had gathered his material for his Mr. Tutt stories from the files of an actual Mr. Tutt." She took solace in knowing that "others in a better position to know than I were equally misinformed." In any event, she felt no hard feelings toward Train or Tutt, noting she still believed *Yankee Lawyer* was "thrilling and absorbing," and she remarked that "if the angels in heaven take cognizance of what we mortals do, I am sure that Mr. Tra[in] must have had a good laugh at my credulity. I hope he did."[17]

The Talking Book Record of *Yankee Lawyer* brought other letters to Scribner's. It would seem that the act of listening to someone read Tutt's narrative had the tendency to make it feel more heartfelt and personal. In January 1946, a gentleman from Massachusetts had just finished listening to his record of *Yankee Lawyer,* and he felt such a personal connection to Tutt's life story and philosophy that he felt an obligation to write to Tutt. This man wrote:

Dear Mr. Tutt:

Your autobiography is a gem. Packed full of that brand of Yankee shrewdness of the kind to be admired. . . .

It is 6:00 A.M. Sunday. I woke up at 5:30 and lay with my hands under my head refreshing memory on some of the many especially good anecdotes and passages in your book which I stayed up till 1:00 A.M. to finish. Incidentally, I had stayed up similarly . . . the night before. The book has given me a great boost. There is so much in your experiences and the way in which you reacted to conditions th[at] is inspiring, adding fuel to the old think-tank. To me it shows a conviction of rightness, yes, righteousness without smugness—and plenty of courage such as we all need.

I needed courage day before yesterday. As "The Great Gildersleeve" says, it was "one of my ba-a-ad days." I went up into my room intending to read my Christian Science Quarterly, in Braille, for I am blind. Felt too rebellious and opened up more Talking Book records of "YANKEE LAWYER" and kept on reading through afternoon, evening, and into the morning. Next day, up early, I put on dust-coat and went at it down in my cellar workshop, feeling like a cat full of your Old Doc's Elixir and ready to tackle tigers.

The writer of this letter explained that he had been blind since 1925, was housebound for eighteen years, and was married to a wonderful, Wellesley-educated woman. He noted that like Tutt, he also "marched here in Boston in one of the feminist parades when participation was not too popular a thing to do." He asked Tutt to send him an autograph for the autograph book he kept for his children, and concluded by thanking Tutt for writing *Yankee Lawyer* and for working with the American Foundation for the Blind to publish a Talking Book Record of his autobiography.[18]

This same gentleman sent another letter to Charles Scribner's, also dated January 6, 1946, but this one was written later in the day, at 4:00 P.M. He stated, "Go ahead. Laugh. I have laughed at myself since writing early this morning." He explained that he had enthusiastically telephoned a friend of his, urging that he, too, read *Yankee Lawyer*. His friend then read an article over the telephone from the *Saturday Evening Post* "giving Train's account of that fictitious autobiography." Being a good sport, he noted that if his friend's wife had not kept "all of their reading matter," he would have "challenged [his] friend to produce his proofs, for I would not have believed this autobiography was a pure piece of fiction. It is superb." Before signing off once again, this time, as "Shamefacedly yours," the writer of this letter noted, "Poor Train is no more. If he were I should ask that he sign one of my loose-leaf sheets. Clever lawyer-writer, great entertainer."[19] At least this Tutt fan found amusement from the publication of Tutt's auto-biography and admired Train despite having been quite duped by him.

While some letters seemed to convey nothing more than sheer admi-ration for Tutt, there was an occasional letter that seemed to cross the line past admiration, possibly toward amorousness. In February 1947, a woman wrote to her "dear Mr. Tutt," and informed him: "I just finished reading your autobiography and laid the book down with the comment (to myself), 'Oh isn't that wonderful! I love him!'" She explained, "I ad-mire Abraham Lincoln, and sometimes I got the impression that I was reading the life of Lincoln"; she noted that Tutt's autobiography resonated with her "because it was so human and so full of compassion and under-standing for Lincoln's 'the common people.'" This reader wrote to Tutt that she had never written a fan letter before, but she could not resist the urge to tell him how much she loved his book. "I really was not aware men of such honesty and caliber were circulating today, especially in the legal profession. I'm glad you wrote the book to correct the impression, and to bring before the public the life of such a delightful personality." The remainder of this woman's letter is rather sad, as she reflected that she felt a "common bond" with Tutt and admired his "loving and cling-ing to an unattainable ideal throughout life," as it made her "love [him] more," since she could "understand [his] days of loneliness." Apparently, this woman had experienced "something rather tragic" and had consid-ered speaking with Tutt about what had happened to her, but she dropped the issue, noting only that she wished she lived closer to New York, "so that I might have the courage to call and tell you."[20] The woman obvi-ously felt a close connection with Tutt, as she was on the brink of confid-ing in him about her personal strife. This letter demonstrates how Tutt's readers placed their trust and faith in the existence of this character, and that some would have even entrusted their most difficult problems to him (if he had actually lived).

Besides letters written to Tutt, there were also letters sent to Charles Scribner's Sons, seeking the usual information. "Is Ephraim Tutt a ficti-tious character, the imagination of Arthur Train, or is Mr. Train writing of

his own experience? From all that is written in the book, one might conclude most anything because it gives one many differing reactions to the
identity of Mr. Tutt," wrote a young woman living in Chicago, Illinois,
in March 1946. A New Jersey librarian inquired, in July 1946, if the book
was a true autobiography, and noted, "if it was an autobiography by Tutt,
would he not [be] listed in Who's Who?"[21]

Friendly squabbles and bets continued, as the matriarch of one Michigan family wrote to Scribner's in July 1946: "Will you please help settle
a . . . family feud?" She explained: "We have just finished—some are still
at it—'Yankee Lawyer,' and have all enjoyed it!"; however, "some of us
maintain there is a living Ephraim Tutt as well as Train's fictional Tutt,"
and "part of the family, including a college professor brother, stau[nch]ly
claims [its] *entirely fiction*—even that 'Yankee Lawyer' is part of the game."
A woman living in Pennsylvania wrote to Scribner's in May 1947, noting
that she had "thoroughly enjoy[ed]" the book, but "quite a heated controversy arose among some of my friends as to the reality of Eph Tutt." In
July 1952, a lieutenant in the US Naval Reserves, stationed at a naval air
station in Kansas, reported that he had become involved in a "minor dispute" over who had written *Yankee Lawyer*. He explained that it was his
"conviction that this book was written by Ephraim Tutt and not by Arthur
Train," since, "having read the book, it is very hard for me to believe that
it was written by someone other than Tutt." In 1950 Scribner's received
word that students attending Michigan Law School were entrenched in
a debate over whether Tutt was real or not. Finally, they determined to
write to Scribner's: "We have as many on one side . . . as on the other,"
and "are at a loss on a final decision."[22]

Attorneys were still unsure of the elusive Ephraim Tutt of the New York
bar; an attorney from Brooklyn, New York, wrote in 1947 that a "discussion was had amongst several associates in my office concerning [*Yankee
Lawyer*] which several of us have read and enjoyed immensely." After asking if Tutt actually wrote the book, the attorney also inquired, "Is Mr. Tutt
still alive and did he practice under that name in New York?" One dutiful son, writing in June 1953 from New York City, asked Scribner's if they

could assist him in getting "in touch with Ephraim Tutt." He explained that he was acting on "a whim of my father whom I like to please. He is 83 years old and has finished the book."[23]

In looking at one final letter, it becomes apparent how significant a role Arthur Train and Ephraim Tutt played in the lives of their readers. This letter demonstrates both the lasting impact of Train's literary mischief and the adaptability of Tutt's stories to real-life predicaments. In April 1946, C. Hugh Woodbury of California wrote to Charles Scribner's Sons noting that he had "long been an admirer of Arthur Train and his tales of Mr. Ephraim Tutt," and that he had purchased Train's book *Tutt and Mr. Tutt* in 1945, which had since been read by nearly everyone in his office. When one of his friends was in the "doldrums," the book was passed on to him; Woodbury reported that Mr. Tutt changed his friend's mood entirely. In fact, Train's "stories . . . tickled his riseabilities to such an extent his daughter threatened to throw him out of the house for making such unseemly noises." When another attorney was depressed and in the midst of a difficult case, it was determined that he should be the next to read *Tutt and Mr. Tutt*. Five days later, the attorney returned it with "his face beaming with joy." When the other attorneys asked him how his lawsuit had come out, the attorney replied, "Why, hell, I won it!"

Woodbury explained that before Train's death, he thought Train "might like to hear of the adventures of "Tutt and Mr. Tutt, [and so he] wrote [Train] much as above and stated that while I esteemed Mr. Tutt as a great and learned lawyer, I was just hankering to get him into a Cribbage contest, where, against my skill (and) luck, his finely drawn legal points wouldn't get him nowhere, no how!" The response he received was rather unusual: "In due time I received a Postal Card, dated Bar Harbor, Maine, July 29, 1945. On the back thereof, was a picture of Mr. Tutt, tall, hat, stogy, and sulphurous smoke rings, (phew). Written there-on was 'Thank you for your interesting letter which is much appreciated.' Signed 'Ephraim Tutt.' This card has been nicely framed and will be shown to any 'doubting Thomases' who barge in here and say that Mr. Tutt was never in the flesh.

How could a postal [card] have been signed if Mr. Tutt had not been a live one?"

In the end, all that Woodbury inquired of Scribner's was whether it planned to publish a book collecting the wonderful stories Train had written about Tutt. It seems his whole office was interested in the answer to this question.[24]

As these letters from the late 1940s and 1950s demonstrate, Ephraim Tutt lived on. Although Train tried before his death to right the rampant misbelief in Tutt's existence, the letters that continued to be written during this period establish that Train's efforts were in vain. Ephraim Tutt gave people a vision of society and law that they wanted to believe in, and many readers maintained faith that such a figure not only could exist, but actually did.

Mr. Tutt at His Best

Why does Ephraim Tutt survive, after all these years?

I think the reason is that he touches our hearts so closely and because he represents the ideal of what lawyers and those who are not lawyers think lawyers ought to do. Above all he has a sense of humor, and with it a tenderness and a kindliness that go well with his profound knowledge of the law and his wily ways and stratagems.

—Honorable Harold R. Medina, *Mr. Tutt at His Best* (1961)

The terrific publicity storm that burst forth with the publication of *Yankee Lawyer* and the resulting chaos over whether Tutt existed caused Tutt's fame to continue to rise, even though Train was not around to continue writing about him. It did not seem to matter whether Tutt was real or not—people loved Tutt for the characteristics and ideals he represented. Although World War II had ended, Tutt still remained a symbol of America, and his character and ideals still resonated with the generation of Americans that had read of his legal adventures for decades. Additionally, some of Train's stories about Tutt were made into television shows and radio programs, keeping Tutt alive in the national consciousness. In fact, more than a decade after Train's death, Charles Scribner's Sons decided to publish a memorial edition of Tutt stories, since Tutt continued to attract a wide audience of fans. By the time this volume was stocked on bookstore shelves, sixteen years had elapsed since Train's death, but the publication of *Mr. Tutt at His Best* in 1961 confirmed that Tutt remained a significant character in American fiction.

The chief priorities of Charles Scribner's Sons in undertaking another Tutt volume were to select Tutt stories that did honor to both the character and his inventor, while also discovering a candidate to write an introduction that would capture the magic, nostalgia, and power of Tutt.

Scribner's needed to find someone who had a true understanding of who Tutt really was and what Train sought to accomplish through this character. Meanwhile, Scribner's certainly wanted the writer of the introduction to be a public figure whose prologue would be one the public would be interested in reading. While it appears that the staff at Scribner's was unable to reach a consensus on a nominee best suited for the job, an offer was made to a certain federal judge whose chambers in downtown Manhattan were a stone's throw from the old district attorney's office where Train had spent some of his happiest years practicing law. In December 1959 the Honorable Harold R. Medina, a judge sitting on the US Court of Appeals for the Second Circuit, wrote to T. J. B. Walsh, the editor at Charles Scribner's Sons who was overseeing the publication of the memorial Tutt volume. Judge Medina's letter stated, "I shall be glad to try my hand at an introduction to your new book of Mr. Tutt stories," and noted that he was "anxious to get started as soon as possible."[1]

As explored briefly below, Judge Medina's childhood and background mirrored Tutt's—both were underdogs who felt like social outcasts as they went through school, pursued education so as to achieve academic greatness, and ultimately found success in serving the public. They were both admirers of the law and devotees to the concept of "justice." These similarities created a bond between Judge Medina and Tutt; in fact, by the time he finished his introduction, Judge Medina was a full-fledged Tutt enthusiast. Although it is doubtful that Scribner's initially recognized the value of securing Judge Medina as the author of the introduction for *Mr. Tutt at His Best,* it would soon become clear that there was no better candidate for the job.

Harold Raymond Medina was born in Brooklyn, New York, in 1888, to Joaquin Medina and Elizabeth Fash. He attended public school, where he recalled encountering some harassment during the Spanish-American War, when his classmates teased him because of his Mexican heritage. Medina later attended Holbrook's Military Academy and was admitted to Princeton University. Described as an "indefatigable young man," Me-

dina led a very active life during his college years, yet "somehow he always fell just short of glory." For example, he joined the freshman football
team, but when, in his own words, a "big hyena jumped on me," he was
left with a misplaced vertebra that kept him from playing football thereafter. He tried his hand at water polo, fencing, and writing for Princeton's
Tiger, but despite all of his efforts, he "was not a great social success." On
the other hand, he thrived academically, graduating in 1909 summa cum
laude. After college, Medina attended Columbia Law School, and during his time there married Ethel Hillyer. Graduating in 1912, Medina was
honored with the Ordonneaux Prize, which was awarded to Columbia
Law School's third-year student with the most outstanding scholastic record throughout his or her law school career.

Upon graduation, Medina secured employment as a law clerk in a small
Manhattan law office. Medina also taught courses at Columbia Law School
and organized and taught "cram courses" to help students prepare for bar
examinations. The latter enterprise was a striking success, with 39,788 law
students having taken Medina's bar preparation course by 1940, when he
stopped offering it. As to his teaching career, Medina was a member of
Columbia Law School's faculty from 1915 until 1940, during which time
he wrote several law books.

As impressive as these ancillary endeavors were, Medina's legal practice
was also marked by greatness. Early in his law career, Medina opened his
own firm and focused on appellate litigation. Over the years he argued
approximately 1,400 cases before the New York State Appellate Division
and achieved an impressive record of not losing a single case from 1931 to
1945. Making a small fortune with his thriving private practice, Medina
sustained a comfortable living. However, in 1947, when he was offered
a position as a federal judge, Medina relinquished his annual income of
$100,000 in lieu of a black robe and a yearly salary of $15,000.

Why, after achieving such success in the private sector, would a man
accept "an assignment that would cut his annual income by 85 percent,
subject his performance to intense national scrutiny and project him into
the circle reserved for famous men?" "I've made plenty of money," Me-

dina explained, "now I'd like to do something for my country. I guess the best I have to contribute is law." With this spirit of working as a servant of the public, in 1947 Harold Medina became a federal judge for the US District Court for the Southern District of New York, a federal trial court. Two years later, Judge Medina was assigned a case that truly challenged his dedication and devotion to the law and justice. Described as "one of the longest, bitterest, most controversial criminal jury trials in the history of the Federal Court," Judge Medina oversaw a lengthy trial of eleven "Communist leaders" who were charged with "conspiring to teach and advocate the overthrow of the Government by violence."[2]

The pressures and stress on Medina were significant. "Day after day pickets marched before the courthouse carrying placards, shouting epithets, many of them directed at Medina himself: 'How do you spell Medina? RAT.' 'Medina will fall like Forrestal.' 'Jump, jump. You've got to jump.'" In addition, the defense attorneys in the case had a habit of periodically accusing Judge Medina of bias, being unfit to try the case, and possessing other negative traits in order to try to poison the case in the press. Although Judge Medina withstood the various personal attacks levied against him, the comments that bothered him most involved rumors that he was racist, anticommunist, or held any other type of bias. Judge Medina explained: "I wasn't anti-Communist or anti-anything," and that he "had tried only to be fair." As to the comments on race discrimination, Judge Medina noted that such statements "annoyed [him] most," since "if there ever was in this world a man who never had a particle of [race discrimination] in his make-up, I'm that man." When the trial was finally over, Medina reported that he "felt that the triumph was basically spiritual," as his "faith in freedom had been affirmed." Medina explained, "I would rather see every Communist go scot free than abandon or water down or in any way diminish the force and vigor of a single one of our precious freedoms."[3]

Whatever adversity he may have faced while sitting on trial, Judge Medina's professional reputation only grew. In 1951 he filled what had been Judge Learned Hand's seat on the bench of the US Court of Appeals for the Second Circuit. Judge Hand was an admired jurist, and Medina found him to be a "great mentor," whose example he wished to follow. Medina explained: "[Judge Hand] sat on the court until the day he died. He was in his 90th year. I love the work, and as long as I'm able to do it, I'm going to keep it up." Medina remained true to this pledge; he served his country as a federal judge for over three decades, retiring in 1980. Judge Medina lived to be 102 years old, never losing his wit, humor, or love of the law.[4]

When Judge Medina agreed to write the introduction to the latest collection of Tutt stories, Scribner's could not anticipate how perfect Judge Medina was for this task. For Judge Medina, this project quickly lost any semblance of being a "job" or "assignment." He devoted himself to this undertaking and the dilemma of finding words that would adequately capture the spirit of Tutt—after all, this was a character so complicated that professional scriptwriters could not manage to write him onto Broadway. Yet as time will show, Judge Medina seemed to have a special understanding of Tutt, as well as the appeal and value of the Tutt character to the American public. He was not only a bona fide Ephraim Tutt fan, but he also felt a special affinity with Tutt—both rose from humble backgrounds to become successful litigators who strove to bring justice into the world in their own ways (with Tutt's cagey ways being distinguishable from the esteemed jurist's). As he submerged himself into the world of Tutt, a relationship developed between Judge Medina and Tutt that made the project a personal one. The bond Judge Medina felt was essential to the success of the project since part of the magic of Tutt was his ability to connect with his readers so as to feel like a friend rather than a mere character.

Judge Medina began researching Tutt immediately—noting that he "like[d] to give ideas time to ripen in the back of [his] mind before writing." Thus in January 1960 he wrote to Walsh asking if he could borrow copies of the Tutt books so he could begin the process of orienting himself with the hundreds of stories Train had written (Judge Medina explained that he had copies of the Tutt books in his summer home but did not plan to go there during the winter). Judge Medina also was concerned with ensuring that the Tutt stories chosen for the memorial volume were those that captured the Tutt character most poignantly. Even at the outset, Judge Medina was dedicated to writing a worthy preface for Tutt and noted to Walsh that although it might seem "silly for me to take all this trouble for $500 . . . I am a little like Mr. Tutt myself, I hope, and the money doesn't make a particle of difference." As Judge Medina poured his energy into the project, Charles Scribner's Sons elected to double the fee to be paid to him. In response to this unexpected news, Judge Medina wrote to Walsh, "it was really quite unnecessary to increase the honorarium as this is a labor of love for me and I am having a gorgeous time." In fact, Judge Medina had begun creating "a card index system with a card for each story, so that I can come back to it and make further notes and memoranda as I go on." Although he felt as though he had "Mr. Tutts running out of [his] ears," he was enjoying the project immensely, and found that he "like[d] [Tutt] more every day."[5]

By the end of February 1960 Judge Medina had created a rather lengthy "interim report" summarizing his progress through the Tutt stories and how he envisioned the book to be. First, Judge Medina had discovered that "there was never any development of Mr. Tutt's character from first to last," in other words, he was the "same Mr. Tutt in the beginning, in the middle and at the end." Therefore, he concluded the order of the stories did not make a whit of difference. Second, Judge Medina declared that it was "now clear to [him] that [he] did not agree with [Charles Scribner's Sons'] selection of stories" and stated that he was assembling his own "number of suggestions" about which stories would be most appropriate and representative of Tutt. One of the other concerns Judge Medina raised in this letter was how he could finish his research and write a thoughtful introduction before a planned vacation. "I thought I could take all the books with me but Mrs. Medina is raising hell about this as well as about the French and Spanish books and dictionaries I want to take along, so I have my problems," Judge Medina explained. However, he reiterated that "this certainly is an interesting job and I don't mind telling you that the more I get to know Mr. Tutt the better I like him." But even in this,

Judge Medina cautioned that "one of our problems is going to be that he does so many shady things that we do not want to give the public the idea that good lawyers are a bunch of crooks and all the judges and district attorneys are a crowd of blackguards, but I hope to work this out in due time."[6]

Luckily, Judge Medina was going to have the time he needed to fully investigate and hone his contribution to the project, and Scribner's informed him that as to the selection of stories, "the final choice . . . of course, will be yours." Upon receiving this news, Judge Medina felt a "great relief," particularly with regard to the issue of his deadline, since he felt that he "really need[ed] more time to do the kind of job I want to do." As for Mrs. Medina, it appears that she may not have gotten her way with regard to the quantity of books her husband planned to bring on their vacation, for Judge Medina noted, in closing, "I rather suspect that when we get back from our trip I will have a proposed order and selection of stories to submit to you and a draft of the introduction itself."[7]

By June 1960 Judge Medina submitted to Scribner's a list of stories he believed were most appropriate for the memorial volume, as well as his completed introduction. "This has turned out to be more of a job than I anticipated, but it has very distinctly been a labor of love and I have enjoyed every minute of it." Perhaps to ease any angst on the side of Walsh, in editing the work of an esteemed federal judge, Judge Medina graciously noted, "I am one of those peculiar persons who really enjoys criticism and I can assure you that not only will I not be offended but I shall be overjoyed to receive comments and suggestions for changes both in the list and in the Introduction." In fact, Judge Medina even invited Walsh to his summer home in Long Island, New York, to "spend an hour or two with me in my library" and to see the judge's research for his introduction— "you will smile when you see my card index system—it was the only way I could do a thorough job."[8]

Through the fall of 1960 Judge Medina and Walsh exchanged letters, as the book entered a refined state, and by December 1960 the book was distributed and available for sale. As Judge Medina had requested, the first edition's dust jacket featured a large sketch of Mr. Tutt, drawn by Arthur William Brown. Tutt is posed in a classic stance, tugging the lapels of his jacket, wearing a bowtie (and what appears to be a wedding ring—this is a mystery since there is no documented tale of Tutt ever loving any other than the already betrothed Esther Farr), with his hair parted to one side and an expression of deep concentration lining his face. A courtesy copy of the book was sent to Judge Medina, who, upon seeing it, could not help but pick up his pen to write Walsh: "'Mr. Tutt At His Best' looks gorgeous to me and I find that nothing whatever has gone wrong, so far as I can see. Indeed, I am happy to convey to Charles Scribner's Sons and to yourself my heartiest congratulations on bringing out such an attractive volume."[9]

The book proved to be a great success. In fact, in March 1961 Walsh happily reported that another printing of *Mr. Tutt at His Best* was forthcoming. While the book's success was attributable almost entirely to the public's continued affection for one of the most popular literary characters of the twentieth century, Judge Medina's introduction also provided a warm reminder of the importance of Ephraim Tutt to American life, literature, and the law. It also was a glowing tribute to what Train accomplished by inventing this beloved character. The introduction began with a brief explanation of how Judge Medina's relationship with Tutt first began. Judge Medina explained that he decided to start his own private practice in 1919, which happened to be the same year that the Tutt stories began to appear in the *Saturday Evening Post*. However, to Judge Medina—and many other readers—they were not just "stories." In fact, Judge Medina "read them over and over," as they "fascinated [him], as they did thousands of other young lawyers eager to believe that justice was not necessarily at the mercy of prosecutors who wanted convictions, sometimes from motives that were none too pure, or of the large number of unscrupulous persons in various categories connected or not connected with the law, who seemed so often in real life to prevail over the righteous and the just."

Medina next discussed the importance of Ephraim Tutt—what wisdom could be gained by learning from Tutt's life and legal practices, and how the Tutt stories, though fiction, were applicable and relevant to real-life practice. He noted that "every lawyer should know that his function in society cannot be fully or properly performed unless he has sympathy for those in trouble and distress and puts his sympathy into action by representing in or out of court those who need the services of a lawyer, even if particular situations are sordid and unpleasant, even if those who need his services are not possessed of much in the way of worldly goods and money in the bank." On this matter, both Tutt and Medina provided solid examples of using one's legal knowledge to serve the public; Tutt used the Pidgeon Fund and represented deserving clients for free, and Medina relinquished his lucrative private practice to serve his country as a federal judge.

In commenting on Tutt's publication of his own autobiography, Judge Medina noted that Tutt became a "tour de force" and the book proved to be "a glorious hoax." Judge Medina described the widespread confusion over Tutt's existence and praised the role of the press in causing people to wonder whether they should cast aside their doubts and believe that Ephraim Tutt was real. In particular, Judge Medina could not help but mention *Yale Law Journal*'s publication of Train's book review on *Yankee Lawyer*—"It is to the everlasting credit of the scholarly and hardly-ever-stuffy Yale Law Journal that it published the review," he remarked.

Turning to Tutt's creator, Medina noted that Arthur Train saw the ugly side of the law and credited Train's experience as an assistant district attorney of New York County as providing Train with the insight needed to capture the spirit and energy of the courtroom in his Tutt stories. Judge Medina also praised Train's ability to capably cast Tutt in scenes in and around New York City, while juxtaposing Tutt's city life with the idyllic world of Pottsville, that "peaceful, quiet little hamlet in the Mohawk Valley in up-state New York where the fishing was good . . . the people were different, so was the scenery; but good old human nature turned out to be just about the same as in the big city."

As for Judge Medina's concern that some of Tutt's methods were sly, and perhaps subversive, he noted that "the reader may be surprised at some of the seemingly strange procedures followed in some of Mr. Tutt's famous trials. . . . It is well to remember, however, that practically anything can happen in real life and in real courtrooms and these unorthodox happenings more often than not actually do smooth the road to justice, even in this day and age." However, in order to avoid any sense that Tutt was a "shyster," Judge Medina turned to the characteristics Tutt possessed that ensured he was anything but. Noting that Tutt's motto was "never turn down a case," Judge Medina showed that Tutt's interest in practicing law was not founded in the fees he could collect—albeit, he did take some cases for fees. What drove Tutt's passion for the law was the value he placed on protecting those unwitting souls who found themselves in the unfortunate position of having committed a seemingly innocent and beneficial act that the law found to be entirely illegal. Judge Medina aptly noted: "A miscarriage of justice was something he just could not stomach. And when this sagacious, astute, wily and resourceful old lawyer girded his loins, he was hard to beat. The human heart was an open book to him and when the jurors looked to Mr. Tutt to find a way to give the wretched prisoner at the bar another chance they never looked in vain. He was Robin Hood and Don Quixote and Sir Galahad all rolled into one; and he did not give a continental who his adversary was or how much money or influence might be used against him. He meets the most desperate situations with a smile and with amazing wit and good humor."

Judge Medina explained that Tutt's everlasting appeal was rooted in his ability to enter a situation just when it seemed that it could become no worse, and find a way for that which was appropriate and fair to triumph. "Every lawyer, good, bad and indifferent, at some time in his life dreams of himself as a knight in shining armor fighting for right and justice, protecting the poor and the helpless, humbling the rich and the powerful, and making the world a better place to live in." Judge Medina stated that when the stakes are at their highest, and the chance of justice prevailing seems the most unlikely, attorneys may sometimes wish to pull "a few fast ones ourselves" and fight "fire with fire in the interest of justice." However, "in real life we don't do these things, because we are afraid the influential members of the bar will call us shysters—and that is precisely what they will do whenever their fingers are burned and they lose a case they thought was in the bag."

In concluding, Judge Medina addressed Tutt's boundless appeal and popularity and answered the question of why Tutt survived over the years. "I think the reason is that he touches our hearts so closely because he represents the ideal of what lawyers and those who are not lawyers think lawyers ought to do. Above all he has a sense of humor, and with it a tenderness and kindliness that go well with his profound knowledge of the law and his wily ways and stratagems."[10]

Mr. Tutt at His Best was a beloved addition to the reading lists of American readers. The press found Judge Medina's story selections to be "excellent" and "every bit as delectable as when they first appeared to delight Post readers." The public agreed. One New Yorker sent a letter to Charles Scribner's Sons, noting that it was "swell having Mr. Tutt around again." He explained, "I'm in my late fifties and well remember the stories when they came out in the Post. They gave me such pleasure then and I am reliving that pleasure in reading the stories just issued."[11] In a handwritten postscript, it was noted, "And of course 'The Autobiography' was simply swell."

Ephraim Tutt—though he never graced this world with his physical presence—served a prominent role in American culture during the decades he appeared in print. In fact, during the course of the fifty years he spent as the most recognized character in American literature, Tutt transformed from a beloved character to a literary legend. He guided a generation of Americans through some of the most devastating and frightening events of the twentieth century—the stock market crash of 1929, the Great Depression of the 1930s, and America's entrance into World War II—while representing a figment of an idealized American way of life. Many people were inspired by Tutt's example and believed that they could, like Tutt, face whatever ominous foe or unpleasant circumstance life had dealt them and overcome their predicament. Although many were fooled into believing he existed, in the end, whether he did or not was of no matter. The example he set, the principles upon which he stood, and the qualities he symbolized, gave spirit and courage to Americans during their darkest hours, while his wit and clever legal strategies were a constant source of amusement and entertainment. For these contributions, Ephraim Tutt was—and remains to be—a significant figure in American literary history. Perhaps Arthur Train said it best when he once observed: "If Mr. Tutt did not exist, it would be necessary to invent him."[12]

Epilogue

Several years ago, on a Sunday evening in the early summer, I walked at twilight to my friend's home on West Sixty-Third Street. It was a gorgeous night. The temperature was mild and comfortable, and a breeze stirred the air every so often to diminish the heat that languished earlier in the day. As I approached the block on which my friend's little brownstone was located, I noticed how it did not seem to fit with the rest of the neighborhood any longer. Against a backdrop of skyscrapers and new high-rise apartment buildings, this quaint string of private homes, with handsome wrought-iron fences cordoning off miniature front yards, looked a little out of place. They may have been from a bygone era, but I was glad they were there—they gave character and history to the neighborhood, and just like my friend, I cherished their very presence. I rang the bell to his home, and as I waited I heard a muffled "thump" followed by a crescendoing "shhhh," which signaled he was approaching the foyer. A few seconds later the door flew open, and Mr. Tutt greeted me, with shining eyes and a broad smile.

His brownstone had not changed much from the way it was described in his autobiography. My two favorite places to sit with him were in his front parlor—filled with interesting books, photographs, and sketches of people and places that meant a great deal to him—and on his patio, where his dog, CJ (short for Chief Justice), loved to run around (and in later years, lie complacently in the sun). Both were perfect for chatting over a cup of tea and basking in the happiness that an evening spent with a good friend can provide.

After I entered his home, I offered to put a kettle of water on the stove since it was approaching six o'clock, and though it was a little late in the day for this ritual, I knew Mr. Tutt enjoyed the habit of an afternoon tea break—a custom he picked up while working on a case in London. But to my surprise, Mr. Tutt told me he thought it was one of those days that "something stronger" was warranted, as he winked mischievously and gravitated toward the cart where he kept his liquor. As Mr. Tutt prepared my drink, I took a seat in his parlor on one of his old-fashioned couches. A moment later, Mr. Tutt handed me a generous glass of his favorite sherry along with a silver-plated bowl of cashews, "these are just marvelous, you should try them in combination with the sherry," he said. Then Mr. Tutt took his usual seat in a well-worn armchair, which was probably his most beloved piece of furniture. The chair looked a little shabby, and the upholstery where his right hand rested was threadbare, but he was the picture of contentment as he sat, swirling his sherry and then taking a long sip. We quickly settled into our normal routine of discussing the cases that had fascinated us since our last visit. As I chatted about some of the cases I had recently worked on, I noticed that there seemed to be something on Mr. Tutt's mind. I knew something was amiss when Mr. Tutt barely reacted to a story I was telling him about a legal technicality I had encountered that would have normally led to a lengthy diatribe about how law was not justice.

"All right, what is it?" I asked, trying to break the ice.

Mr. Tutt seemed surprised by my question, but then a look of relief passed over him.

"I'm so sorry to be telling you this, my dear, as it has always been such a joy to meet with you, and I would like to think that you've enjoyed my company nearly as much as I've enjoyed yours."

I placed my sherry on the coaster in front of me, and leaned a little closer.

"It just seems that it's time for me to get a change of scenery and to move away from the city," he told me rather plaintively, as if he were seeking my approval.

I nodded my head as if I understood, but we both knew my acquiescence was not genuine.

"Despite my youthful looks," he paused and smiled at his own joke, "I am getting older, and I feel that I could benefit from spending more of my time in a slower-paced place, even though I love this city very much. It's just the rush of it all, and the noise. Plus, I cannot even express how much I would love to get in some fishing before the winter," he said.

Mr. Tutt paused for a moment and then added, "I want to hear the birds singing when I awake, hear the June bugs humming in the mid-afternoon, and spend some time out on the lake."

I was not thrilled by the idea of Mr. Tutt leaving the city, and I think my expression told him so. I could not think of a thing to say in response to this unwelcome news, so I just sat thoughtfully.

"Besides, I think little Henry could use my guidance, and nothing gives either of us more pleasure than when Esther lets us take the boat out for a day's fishing."

I smiled, since I knew Henry, Esther Farr's son with her late husband, Richard, had become Tutt's pride and joy. The two were inseparable whenever Tutt visited, and Esther could not hide her delight that she and Tutt were together again after so many years.

"Well, what will become of your home here?" I timidly asked.

"This place," he laughed, "well, I don't plan to take it with me, but it will be here as it always has been."

I cocked my head to the side and gave him an expression that aimed to get a little more information out of him.

"This is my home. I am not going to change a thing about it. When I visit, I want it ready for me, and for it to be that old familiar place I've returned to for twenty years," he assured me.

"So, it's Pottsville that you're running off to," I mumbled as I was piecing his plan together.

"Of course, where else is there better fishing, except for some of the salmon streams in New Brunswick, but who has the time to travel all the way to Canada for some fishing?"

"Henry will love having you there," I offered, in an effort to warm to his plan, though I think he could sense my poorly hidden disappointment for losing one of my favorite friends to the countryside.

"Pottsville isn't so far, and, I assure you it is much easier to get to than you think," Mr. Tutt offered.

"I'd rather not try again," I replied, as we both laughed. (The last—and only—time I tried to visit Mr. Tutt in Pottsville, I became so lost in what seemed a never-ending wilderness, I gave up on Pottsville when I saw the first sign directing me back to civilization.)

The room turned quiet, and feeling this was a fine time for another sip of my sherry, I took a generous gulp of the sweet liquor and set my glass down again.

"When do you leave?"

"Tomorrow morning," he replied.

"You can't be serious!" I gasped.

"I am sorry for the short notice," he replied, looking a little pained for having shocked me. "Once the idea settled in my mind, my desire to take leave of the city right away has only grown the greater."

"I am just a little surprised, that is all," I replied.

"Promise you will stay in touch," I half-asked, half-demanded.

"Certainly. And I will be relying on you to keep me abreast of what's happening in this great city of ours."

I nodded and smiled. Maybe this wouldn't be so bad after all.

"Well, enough of this suffocatingly dull conversation. I have half a mind to forbid another word about my trip for the rest of the evening so we can spend our time talking about that crooked attorney handling—or should I say botching—that triple-homicide case."

"Are you talking about the Walcott case?"

"Of course. What other triple-homicide trial has been splashed across the front page of all the newspapers this past week?"

"I think I liked you better when you were sentimental," I joked.

The evening passed pleasantly enough, but as time wore on, the more bittersweet the night felt. As Tutt's grandfather clock rang in the nine o'clock hour, we both became rather pensive. It was time for me to leave.

I looked over at Mr. Tutt and took in the scene before me. He sat amiably in his old armchair, removed his eyeglasses and set them on the small table that was beside him, next to a book that he had been reading earlier in the day and a stogie that he must have been saving for later. He glanced across the room, looking absently at the space, and his mouth parted into a slight smile.

Before gathering my things to leave, he said that he had something he would like to give me; he reached for his cane, exerted a bit more effort than I'd like to see him undergo, ejected himself from his chair, and walked out of the room. I heard him moving things around in the adjoining room, and then that familiar "thump . . . shhhh" of his cane hitting the floor and his feet shuffling across it. As he walked toward me, he held out a small package wrapped in brown paper with a bit of string tied around it.

"I think you might like to have this," he said. "And, for goodness sake, open it later."

"What's the fun in that?" I asked. He hesitated for a moment and then changed his mind.

"Fine, you may open it now, but please don't make a fuss over it. I was rummaging through some old books earlier and came across one that I thought you should have," Tutt said.

As I unwrapped the paper enveloping it, touched that he had bothered to wrap it, I was baffled to find that the book he wanted to give me was his own autobiography, *Yankee Lawyer.* Mr. Tutt knew I had a copy of the book already; I looked up at him, not knowing what I was to make of it, and Mr. Tutt laughed.

"Good thing you are opening it in front of me," he chuckled. "Look inside the cover."

As I opened the book, I saw two inscriptions. The first was by Tutt's old friend, who merely wrote, "Signed by the author, Arthur Train." A few inches below Train's autograph, I saw the familiar handwriting of Mr. Tutt, who wrote "What a hack! He always wrote whatever a reader wanted!" On a more serious note, Tutt continued: "For my biographer and friend, thank you for listening as I relived the incredible adventures I had with the character whose name appears above. Affectionately, Ephraim Tutt."

I thanked him repeatedly for both the book and the hours he spent with me, which were some of the most memorable and enjoyable I've had. As we walked toward the door, we did so with heavy hearts.

"I am going to miss this place," he said, as we both looked back into the room we were vacating. My chest tightened and my eyes stung as tears welled within them; I had spent so many wonderful hours with Mr. Tutt in this room, talking about his life and cases, hearing about how he rekindled his romance with Esther after her husband died, and listening to Tutt as he recounted many stories about his late friend, Arthur Train. As these memories flooded my mind, I turned to Mr. Tutt, who seemed just as lost in the bitterness of the moment as I was. I slowly gathered my strength to say goodbye, but before leaving, a few questions came to mind that I had wanted to ask him for some time.

"Before I go, would you mind if I ask you about your old law practice?" I asked.

He nodded his assent, perhaps relieved that I was stalling my inevitable departure.

"Looking back at your legal career, is there anything you would change about the choices you made and the type of work you did?"

"Not a thing," he stated without the slightest pause. "I am proud of the cases I took, and I believe I fulfilled my oath as a lawyer—to serve the public and abide by the law."

"I know there were times when you were annoyed by the way Arthur Train characterized you in his stories, but if Train were alive today and asked you anew if he could document your legal career and dramatize your cases in books and stories, would you let him?"

"I have wondered about that a great many times," Mr. Tutt replied, with a bit of a sigh. He thought about my question for a moment, and then, leaning back onto his cane and looking directly into my eyes, he said emphatically:

"Train once told me that the reason he wrote so many stories about me was because they touched his readers in a very personal way—renewing their faith in humanity and inspiring lawyers to practice in a public-spirited way. If that's the truth, then any embarrassment I have suffered from his romanticized accounts about myself would be but a small price to pay. So, if he asked me again, I would still permit him to write his stories." He then glanced over to a small picture frame that contained a picture of his old confidant, Train. Although the two had certainly exchanged some harsh words over the years, upon Train's death, Tutt vowed to never speak ill of his longtime friend.

"When it came to my cases, I merely ensured that justice was done, whether the law dictated it, or, if it needed a little finagling, I finagled it so that it would," Mr. Tutt added.

"I was never a shyster, and I never manipulated the law to serve my own selfish needs. If I lost a case, I deserved to lose. When I won a case, it's because justice was on my side, and, by George, I would make sure that it would triumph!" His eyes twinkled as he delivered this final phrase.

"Counselor, it's been a pleasure," I stated, holding out my hand.

Mr. Tutt took my hand and gave it a confident shake.

Appendix

Arthur Train's Books

1905	*McAllister and His Double*
1906	*Mortmain*
1907	*The Prisoner at the Bar*
1908	*True Stories of Crime*
1909	*The Butler's Story*
1911	*The True Confessions of Artemas Quibble*
1912	*Courts, Criminals and the Camorra*
1912	*"C.Q." or, in the Wireless House*
1914	*The Goldfish*
1915	*The Man Who Rocked the Earth*
1917	*The World and Thomas Kelly*
1918	*The Earthquake*
1919	*Tutt and Mr. Tutt*
1920	*As It Was in the Beginning*
1921	*By Advice of Counsel*
1921	*The Hermit of Turkey Hollow*
1923	*His Children's Children*
1923	*Tut, Tut! Mr. Tutt*
1924	*The Needle's Eye*
1925	*The Lost Gospel*

1925   *On the Trail of the Bad Men*

1926   *The Blind Goddess*

1926   *Page Mr. Tutt*

1927   *High Winds*

1927   *When Tutt Meets Tutt*

1928   *Ambition*

1928   *The Horns of Ramadan*

1929   *Illusion*

1930   *The Adventures of Ephraim Tutt*

1930   *Paper Profits*

1931   *Puritan's Progress*

1931   *Tutt for Tutt*

1932   *The Strange Attacks on Mr. Hoover*

1932   *Princess Pro Tem*

1933   *No Matter Where*

1935   *Jacob's Ladder*

1936   *Manhattan Murder*

1936   *Mr. Tutt Takes the Stand*

1936   *Mr. Tutt's Case Book*

1938   *Old Man Tutt*

1939   *My Day in Court*

1939   *From the District Attorney's Office*

1940   *Tassels on Her Boots*

1941   *Mr. Tutt Comes Home*

1943   *Yankee Lawyer*

1945   *Mr. Tutt Finds a Way*

1961   *Mr. Tutt at His Best*

Notes

Introduction

1. "Marines Force River Line; 7th Takes Strategic Hills," *New York Times,* May 24, 1945, 1, 4.

2. Letter, Sgt. Peter Ragan, Cpt. K. P. MacEachern, T/5 Robert Kopplen, to Charles Scribner's Sons, May 24, 1945. Archives of Charles Scribner's Sons, 1786–2003, No. C0101, Boxes 154–55, Manuscripts Division, Department of Rare Books and Special Collections, Princeton University Library (hereinafter MD, RBSC, PUL).

3. Letters, C. F. Orofino to Charles Scribner's Sons, February 6, 1945; Clara Lichtenstein to Charles Scribner's Sons, December 3, 1943. Archives of Charles Scribner's Sons, 1786–2003, No. C0101, Boxes 154–55, MD, RBSC, PUL.

4. Letters, Howe to Arthur Train, September 1943; Mrs. C. W. Hollowell [not addressed to any party], March 29, 1944. Archives of Charles Scribner's Sons, 1786–2003, No. C0101, Boxes 154–55, MD, RBSC, PUL.

5. Letter, Lyle T. Hammond to Dr. Ephraim Tutt, January 6, 1946, 4:00 P.M. Archives of Charles Scribner's Sons, 1786–2003, No. C0101, Boxes 154–55, MD, RBSC, PUL.

6. Letter, Mrs. F. W. Boley to Chas. Scribner's Sons, November 6, 1945. Archives of Charles Scribner's Sons, 1786–2003, No. C0101, Boxes 154–55, MD, RBSC, PUL.

Chapter 1

Epigraph: *My Day in Court* (New York: Charles Scribner's Sons, 1939), 6 (hereinafter *My Day in Court*).

1. Interview by Molly Guptill with John Train, September 27, 2009.

2. See "Arthur Train Dead; Created 'Mr. Tutt,'" *New York Times,* December 23,

1945, 17; see also John A. Garraty and Mark C. Carnes, *American National Biography,* vol. 21 (New York: Oxford University Press, 1999), 800.

3. "Charles Russell Train," *Boston Daily Globe,* July 30, 1885, 6; see also Arthur Train, *Puritan's Progress* (New York: Charles Scribner's Sons, 1931), 150, 170 (hereinafter *Puritan's Progress*); *Biographical Directory of the United States Congress, 1774–1989* (Washington, DC: United States Government Printing Office, 1989), 1952.

4. *Biographical Directory of the United States Congress, 1774–1989,* 1952.

5. *Puritan's Progress,* 326–27, 330–37.

6. William Whitman, "They Write Books" column, "Law and Society," *Boston Evening Globe,* April 6, 1929; *My Day in Court,* 5; *Puritan's Progress,* 329.

7. *Puritan's Progress,* 151, 339–40, 349–50, 358; see also "Arthur Train Dead; Created 'Mr. Tutt,'" 17.

8. *My Day in Court,* 6; see also "Arthur Train Dead; Created 'Mr. Tutt,'" 17; "Married," *New York Times,* April 22, 1897, 7.

9. *My Day in Court,* 6, 7.

10. "Col. Gardiner Is Removed," *New York Times,* December 23, 1900, 1.

11. *My Day in Court,* 7–8, 12.

12. *My Day in Court,* 253, 261; see also "Mrs. Blake's Fault, Mrs. Mackay Says," *New York Times,* October 16, 1913, 7; "No Blake-MacKay Suit," *New York Times,* November 11, 1913, 1; "Mackays Obtain Divorce in Paris," *New York Times,* February 19, 1914, 1; "Dr. Blake Marries Mrs. Mackay in Paris," *New York Times,* November 29, 1914, 1.

13. *My Day in Court,* 308–10.

14. Ibid., 310–13; see also "Authors' League Launched," *New York Times,* December 17, 1912, 12, 9; "Proposes Prizes for Literary Works," *New York Times,* November 19, 1928, 11.

15. *My Day in Court,* 369.

16. "Books for Lawyers," reviewing "Mr. Tutt at His Best," *American Bar Association Journal* 47, no. 7 (1961): 719; Robert van Gelder, "An Interview with Mr. Arthur Train," *New York Times,* April 13, 1941, BR2; *My Day in Court,* 3–6.

17. Letter, from Marshall Bond to Arthur Train, May 29, 1922, Beinecke Rare Book and Manuscript Library, Yale University Library, Marshall Bond Papers.

18. Letter, Arthur Train to Marshall Bond, January 26, 1923, Beinecke Rare Book and Manuscript Library, Yale University Library, Marshall Bond Papers; "New Brunswick Honors Train," *New York Times,* July 28, 1931, 28.

19. *My Day in Court,* 505–9.

20. A. Scott Berg, *Max Perkins, Editor of Genius* (New York: Dutton, 1978), 37, 57.

21. Ibid., 6, 32–33, 36–37, 56–57; see also "M. E. Perkins, 62, Scribner's Editor," *New York Times,* June 18, 1947, 25.

22. Berg, *Max Perkins Editor of Genius,* 3–5, 58–59; "M. E. Perkins, 62, Scribner's Editor," 25.

23. "The Mill of Justice," *New York Times,* January 6, 1908, SM4; "Latest Works of Fiction," *New York Times,* March 24, 1918, BR 122.

24. Arthur Train, *Mr. Tutt's Case Book* (1936; repr. New York: Charles Scribner's Sons, 1952), ix.

25. Berg, *Max Perkins Editor of Genius,* 57–58.

26. Arthur Train, *Tutt and Mr. Tutt* (New York: Charles Scribner's Sons, 1925), 5–8.

27. Ibid., 6–7.

28. Ibid., 1–16, 20, 28.

29. Ibid., 26–41.

30. Ibid., 35–48.

31. See Train, *Tutt and Mr. Tutt;* see also "Latest Works of Fiction," *New York Times,* April 18, 1920, BR189.

32. Grant Overton, *American Nights Entertainment* (New York: J. J. Little and Ives, 1923), 100; see also *Puritan's Progress,* 339.

33. "Latest Works of Fiction," *New York Times,* September 30, 1923, XX4.

34. "Latest Works of Fiction," *New York Times,* February 18, 1923, BR11.

35. Arthur Train, *His Children's Children* (New York: Charles Scribner's Sons, 1923).

36. "The Screen," *New York Times,* November 5, 1923, 15; *My Day in Court,* 384.

37. See "'Noah's Ark' and Other Recent Works of Fiction," *New York Times,* March 7, 1926, BR8; "The Screen," *New York Times,* September 28, 1929.

38. "Latest Works of Fiction," *New York Times,* December 12, 1926, BR37.

39. Conrad Black, *Franklin Delano Roosevelt* (New York: Public Affairs, 2003), 211–12.

40. "'Yonder Lies Jericho' and Other Recent Works of Fiction," *New York Times,* August 13, 1933, BR6.

41. "Revival of Fantasy in Books Foreseen," *New York Times,* July 15, 1932, 13.

42. Beatrice Sherman, "Fiction in Lighter Vein," *New York Times,* March 18, 1934, BR12.

43. Beatrice Sherman, "Mr. Tutt Takes the Stand. By Arthur Train," *New York Times,* August 30, 1936, BR18; Arthur Train, *Old Man Tutt* (New York: Charles Scribner's Sons, 1938), 213–42.

44. Train, *Old Man Tutt,* 243–69.

45. Ibid., 119, 131.

46. Letter, Charles Scribner's Sons to Eugene Connett, March 2, 1938. Archives of Charles Scribner's Sons, 1786–2003, No. C0101, Boxes 154–55, MD, RBSC, PUL; *My Day in Court,* 487; Van Gelder, "An Interview with Mr. Arthur Train," BR2.

47. *My Day in Court,* 487–88.

48. Letter, James Goode to Arthur Train, September 2, 1944. Archives of Charles Scribner's Sons, 1786–2003, No. C0101, Boxes 154–55, MD, RBSC, PUL.

49. See *Puritan's Progress; My Day in Court;* and Arthur Train, *From the District Attorney's Office* (New York: Charles Scribner's Sons, 1939).

50. "Rationing Cuts Down Greatest Book Sales in History," *New York Times,* August 8, 1943, BR4.

51. "Legal Fiction," *Time Magazine,* September 20, 1943, 98.

52. Van Gelder, "An Interview with Mr. Arthur Train," BR2.

Chapter 2

Epigraph: Letters, Maxwell Perkins to Arthur Train, May 5, 1942; Arthur Train to Maxwell Perkins, October 5, 1942. Archives of Charles Scribner's Sons, 1786–2003, No. C0101, Boxes 154–55, MD, RBSC, PUL.

1. Doris Kearns Goodwin, *No Ordinary Time* (New York: Simon and Schuster, 1994), 357–59; see also Bennett Cerf, "Auto Curbs Bring New Book Demand," *New York Times,* January 3, 1943, A51.

2. Cerf, "Auto Curbs Bring New Book Demand," A51.

3. "Rationing Cuts Down Greatest Book Sales in History," BR4; Pat Beaird, "Religious Books and the War," *New York Times,* March 28, 1943, BR6.

4. Austin Stevens, "Notes on Books and Authors," *New York Times,* December 13, 1942, BR9; "Books Called Weapons," *New York Times,* December 7, 1942, 19.

5. "Willkie Uneasy over Censorship," *New York Times,* January 13, 1943, 20; Frederic G. Meloher, "Signs in the Publisher's Zodiac," *New York Times,* March 21, 1943, BR12.

6. "Legal Fiction," *Time Magazine,* September 20, 1943, 98; "Arthur Train," *Hartford Courant,* December 26, 1943, 6.

7. "U.S. Urged to Train Boys to Be Officers," *New York Times,* May 13, 1942, 17.

8. Edward Streeter, "The Life and Times of Mr. Tutt," *New York Times,* August 29, 1943, BR1.

9. Display Ad., 129, *New York Times,* October 24, 1943, BR14.

10. See e.g., "The Best Selling Books, Here and Everywhere," *New York Times,* December 19, 1943, B11.

11. Arthur Train, *Yankee Lawyer: The Autobiography of Ephraim Tutt* (New York: Charles Scribner's Sons, 1945), xi–xiii (hereinafter *Yankee Lawyer*).

12. Ibid., 1–8.

13. Ibid., 1–22.

14. Ibid., 22–44.

15. Ibid., 47–57.

16. Ibid., 67, 73–80.

17. Ibid., 80–82.

18. Ibid., 61, 82–87.

19. Ibid., 89, 103, 107–11.

20. Ibid., 110, 396–401.

21. Ibid., 111, 142–49.

22. Ibid., 152, 156, 169–75, 185–87.

23. Ibid., 189–95.

24. Ibid., 202, 204–16, 220.

25. Ibid., 221–30.

26. Ibid., 231–34.

27. Ibid., 235–36.

28. Ibid., 253, 260–302.

29. Ibid., 304–21.

30. Ibid., 309–12, 321–23.

31. Ibid., 349–52, 362, 373–74.

32. Ibid., 381–86, 391–95.

33. Ibid., 434–39.

34. Ibid., 434–48.

Chapter 3

Epigraph: Reginald Heber Smith, "Books for Lawyers," *American Bar Association Journal* 30 (1944): 630 (reviewing *Yankee Lawyer*).

1. See Arthur Train, *Yankee Lawyer* (New York: Grosset and Dunlap, 1943), dust jacket.

2. Smith, "Books for Lawyers," 630.

3. Arthur Garfield Hays, "Current Books," *Lawyers Guild Review* 3, no. 6 (1943): 57.

4. Arthur Train, "Yankee Lawyer: The Autobiography of Ephraim Tutt," *Yale Law Journal* 52 (1943): 945–46 (reviewing *Yankee Lawyer*).

5. J. M. Maguire, "Book Reviews," *Harvard Law Review* 57 (1944) (reviewing *Yankee Lawyer*).

6. Edward Streeter, "The Life and Times of Mr. Tutt," *New York Times,* August 29, 1943, BR1.

7. John Chamberlain, "Books of the Times," *New York Times,* September 2, 1943, 17.

8. "The Executive's Bookshelf," *Wall Street Journal,* August 28, 1943, 4.

9. Paul Engle, "Mr. Tutt's Incident Packed Life Is Fun to Read About," *Chicago Daily Tribune,* September 5, 1943, E12.

10. Benjamin Howden, "Mr. Tutt Throws Bricks in His Autobiography," *Los Angeles Times,* September 5, 1943, C4.

11. "Marginal Notes on Some Recent Books," *Berkeley Daily Gazette,* November 26, 1943.

12. Albert Lernard, "The Law & The Profits," *Washington Post,* September 5, 1943, L4.

13. R. D. B., "Lawyer Tutt," *Hartford Courant,* September 5, 1943, SM15.

14. "Hoaks," *Newsweek,* September 13, 1943, 90.

15. "Legal Fiction," *Time Magazine,* September 20, 1943, 98.

Chapter 4

Epigraph: Letter, MHS to Mr. Tutt, April 9, 1946. Archives of Charles Scribner's Sons, 1786–2003, No. C0101, Boxes 154–55, MD, RBSC, PUL.

1. John Darnton, "Literary Hoaxes out of the Past," *New York Times,* February 13, 1972, 56.

2. Ibid.; B. A. Botkin, "A Tall Tale Himself," *New York Times,* September 2, 1956, BR2.

3. Motoko Rich, "A Family Tree of Literary Fakers," *New York Times,* March 8, 2008, B7; "A Sea-Going Lass Whose Nurse Was a Sailmaker," *New York Times,* March 10, 1929, 65; "Hoaxes Recurrent in All Literature," *New York Times,* November 15, 1953, 44; "Current Magazines," *New York Times,* June 16, 1929, BR11.

4. Darnton, "Literary Hoaxes Out of the Past," 56; "Book-of-Month Club Sues Dutton Head," *New York Times,* May 11, 1929, 14.

5. Michael Crichton, "Cloning Around," *New York Times,* April 23, 1978, BR2.

6. See Richard Haitch, "Follow-Up on the News, Cloning," *New York Times,* January 14, 1979, 33 (internal quotation marks omitted); *Bromhall v. Rorvik,* 478 F. Supp. 361 (E. D. Pa., 1979); Richard L. Hudson, "Blurring the Line," *New York Times,* November 15, 1978, 1; "Cloning Book Suit Is Settled," *New York Times,* April 8, 1982, C2.

7. Hudson, "Blurring the Line," 1.

8. Edward Wyatt, "Live on 'Oprah,' a Memoirist Is Kicked Out of the Book Club," *New York Times,* January 27, 2006, A1.

9. Letters, Alice Sweeney to Charles Scribner's, September 11, 1943; Charles Scribner's Sons to Alice Sweeney, September 14, 1943. Archives of Charles Scribner's Sons, 1786–2003, No. C0101, Boxes 154–55, MD, RBSC, PUL.

10. Letter, Howe to Arthur Train, September 1943. Archives of Charles Scribner's Sons, 1786–2003, No. C0101, Boxes 154–55, MD, RBSC, PUL.

11. Letters, Arthur Train to Maxwell Perkins, September 15, 1943; Maxwell Perkins to Arthur Train, September 20, 1945. Archives of Charles Scribner's Sons, 1786–2003, No. C0101, Boxes 154–55, MD, RBSC, PUL.

12. Letter, Maxwell Perkins to Arthur Train, August 31, 1943. Archives of Charles Scribner's Sons, 1786–2003, No. C0101, Boxes 154–55, MD, RBSC, PUL.

13. Letters, Gordon Pook to Charles Scribner's Sons, September 26, 1943; Charles Scribner's Sons to Gordon Pook, September 28, 1943; Maxwell Perkins to Arthur Train, October 4, 1943. Archives of Charles Scribner's Sons, 1786–2003, No. C0101, Boxes 154–55, MD, RBSC, PUL.

14. Letter, W. Prior to Charles Scribner's Sons, November 8, 1943. Archives of Charles Scribner's Sons, 1786–2003, No. Co101, Boxes 154–55, MD, RBSC, PUL.

15. Letters, Clara Lichtenstein to Charles Scribner's Sons, December 3, 1943; H. L. Austin to Charles Scribner's Sons, November 22, 1944; Ira Goldberg to Charles Scribner's Sons, February 9, 1944. Archives of Charles Scribner's Sons, 1786–2003, No. Co101, Boxes 154–55, MD, RBSC, PUL.

16. Letter, Josephine Hussey to Charles Scribner's Sons, n.d. Archives of Charles Scribner's Sons, 1786–2003, No. Co101, Boxes 154–55, MD, RBSC, PUL.

17. Letter, Inez C. Ader to Charles Scribner's Sons, December 1, 1943. Archives of Charles Scribner's Sons, 1786–2003, No. Co101, Boxes 154–55, MD, RBSC, PUL.

18. Letter, Judge Archie Cohen to Scribner & Sons, December 9, 1943. Archives of Charles Scribner's Sons, 1786–2003, No. Co101, Boxes 154–55, MD, RBSC, PUL.

19. Letters, Daniel Grady to "Scribner & Company," December 31, 1943; J. Howard Payne to Charles Scribner's & Sons, February 1, 1944; Julia L. Seider to Charles Scribner's Sons, February 17, 1944; Julia L. Seider to Charles Scribner's & Sons, February 21, 1944. Archives of Charles Scribner's Sons, 1786–2003, No. Co101, Boxes 154–55, MD, RBSC, PUL.

20. Letter, William A. Jacobs to Charles Scribner's Sons, January 15, 1944. Archives of Charles Scribner's Sons, 1786–2003, No. Co101, Boxes 154–55, MD, RBSC, PUL.

21. Letter, Randolph R. Conners to Charles Scribner's Sons, January 11, 1944. Archives of Charles Scribner's Sons, 1786–2003, No. Co101, Boxes 154–55, MD, RBSC, PUL

22. Letter, Carl F. Nitto to Chas. Scribner & Sons, December 14, 1943. Archives of Charles Scribner's Sons, 1786–2003, No. Co101, Boxes 154–55, MD, RBSC, PUL.

23. Letter, Colonel Louis C. Wilson to Arthur Train, February 29, 1944. Archives of Charles Scribner's Sons, 1786–2003, No. Co101, Boxes 154–55, MD, RBSC, PUL.

24. Letter, Harry D. Nims to Arthur C. Train, January 5, 1944. Archives of Charles Scribner's Sons, 1786–2003, No. Co101, Boxes 154–55, MD, RBSC, PUL.

25. Letters, J. L. Macomber to Chas. Scribner's Sons, January 11, 1944; Mrs. Bruce Caswell to Charles Scribner's Sons, January 21, 1944. Archives of Charles Scribner's Sons, 1786–2003, No. Co101, Boxes 154–55, MD, RBSC, PUL.

26. Letter, L. C. Wolcott to Charles Scribner's Sons, January 24, 1944. Archives of Charles Scribner's Sons, 1786–2003, No. Co101, Boxes 154–55, MD, RBSC, PUL.

27. Letter, C. E. Wright to Charles Scribner's Sons, December 11, 1943. Archives of Charles Scribner's Sons, 1786–2003, No. Co101, Boxes 154–55, MD, RBSC, PUL.

28. Letters, Dr. Painless Parker to Mr. Ephraim Tutt, c/o Charles Scribner's Sons, January 19, 1944; Harry B. Marsh to Arthur Train, c/o Chas. Scribner's Sons, March 4, 1944; Mrs. C. W. Hollowell [not addressed to any party], March 29, 1944.

Archives of Charles Scribner's Sons, 1786–2003, No. C0101, Boxes 154–55, MD, RBSC, PUL.

29. Letters, Gordon Chilson Reardon to Charles Scribner's Sons, January 7, 1943; Ethel Allen to Charles Scribner's Sons, February 16, 1944. Archives of Charles Scribner's Sons, 1786–2003, No. C0101, Boxes 154–55, MD, RBSC, PUL.

30. Letter, [illegible name from Hempstead, NY] to Charles Scribner's Sons, March 7, 1945. Archives of Charles Scribner's Sons, 1786–2003, No. C0101, Boxes 154–55, MD, RBSC, PUL.

31. Letter, G. S. Atkinson to Charles Scribner's & Sons, December 22, 1943. Archives of Charles Scribner's Sons, 1786–2003, No. C0101, Boxes 154–55, MD, RBSC, PUL.

32. Letter, Arthur Hoskille to Ephraim Tutt, n.d. Archives of Charles Scribner's Sons, 1786–2003, No. C0101, Boxes 154–55, MD, RBSC, PUL.

33. Letter, Mrs. F. W. Boley to Chas. Scribner's Sons, November 6, 1945. Archives of Charles Scribner's Sons, 1786–2003, No. C0101, Boxes 154–55, MD, RBSC, PUL.

34. Letters, Mrs. George Franklin Whitley, Jr. to Charles Scribner's Sons, January 21, 1945; Mrs. Lucy Bloomfield to Charles Scribner's & Sons, April 18, 1947. Archives of Charles Scribner's Sons, 1786–2003, No. C0101, Boxes 154–55, MD, RBSC, PUL.

35. "Santa Editorial to Be Reread Today," *New York Times,* December 20, 1933, 23.

36. Smith, "Books for Lawyers," 630.

37. Letters, Arthur Train to Maxwell Perkins, September 15, 1943; Maxwell Perkins to Arthur Train, September 23, 1943. Archives of Charles Scribner's Sons, 1786–2003, No. C0101, Boxes 154–55, MD, RBSC, PUL.

Chapter 5

Epigraph: Frank D. Adams, "As Popular as Pin-Up Girls," *New York Times,* April 30, 1944, BR1.

1. "It's a Woman's War, Too," *New York Times,* March 14, 1943, X15.

2. "Soldiers' Tastes in Books Revealed," *New York Times,* April 12, 1942, 47; "Book Drive Starts Jan. 12," *New York Times,* December 25, 1941, 22; "Books Start to Pour in for Service Men; President and Mrs. Roosevelt Donate," *New York Times,* January 10, 1942, 9; "Victory Book Day," *New York Times,* April 17, 1942, 16; "63% of Volumes Unusable in Brooklyn Book Drive," *New York Times,* March 9, 1942, 17; Elizabeth Morrow, "Letters to the Times, Books—A Symbol of Freedom," March 4, 1942 (letter dated February 28, 1942), 18.

3. "Wanted: Books for Fighters," *New York Times,* April 11, 1942, 12; "Plea for Victory Books," *New York Times,* February 21, 1943, 31; "Victory Book Drive," *New York Times,* January 6, 1943, 24.

4. "Milkmen to Help in Book Campaign," *New York Times,* April 12, 1942, 47; "Roosevelt Makes Victory Book Plea," *New York Times,* April 15, 1942, 18; "Books Start to Pour In for Service Men; President and Mrs. Roosevelt Donate," 9; "Victory Book Drive to Be Closed Dec. 31," *New York Times,* December 11, 1943, 13; "Army to Buy Books in Lots of 50,000," *New York Times,* May 13, 1943, 18.

5. John Y. Cole, "The ASE: An Introduction," *Books in Action: The Armed Services Editions* (Washington, DC: Library of Congress, 1984); Adams, "As Popular as Pin-Up Girls."

6. "Army to Buy Books in Lots of 50,000"; "Books as Weapons," *New York Times,* June 20, 1944, 18; Adams, "As Popular as Pin-Up Girls"; "35,000,000 Books to Be Printed in Year in New Pocket Form for Forces Overseas," *New York Times,* May 18, 1943, 25.

7. "35,000,000 Books to Be Printed in Year in New Pocket Form for Forces Overseas" 5; Adams, "As Popular as Pin-Up Girls."

8. Adams, "As Popular as Pin-Up Girls"; Cole, "The ASE: An Introduction," *Books in Action: The Armed Services Editions.*

9. Cole, "The ASE: An Introduction," *Books in Action: The Armed Services Editions*; Adams, "As Popular as Pin-Up Girls."

10. "35,000,000 Books to Be Printed in Year in New Pocket Form for Forces Overseas."

11. James B. Reston, "Says Army Defeats Hatch Act Intent," *New York Times,* July 11, 1944, 7; "Topics of the Times," *New York Times,* July 14, 1944, 12; see also Cole, "The ASE: An Introduction," *Books in Action: The Armed Services Editions.*

12. "Topics of the Times"; "Should Soldiers Read," *New York Times,* July 18, 1944, 18; Cole, "The ASE: An Introduction," *Books in Action: The Armed Services Editions.*

13. See "Books and Authors," *New York Times,* June 6, 1943, BR10; "35,000,000 Books to Be Printed in Year in New Pocket Form for Forces Overseas."

14. Adams, "As Popular as Pin-Up Girls."

15. Harry Hansen, "Armed Services Editions Enjoy Immense Popularity," *Chicago Daily Tribune,* July 16, 1944, B10.

16. Mel Gussow, "Literature Re-Enlists in the Military; Pilot Project Is Sending Books to American Ships and Troops Abroad," *New York Times,* November 7, 2002, E1; Adams, "As Popular as Pin-Up Girls."

17. "Services to Get 85,000,000 Books," *New York Times,* February 2, 1945, 17.

18. "Books as Weapons"; "War Book Council Gets Review Award," *New York Times,* August 9, 1945, 19; "Service Editions to End," *New York Times,* September 20, 1947, 13.

19. Adams, "As Popular as Pin-Up Girls"; "Books and Authors"; Harry Hansen, "Pocket Size Best Sellers on Their Way to Best Fighters," *Chicago Daily Tribune,* October 3, 1943, F13.

20. "Service Officers to Be Feted at Bar Harbor Estate Today," *New York Times,* July 12, 1942, D1; interview by Molly Guptill Manning with John Train, September 12, 2009; *My Day in Court,* 348.

21. See, e.g., "Bridge, the Jump Rebid," *New York Times,* December 6, 1942, X8; "Bar Harbor Lists Show of Gardens," *New York Times,* July 23, 1939, D1; "Many Members of the Bar Harbor Colony Are Actively Participating in USO Drive," *New York Times,* August 9, 1942, D1.

22. Adams, "As Popular as Pin-Up Girls"; Hansen, "Pocket Size Best Sellers on Their Way to Best Fighters."

23. Letters, Sgt. John H. Gilbert Jr. to Charles Scriber's Sons, February 11, 1944; Alfred Segal to Charles Scribner's Sons, January 24, 1945. Archives of Charles Scribner's Sons, 1786–2003, No. Co101, Boxes 154–55, MD, RBSC, PUL.

24. Letter, Bernard Fox to "Gentlemen," February 19, 1945. Archives of Charles Scribner's Sons, 1786–2003, No. Co101, Boxes 154–55, MD, RBSC, PUL.

25. Letters, Philip M. Rodgers to Charles Scribner's Sons, February 20, 1945; Cooper L. Frazier to Charles Scribner's Sons, n.d. Archives of Charles Scribner's Sons, 1786–2003, No. Co101, Boxes 154–55, MD, RBSC, PUL.

26. Letter, James I. Shaw to Charles Scribner's Sons, June 24, 1945. Archives of Charles Scribner's Sons, 1786–2003, No. Co101, Boxes 154–55, MD, RBSC, PUL.

27. Letters, John B. Farese to William Embree, June 26, 1945; William D. Embree to John B. Farese, July 10, 1945; John Farese to Maxwell Perkins, July 16, 1945. Archives of Charles Scribner's Sons, 1786–2003, No. Co101, Boxes 154–55, MD, RBSC, PUL.

28. Letter, Sam Axelrod to Charles Scribner's Sons, n.d. Archives of Charles Scribner's Sons, 1786–2003, No. Co101, Boxes 154–55, MD, RBSC, PUL.

29. Letter, Sgt. Peter Ragan, Cpt. K. P. MacEachern, T/5 Robert Kopplen, to Charles Scribner's Sons, May 24, 1945. Archives of Charles Scribner's Sons, 1786–2003, No. Co101, Boxes 154–55, MD, RBSC, PUL.

30. Letter, James Miller to Charles Scribner's Sons, July 3, 1945. Archives of Charles Scribner's Sons, 1786–2003, No. Co101, Boxes 154–55, MD, RBSC, PUL.

31. Letter, C. F. Orofino to Charles Scribner's Sons, February 6, 1945. Archives of Charles Scribner's Sons, 1786–2003, No. Co101, Boxes 154–55, MD, RBSC, PUL.

32. Letter, [illegible name, addressed from Landing Craft Base #2] to Mr. Tutt, June 15, 1944. Archives of Charles Scribner's Sons, 1786–2003, No. Co101, Boxes 154–55, MD, RBSC, PUL.

33. Letter, James D. Cargill to Charles Scribner's Sons, September 15, 1945. Archives of Charles Scribner's Sons, 1786–2003, No. Co101, Boxes 154–55, MD, RBSC, PUL.

34. Letter, "At Sea" serviceman to Chas. Scribner's Sons, July 20, 1945. Archives of Charles Scribner's Sons, 1786–2003, No. Co101, Boxes 154–55, MD, RBSC, PUL.

35. Letter, Roger Scott to Arthur Train, December 12, 1946. Archives of Charles Scribner's Sons, 1786–2003, No. Co101, Boxes 154–55, MD, RBSC, PUL.

Chapter 6

Epigraph: Letter, Cigar Institute of America, Inc., to Mr. Geffen, March 20, 1942. Archives of Charles Scribner's Sons, 1786–2003, No. Co101, Boxes 154–55, MD, RBSC, PUL.

1. Arthur Train, *Mr. Tutt Finds a Way* (New York: Charles Scribner's Sons, 1945), 1 (hereinafter *Mr. Tutt Finds a Way*); Edward Streeter, "The Life and Times of Mr. Tutt," *New York Times,* August 29, 1943, BR1; Arthur Train, "Should I Apologize?" *Saturday Evening Post,* February 26, 1944, 9.

2. "Alas, There's No Mr. Tutt, Artist Ruefully Admits," *Toronto Globe Mail,* October 16, 1944; "Arthur William Brown Is Dead; Illustrator and Caricaturist, 85," *New York Times,* October 25, 1966, 45.

3. *Yankee Lawyer,* 401.

4. "Alas, There's No Mr. Tutt, Artist Ruefully Admits."

5. Letter, Cigar Institute of America to Mr. Geffen, March 20, 1942. Archives of Charles Scribner's Sons, 1786–2003, No. Co101, Boxes 154–55, MD, RBSC, PUL.

6. Letters, Charles Scribner's Sons to Train, March 23, 1942; Charles Scribner's Sons to Mr. Geffen, March 26, 1942. Archives of Charles Scribner's Sons, 1786–2003, No. Co101, Boxes 154–55, MD, RBSC, PUL.

7. "New Brunswick Honors Train," *New York Times,* July 28, 1931, 28; "Donald McKay, 80, FISHERMAN'S GUIDE; Said to Have Been Model of Guide in 'Mr. Tutt' Stories," *New York Times,* August 24, 1939, 25. See also George Greenfield, "Wood, Field and Stream," *New York Times,* February 27, 1935, 26.

8. *My Day in Court,* 488.

9. Letters, Eugene V. Connett to Maxwell Perkins, March 4, 1938; Eugene Connett to Maxwell Perkins, c/o Charles Scribner's Sons, March 17, 1938; Charles Scribner's Sons to Mr. Hunt, February 11, 1938. Archives of Charles Scribner's Sons, 1786–2003, No. Co101, Boxes 154–55, MD, RBSC, PUL.

10. John W. Randolph, "Wood Field and Stream," *New York Times,* December 29, 1959, 30; Raymond R. Camp, ed., *The Fireside Book of Fishing: A Selection from the Great Literature of Angling* (New York: Simon and Schuster, 1959).

11. Letters, Karl Koehler to Charles Scribner's Sons, April 1, 1944; Charles Scribner's Sons to Karl Koehler, April 5, 1944. Archives of Charles Scribner's Sons, 1786–2003, No. Co101, Boxes 154–55, MD, RBSC, PUL.

12. "Rialto Gossip," *New York Times,* February 7, 1937, 161; see also "Owen Davis Dies," *New York Times,* October 15, 1956, 25; "News of the Stage," *New York Times,* May 26, 1937, 30.

13. "Owen Davis Dies"; "News of the Stage," *New York Times,* June 1, 1937, 27; "News of the Screen," *New York Times,* June 8, 1937, 30.

14. "News of the Stage," *New York Times,* September 27, 1937, 20; "The News and Gossip of Broadway," *New York Times,* November 14, 1937, 181.

15. Letters, Maxwell Perkins to Arthur Train, June 17, 1937; Maxwell Perkins to Arthur Train, June 16, 1938; Maxwell Perkins to Arthur Train, September, 16, 1938; Arthur Train to "Max," n.d. Archives of Charles Scribner's Sons, 1786–2003, No. C0101, Boxes 154–55, MD, RBSC, PUL.

16. "Gossip of the Rialto," *New York Times,* January 2, 1938, 123.

17. "Gossip of the Rialto," *New York Times,* February 19, 1939, 123; "Cohan Takes Lead in Howard Play," *New York Times,* October 13, 1939, 30.

18. Telegraph, Ray to Arthur, September 2, 1943 (emphasis omitted). Archives of Charles Scribner's Sons, 1786–2003, No. C0101, Boxes 154–55, MD, RBSC, PUL; "Gossip of the Rialto," *New York Times,* January 23, 1944, XI.

19. "Massey to Be Seen as Ephraim Tutt," *New York Times,* November 4, 1943, 27.

20. "Return of 'Porgy' Listed for Feb. 7," *New York Times,* January 29, 1944, 11; "Massey to Be Seen as Ephraim Tutt"; "Some Massey Matters of the Moment," *New York Times,* February 6, 1944, Sec. 2, p. 1; "Gossip of the Rialto," *New York Times,* May 14, 1944, XI.

21. "National Theatre Making Progress," *New York Times,* January 31, 1947, 16; "News and Gossip Gathered on the Rialto," *New York Times,* July 27, 1947, XI.

22. "Massey to Be Seen as Ephraim Tutt."

23. "Radio—TV Notes," *New York Times,* August 6, 1951, 28; J. P. Shanley, "TV: Nat (King) Cole; Singer's New Show Offers Refreshing Fifteen Minutes over Channel 4 'Mr. Tutt Goes West,'" *New York Times,* November 6, 1956, 71.

24. Letters, S. Carter Williams to Charles Scribner's Sons, June 14, 1939; L. A. Brodsky to Charles Scribner's Sons, June 26, 1946. Archives of Charles Scribner's Sons, 1786–2003, No. C0101, Boxes 154–55, MD, RBSC, PUL.

25. Letters, Charles Scribner's Sons to A. N. Marquis Co., December 6 1943; Letter, Elmer F. Weck to Charles Scribner's Sons, December 20, 1943. Archives of Charles Scribner's Sons, 1786–2003, No. C0101, Boxes 154–55, MD, RBSC, PUL; *Mr. Tutt Finds a Way,* 17.

26. Letter, Arthur Train to Maxwell Perkins, December 7, 1943. Archives of Charles Scribner's Sons, 1786–2003, No. C0101, Boxes 154–55, MD, RBSC, PUL.

27. Letters, Charles Scribner's Sons to A. N. Marquis Co., December 8, 1943; Charles Scribner's Sons to A. N. Marquis Company, December 17, 1943; Elmer Weck to Charles Scribner's Sons, December 20, 1943. Archives of Charles Scribner's Sons, 1786–2003, No. C0101, Boxes 154–55, MD, RBSC, PUL.

28. *Mr. Tutt Finds a Way,* 17.

29. Letters, L. W. Babcock to Charles Scribner's Sons, June 19, 1940; Charles

Scribner's Sons to L. W. Babcock, June 25, 1940. Archives of Charles Scribner's Sons, 1786–2003, No. C0101, Boxes 154–55, MD, RBSC, PUL.

30. Letters, John Sutherland to Maxwell Perkins, January 3, 1946; Hal Landers to Burroughs Mitchell, January 41 [*sic*], 1961. Archives of Charles Scribner's Sons, 1786–2003, No. C0101, Boxes 154–55, MD, RBSC, PUL.

31. Letter, Arthur Davies to Chas. Scribner's Sons, January 29, 1946. Archives of Charles Scribner's Sons, 1786–2003, No. C0101, Boxes 154–55, MD, RBSC, PUL.

Chapter 7

Epigraph: Arthur Train, "The Truth about Ephraim Tutt," *Saturday Evening Post,* February 26, 1944 (hereinafter "The Truth"), 55; see also *Mr. Tutt Finds a Way,* 16.

1. "The Truth," 9–11, 52, 54–55 (emphasis added); see also *Mr. Tutt Finds a Way,* chap. 1.

2. Michiko Kakutani, "Bending the Truth in a Million Little Ways," *New York Times,* January 17, 2006, E1.

3. Ibid.

4. Edward Wyatt, "Treatment Description in Memoir Is Disputed," *New York Times,* January 24, 2006, E1; Virginia Heffernan, "Ms. Winfrey Takes a Guest to the Televised Woodshed," *New York Times,* January 27, 2006, A16; Edward Wyatt, "Frey Says Falsehoods Improved His Tale," *New York Times,* February 2, 2006, E1.

5. Kakutani, "Bending the Truth in a Million Little Ways."

6. "The Truth," 9–11; see also *Mr. Tutt Finds a Way,* 1–3, 7.

7. "The Truth," 10–11; *Mr. Tutt Finds a Way,* 3–8.

8. "The Truth," 52–55; *Mr. Tutt Finds a Way,* 8–16.

9. "Sure, Virginia, There's a Mr. Tutt," *Saturday Evening Post,* April 8, 1944, vol. 216 #4, p. 4.

10. Ibid.

11. Letters, MHS to Mr. Tutt, April 9, 1946; Col. Louis C. Wilson to Arthur Train, February 29, 1944; Mrs. F. W. Boley to Chas. Scribner's Sons, November 6, 1945. Archives of Charles Scribner's Sons, 1786–2003, No. C0101, Boxes 154–55, MD, RBSC, PUL.

Chapter 8

Epigraph: Letters, Arthur Train to Maxwell Perkins, July 18, 1943; Maxwell Perkins to Arthur Train, July 20, 1943. Archives of Charles Scribner's Sons, 1786–2003, No. C0101, Boxes 154–55, MD, RBSC, PUL.

1. Letter, J. D. Hatch Jr., to Arthur Train, March 2, 1943. Archives of Charles Scribner's Sons, 1786–2003, No. C0101, Boxes 154–55, MD, RBSC, PUL.

2. "Wins Prize in Oratory," *Bulletin* (February 2, 1923); "Linet Will Direct Orphan Home Drive" (source unknown, 1950, handwritten date); "Northern Liberties Hospital to Be Subject of Radio Talk" (source unknown, 1930, handwritten date), Lewis Linet Scrapbook.

3. "Servicemen to Get Aid on Overcharging" (source unknown, n.d.) Lewis Linet Scrapbook.

4. "Depositors Move to Guard Interests as Bank Is Closed" (source unknown, n.d.); "Report on Closed Bank Awaited by Depositors" (source unknown, n.d.); "3,000 Sign Bank Plan" (source unknown, 1933, handwritten date), Lewis Linet Scrapbook.

5. "Among the Boys" (source unknown, January 1935, handwritten date), Lewis Linet Scrapbook.

6. Article, "Jay Cooke Going to Army Camp," *Philadelphia Bulletin* (July 2 [unknown year]); "Lewis Linet Returns from Good Will Tour" (source unknown, May 1944, handwritten date), Lewis Linet Scrapbook.

7. "Lewis R. Linet Award Established," *Journal Intelligencer,* Philadelphia, July 10, 1978, 1; Letter, Herman Idler to Lewis Linet, January 5, 1979, Lewis Linet Scrapbook; "Candidate for Judge" (source unknown, 1934, handwritten date), Lewis Linet Scrapbook.

8. "Esq. Spotlight: Lewis R. Linet '24," *Temple, Esq.* (Temple Law School, Spring 2001, p. 5); *Commonwealth ex rel. Maurer v. O'Neill,* 368 Pa. 369, 371, 83 A. 2d 382, 382 (Sup. Ct. PA, 1951).

9. "When Lawyer Sues Lawyer" (source unknown, n.d.), Lewis Linet Scrapbook.

10. See New York State Supreme Court, New York County, Index No. 7108-1944, Complaint, 1–9.

11. Letter, Maxwell Perkins to Arthur Train, July 20, 1943. Archives of Charles Scribner's Sons, 1786–2003, No. C0101, Boxes 154–55, MD, RBSC, PUL; H. I. Phillips, "The Once Over," *Washington Post,* July 9, 1944, B4.

12. See New York Supreme Court, New York County, Index No. 7108–1944, Complaint, 9–10.

13. *New York Times,* Display Ad 103, May 28, 1944, BR20; *New York Times,* Display Ad 91, June 18, 1944, BR12.

14. Phillips, "The Once Over."

15. "The Case against Mr. Tutt," *Hartford Courant,* May 18, 1944, 10; "Ideas," *Time Magazine,* May 29, 1944.

16. Letter, Maxwell Perkins to Arthur Train, May 1, 1944. Archives of Charles Scribner's Sons, 1786–2003, No. C0101, Boxes 154–55, MD, RBSC, PUL; William J. Clew, "That's for Tutt's Accusers!" *Hartford Courant,* April 1, 1945, D14.

17. Letter, Charles Scribner to John W. Davis, April 4, 1944. Archives of Charles Scribner's Sons, 1786–2003, No. C0101, Boxes 154–55, MD, RBSC, PUL.

18. Letter, John W. Davis to Charles Scribner, April 6, 1944. Archives of Charles Scribner's Sons, 1786–2003, No. C0101, Boxes 154–55, MD, RBSC, PUL; *Mr. Tutt Finds a Way*, 230; see also New York Supreme Court, New York County, Index No. 7108–1944, Memorandum in Support of Defendants' Motion to Dismiss, 8–9.

19. New York Supreme Court, New York County, Index No. 7108–1944, "Memorandum in Opposition to Defendants' Motion to Dismiss," 5–11.

20. *Mr. Tutt Finds a Way*, 230–31; New York Supreme Court, New York County, Index No. 7108–1944, "Stipulation of Discontinuance."

21. *Mr. Tutt Finds a Way*, 228–33.

22. Motoko Rich, "Publisher and Author Settle Suit over Lies," *New York Times*, September 7, 2006, E1.

23. Henry Raymont, "Howard Hughes' Memoirs Are Bought for Book and Serial in Life Magazine," *New York Times*, December 8, 1971, 65; Wallace Turner, "Handwriting and Language Are Called Keys to Authenticating Hughes Book," *New York Times*, January 11, 1972, 23; Gladwin Hill, "Former Aide Believes Voice Was Hughes's and 'Autobiography' Is Authentic," *New York Times*, January 12, 1972, 30.

24. Douglas Robinson, "Author Is Said to Theorize He Was Duped on Hughes," *New York Times*, January 22, 1972, 1; Douglas Robinson, "Irving Discloses His Wife Is 'Helga Hughes,'" *New York Times*, January 29, 1972, 1; Douglas Robinson, "A U.S.-State Inquiry Announced Here," *New York Times*, February 1, 1972, 1.

25. Peter Kihss, "Life Finds Irving's Manuscript a 'Hoax,'" *New York Times*, February 12, 1972, 1; Wallace Turner, "Portions of Irving's Books Like Hughes Aide's Story," *New York Times*, February 13, 1972, 1; Lawrence van Gelder, "2 Irvings Indicted with Researcher by New York Jury," *New York Times*, March 10, 1972, 1.

26. Lawrence van Gelder, "Irving Sentenced to 2 1/2 Year Term," *New York Times*, June 17, 1972, 1; see also "Mrs. Irving Asserts Swiss Break Pledge," *New York Times*, June 29, 1972, 27.

27. Lesley Oelsner, "Please Cliff, Say It Isn't So; The Hughes Affair," *New York Times*, February 13, 1972, E3.

Chapter 9

Epigraph: *Mr. Tutt Finds a Way*, 16.

1. Letter, Arthur Train to Maxwell Perkins, September 12, 1942. Archives of Charles Scribner's Sons, 1786–2003, No. C0101, Boxes 154–55, MD, RBSC, PUL.

2. Interview by Molly Guptill with John Train, September 12, 2009; Stanley J. Kunitz, *Twentieth Century Authors: A Biographical Dictionary of Modern Literature* (New York: H. W. Wilson, 1955, 1st. supp.), 1005.

3. Telegram, Lucy Train Worcester to Maxwell Perkins, December 22, 1945; Letter, Maxwell Perkins to Mrs. Frederick William Boley, January 18, 1946. Archives of Charles Scribner's Sons, 1786–2003, No. C0101, Boxes 154–55, MD, RBSC, PUL.

4. "Arthur Train," *Hartford Courant,* December 26, 1945, 6.

5. "Man Who Made Ephraim Tutt Live Is Dead," *Chicago Daily Tribune,* December 23, 1945, 10; "Arthur Train, Ephraim Tutt Creator, Passes," *Los Angeles Times,* December 23, 1945, 3.

6. "Mr. Train and Mr. Tutt," *New York Times,* December 24, 1945, 14; Train, "Should I Apologize?"; *Puritan's Progress,* 339.

7. "Mr. Train and Mr. Tutt."

8. "Arthur Train," *Hartford Courant,* December 26, 1943, 6.

9. John A. Garraty and Mark C. Carnes, *American National Biography* (New York: Oxford University Press, 1999), 21:800.

10. *Mr. Tutt Finds a Way,* 16.

11. Thane Rosenbaum, *The Myth of Moral Justice* (New York: Harper Perennial, 2005), 19.

12. Michael Distelhorst, "Teaching a Lawyer's Confessions: Three Virtue Myths," *Legal Studies Forum* 21 (1997): 283.

13. Letters, Mrs. Frederick William Boley to Maxwell Perkins, January 11, 1946; Maxwell Perkins to Mrs. Frederick William Boley, January 18, 1946. Archives of Charles Scribner's Sons, 1786–2003, No. Co101, Boxes 154–55, MD, RBSC, PUL.

14. Letters, Mrs. H. D. Taylor to Charles Scribner's Sons, January 2, 1946; Mrs. John A. Harlow to Ephraim Tutt, 1946. Archives of Charles Scribner's Sons, 1786–2003, No. Co101, Boxes 154–55, MD, RBSC, PUL.

15. Letter, Charles Scribner's Sons to Mrs. John A. Harlow, January 31, 1946. Archives of Charles Scribner's Sons, 1786–2003, No. Co101, Boxes 154–55, MD, RBSC, PUL.

16. Letters, Mrs. David Stevenson to Mr. Tutt, c/o Charles Scribner's Sons, April 19, 1949; Charles Scribner's Sons to Mrs. David Stevenson, April 26, 1949. Archives of Charles Scribner's Sons, 1786–2003, No. Co101, Boxes 154–55, MD, RBSC, PUL.

17. Letter, Mrs. David Stevenson to Mr. Wallace Meyers, n.d. Archives of Charles Scribner's Sons, 1786–2003, No. Co101, Boxes 154–55, MD, RBSC, PUL.

18. Letter, Lyle T. Hammond to Dr. Ephraim Tutt, January 6, 1946, 6:00 A.M. Archives of Charles Scribner's Sons, 1786–2003, No. Co101, Boxes 154–55, MD, RBSC, PUL.

19. Letter, Lyle T. Hammond to Dr. Ephraim Tutt, January 6, 1946, 4:00 P.M. Archives of Charles Scribner's Sons, 1786–2003, No. Co101, Boxes 154–55, MD, RBSC, PUL.

20. Letter, Wyncote, PA, February 17, 1947. Archives of Charles Scribner's Sons, 1786–2003, No. Co101, Boxes 154–55, MD, RBSC, PUL.

21. Letters, Miss Katherine Little to Charles Scribner's Sons, March 18, 1946; Genevieve Ford to Charles Scribner's Sons, July 22, 1946. Archives of Charles Scribner's Sons, 1786–2003, No. Co101, Boxes 154–55, MD, RBSC, PUL.

22. Letters, Mildred E. Davis to Charles Scribner's Sons, July 27, 1946; Catherine Jarrett to Charles Scribner's Sons, May 19, 1947; Lt. Stanley R. Sterbenz to Charles Scribner's Sons, July 29, 1952; M. M. Sackett to Consolidated Book Publishers, February 7, 1950. Archives of Charles Scribner's Sons, 1786–2003, No. C0101, Boxes 154–55, MD, RBSC, PUL.

23. Letters, Isidore Okun to Charles Scribner's Sons, April 7, 1947; Fred Strauss to Charles Scribner's Sons, June 13, 1953. Archives of Charles Scribner's Sons, 1786–2003, No. C0101, Boxes 154–55, MD, RBSC, PUL.

24. Letter, C. Hugh Woodbury to Messrs Charles Scribner's and Sons, April 6, 1946. Archives of Charles Scribner's Sons, 1786–2003, No. C0101, Boxes 154–55, MD, RBSC, PUL.

Chapter 10

Epigraph: Arthur Train, *Mr. Tutt at His Best* (New York: Charles Scribner's Sons, 1961), xii (introduction by Judge Harold R. Medina).

1. Letter, Judge Harold Medina to T. J. B. Walsh, December 27, 1959. Archives of Charles Scribner's Sons, 1786–2003, No. C0101, Boxes 154–55, MD, RBSC, PUL.

2. "Communists: The Presence of Evil," *Time Magazine,* October 24, 1949; "Harold Medina, U.S. Judge, Dies at 102," *New York Times,* March 16, 1990, B7; "Harold Medina, at 89, Still Loves Law, Columbia and Telling Tales," *New York Times,* January 20, 1978, B15.

3. Alpheus Mason, "The Triumph Is Spiritual," *New York Times,* September 20, 1959, BR3; "Harold Medina, U.S. Judge, Dies at 102"; "Medina Recalls Trial's Bad Day," *New York Times,* October 15, 1949, 2.

4. "Harold Medina, at 89, Still Loves Law, Columbia and Telling Stories"; "Harold Medina, U.S. Judge, Dies at 102."

5. Letters, Judge Harold Medina to T. J. B. Walsh, December 27, 1959; Judge Harold Medina to T. J. B. Walsh, January 6, 1960; T. J. B. Walsh to Judge Harold Medina, January 4, 1960; Judge Medina to T. J. B. Walsh, January 19, 1960; Judge Medina to T. J. B. Walsh, January 26, 1960. Archives of Charles Scribner's Sons, 1786–2003, No. C0101, Boxes 154–55, MD, RBSC, PUL.

6. Letter, Judge Medina to T. J. B. Walsh, February 25, 1960. Archives of Charles Scribner's Sons, 1786–2003, No. C0101, Boxes 154–55, MD, RBSC, PUL.

7. Letters, T. J. B. Walsh to Judge Medina, February 29, 1960; Judge Medina to T. J. B. Walsh, March 3, 1960. Archives of Charles Scribner's Sons, 1786–2003, No. C0101, Boxes 154–55, MD, RBSC, PUL.

8. Letters, Judge Medina to T. J. B. Walsh, June 17, 1960; Judge Medina to T. J. B. Walsh, June 25, 1960. Archives of Charles Scribner's Sons, 1786–2003, No. C0101, Boxes 154–55, MD, RBSC, PUL.

9. Letter, Judge Medina to T. J. B. Walsh, December 15, 1960. Archives of Charles Scribner's Sons, 1786–2003, No. C0101, Boxes 154–55, MD, RBSC, PUL.

10. Train, *Mr. Tutt at His Best.*

11. "Books and Authors," *Lewiston Daily Sun,* April 24, 1961; Letter, Spencer Brock Jr., to Charles Scribner's Sons, March 11, 1961. Archives of Charles Scribner's Sons, 1786–2003, No. C0101, Boxes 154–55, MD, RBSC, PUL.

12. Arthur Train, "Yankee Lawyer: The Autobiography of Ephraim Tutt," *Yale Law Journal* 52 (1943): 945, 947 (reviewing *Yankee Lawyer*).

Selected Bibliography

Archival Collections

Bond, Marshall. Papers. Beinecke Rare Book and Manuscript Library, Yale University Library, New Haven, Connecticut.

Charles Scribner's Sons Records. Arthur Train Author File. Manuscripts Division, Department of Rare Books and Special Collections, Princeton University Library, Princeton, New Jersey.

Books and Journal Articles

Berg, A. Scott. *Max Perkins, Editor of Genius.* New York: Dutton, 1978.

Biographical Directory of the United States Congress, 1774–1989. Washington, DC: United States Government Printing Office, 1989.

Black, Conrad. *Franklin Delano Roosevelt.* New York: Public Affairs, 2003.

"Books for Lawyers," reviewing "Mr. Tutt at His Best." *American Bar Association Journal* 47, no. 7 (1961): 719.

Camp, Raymond R., ed. *The Fireside Book of Fishing: A Selection from the Great Literature of Angling.* New York: Simon and Schuster, 1959.

Cole, John Y. *Books in Action: The Armed Services Editions.* Washington, DC: Library of Congress, 1984.

Distelhorst, Michael. "Teaching a Lawyer's Confessions: Three Virtue Myths." *Legal Studies Forum* 21 (1997): 283.

"Esq. Spotlight: Lewis R. Linet '24." *Temple, Esq.* (Spring 2001): 5.

Garraty, John A., and Mark C. Carnes. *American National Biography.* Vol. 21. New York: Oxford University Press, 1999.

Goodwin, Doris Kearns. *No Ordinary Time.* New York: Simon and Schuster, 1994.

Harbaugh, William. *Lawyer's Lawyer: The Life of John W. Davis.* Charlottesville: University Press of Virginia, 1990.

Hays, Arthur Garfield. "Current Books." *Lawyers Guild Review* 3, no. 6 (November–December 1943): 57.

Kunitz, Stanley J. *Twentieth Century Authors: A Biographical Dictionary of Modern Literature.* New York: H. W. Wilson, 1955, 1st. Supp.

Lowell, Joan. *Cradle of the Deep.* New York: Simon and Schuster, 1929.

Maguire, J. M. "Book Reviews." *Harvard Law Review* 57 (1944): 261–62.

Newman, John Henry. *Apologia Pro Vita Sua.* London: Penguin, 1994.

Overton, Grant. *American Nights Entertainment.* New York: J. J. Little and Ives, 1923.

Rosenbaum, Thane. *The Myth of Moral Justice.* New York: Harper Perennial, 2005.

Smith, Reginald Heber. "Books for Lawyers." *American Bar Association Journal* 30 (1944): 630.

Train, Arthur. *The Adventures of Ephraim Tutt.* New York: Charles Scribner's Sons, 1930.

———. *The Blind Goddess.* New York: Charles Scribner's Sons, 1926.

———. *From the District Attorney's Office.* New York: Charles Scribner's Sons, 1939.

———. *His Children's Children.* New York: Charles Scribner's Sons, 1923.

———. *Illusion.* New York: Charles Scribner's Sons, 1929.

———. *Mr. Tutt at His Best.* With a new introduction by Harold R. Medina. New York: Charles Scribner's Sons, 1961.

———. *Mr. Tutt Finds a Way.* New York: Charles Scribner's Sons, 1945.

———. *Mr. Tutt's Case Book.* New York: Charles Scribner's Sons, 1952. First published in 1936.

———. *My Day in Court.* New York: Charles Scribner's Sons, 1939.

———. *Old Man Tutt.* New York: Charles Scribner's Sons, 1938.

———. *Puritan's Progress.* New York: Charles Scribner's Sons, 1931.

———. *Tutt and Mr. Tutt.* New York: Charles Scribner's Sons, 1925.

———. *Yankee Lawyer: The Autobiography of Ephraim Tutt.* New York: Charles Scribner's Sons, 1945.

———. "Yankee Lawyer: The Autobiography of Ephraim Tutt." *Yale Law Journal* 52 (1943): 945–46.

Court Cases and Legal Documents

Bromhall v. Rorvik, 478 F. Supp. 361 (E. D. Pa., 1979).

Commonwealth ex rel. Maurer v. O'Neill, 368 Pa. 369, 371, 83 A. 2d 382, 382 (Sup. Ct. Pa., 1951).

Linet v. Train, et al., New York State Supreme Court, New York County, Index No. 7108–1944, Summons with Notice, Complaint, Memorandum in Support of Defendants' Motion to Dismiss the Alleged Second Cause of Action Set Forth in the Complaint, Memorandum in Opposition to Defendants' Motion to Dismiss Second Cause of Action, Stipulation of Discontinuance.

Interviews

Interviews by Molly Guptill Manning with John Train, conducted September 12, 2009, and September 27, 2009, in New York, New York.

Periodicals and Newspapers

Berkeley Daily Gazette
Boston Daily Globe
Boston Evening Globe
Chicago Daily Tribune
Hartford Courant
Jewish World
Journal Intelligencer
Lewiston Daily Sun
Los Angeles Times
New York Herald Tribune
New York Times
Newsweek
Philadelphia Bulletin
Philadelphia Evening Ledger
Philadelphia Review
Saturday Evening Post
Time Magazine
Toronto Globe Mail
Wall Street Journal
Washington Post

Scrapbook

Scrapbook of Lewis R. Linet, courtesy of Lewis R. Linet Jr.

Websites

"A Brief History of the Armed Services Editions." http://www. armedserviceseditions .com.

Koestler, Frances A. *The Unseen Minority.* Electronic Publication, American Foundation for the Blind, 2004, chap. 10 (discussing the advent of the Talking Book Records). http://www.afb.org/unseen/book.asp?ch=Koe-00toc.

Library of Congress. Selected Special Collections, Armed Services Editions Collection. www.loc.gov/rr/rarebook/coll/020.html.

Index